Calendars and Years II

Astronomy and Time in the Ancient and Medieval World

edited by

John Steele

Oxbow Books
Oxford and Oakville

Published by
Oxbow Books, Oxford, UK

ISBN 978-1-84217-987-1

This book is available direct from:

Oxbow Books, Oxford, UK
(Phone: 01865-241249; Fax: 01865-794449)

and

The David Brown Book Company
PO Box 511, Oakville, CT 06779, USA
(Phone: 860-945-9329; Fax: 860-945-9468)

or from our website

www.oxbowbooks.com

A CIP record for this book is available from the British library

Library of Congress Cataloging-in-Publication Data

Calendars and years II : astronomy and time in the ancient and medieval world / edited by John Steele.
p. cm.
ISBN 978-1-84217-987-1 (pbk.)
1. Calendars--History--To 1500. 2. Chronology, Historical. 3. Astronomy, Ancient. 4. Astronomy, Medieval. 5. Time measurements--History--To 1500. I. Steele, John M.
CE21.C35 2011
903--dc22
2010050030

Printed and bound in Great Britain by
Hobbs the Printers, Totton, Hampshire

Contents

Preface

Understanding ancient calendars is an essential tool in the writing of history: without dates how are we to know which event preceded another? Dates given in most ancient and medieval calendars can be readily converted into the Julian or Gregorian calendar using tables found in many handbooks. But how did those handbooks come about? It was in order to address this question, and in particular the issue of whether any unjustified assumptions have become embedded within our current understanding of ancient calendars, that Henry Zemel and I organised a session at the Seventh Biennial History of Astronomy Workshop held at Notre Dame University in July 2005, the papers from which formed the basis for the volume *Calendars and Years: Astronomy and Time in the Ancient Near East*, published in 2007. The present volume complements that collection by considering calendars and time-reckoning in other important ancient and medieval cultures: China, India, the Jewish world, the Islamic world, and Mesoamerica. As with the previous volume, the focus in these papers is on the evidence for understanding the ancient and medieval calendars and the year lengths they use, whether through a historiographical study of the state of current research on a particular calendar or a detailed presentation of the preserved textual material that provides evidence for the workings of a calendar.

John M. Steele
July 2010

The Chinese Sexagenary Cycle and the Ritual Foundations of the Calendar

Adam Smith

From the earliest appearance of literacy in East Asia, around 1250 BC, there is evidence of the routine use of a system for recording dates using cycles of named days. The more fundamental of these consists of ten terms and will be referred to here as the '10-cycle' (table 1). By running the 10-cycle concurrently with a second cycle twelve days in length, the '12-cycle' (table 2), a longer cycle of sixty days is generated, sixty being the lowest common multiple of ten and twelve. We will refer to this compound cycle as the '60-cycle'.[1] At the time of their first attestation, the day was the only unit of time that the three cycles were used to record.[2] Days within these cycles will be referred to in this chapter with the formulae n/60, n/10 and n/12. So, for example, 3/10 refers to the third day of the 10-cycle.

There are many ways of visualizing the compound 60-cycle.[3] A comparativist might think of it as a pair of toothed wheels engaged with one another (figure 1), by analogy with the representations of the Mesoamerican Tzolk'in cycle, with which the Chinese 60-cycle has certain similarities. However, in the centuries after its first appearance it was conceived by its users in terms of a simple tabular format, with the sixty compound terms arranged in six vertical columns of ten terms each, one for each round of the 10-cycle. The first (rightmost) column began with the pair of terms for day 1/60 (1/10 paired with 1/12), below which followed 2/60 (2/10 and 2/12), 3/60 (3/10 and 3/12), and so on down to 10/60 (10/10 and 10/12) at the bottom. The beginning of a new column, as at 11/60 (1/10 and 11/12), coincided with the recommencement of the 10-cycle. The first repeat in the 12-cycle occurred on day 13/60 (3/10 and 1/12), at the third position in the second column. Many examples of this tabular format survive among the earliest remains of scribal training.[4]

The mathematical principles of the compound 60-cycle, and its timekeeping function, have obvious parallels in the calendars of other cultures. In addition to the 260-day Mesomerican Tzolk'in, a compound cycle of 13 × 20 days, there is a similarly direct parallel with the form and function of the 42-day round of the Akan calendar, a compound cycle of 6 × 7 days.[5]

The origins of the Chinese cycles are largely obscure.[6] No compelling etymology for the names of the terms in the 10- and 12-cycles has ever been constructed, in Chinese, or any other language. They show no connection to the system of decimal numbers that also appears with the first evidence of the script. The 10-cycle is, fundamentally, the early Chinese week. The 12-cycle may have had a similar status among certain groups or in particular contexts but they have left no evidence of their existence. The well-known correlation of the 12-cycle with a list of animals is not attested within the first one thousand

	1	2	3	4	5	6	7	8	9	10
Modern Graph	甲	乙	丙	丁	戊	己	庚	辛	壬	癸
Pinyin	jia	yi	bing	ding	wu	ji	geng	xin	ren	gui
Shang Graph (ca. 1200 BC)										

TABLE 1. The 10-cycle.

	1	2	3	4	5	6	7	8	9	10	11	12
Modern Graph	子	丑	寅	卯	辰	巳	午	未	申	酉	戌	亥
Pinyin	zi	chou	yin	mao	chen	si	wu	wei	shen	you	xu	hai
Shang Graph (ca. 1200 BC)												

TABLE 2. The 12-cycle.

years of the cycle's use.

The graphs used to write the terms of the 10-cycle may have been created for that purpose. That is, they are not obviously borrowings of graphs used to write other words. This is not the case for some terms in the 12-cycle. The writings for the sixth and tenth terms, for example, are phonologically motivated secondary uses of pictograms created to write 'child' (*zi* 子)[7] and 'beer' (*jiu* 酒), employed as approximate phonetic spellers. This suggests that certain fundamental properties of the script were already established before they were applied to writing the 12-cycle.

In addition to their role in the calendar, terms in the 10-cycle, at the time of their first appearance and for several centuries after, were employed in names referring to dead kin. The 10-cycle and 60-cycle also underlay the calendrical apparatus that was used to schedule sacrificial performances directed towards these same dead kin, a central religious preoccupation of elites and probably the early Chinese population more broadly during the late second millennium.

The use of the 60-cycle to record dates was retained after the practice of naming dead kin with cyclical terms came to be abandoned, and the legacy of its role in scheduling ritual events continued to be felt, in elite funeral arrangements for example, into the mid first millennium BC. However, this break with the earlier ritual significance of the cyclical terms, as a means of referring to and commemorating dead family members, allowed them to be reinterpreted as a more abstract system of ordinals, one that could be creatively redeployed to label sequential or cyclical phenomena of many kinds in addition to days. Many of these new uses in their turn attracted a religious or magical focus.

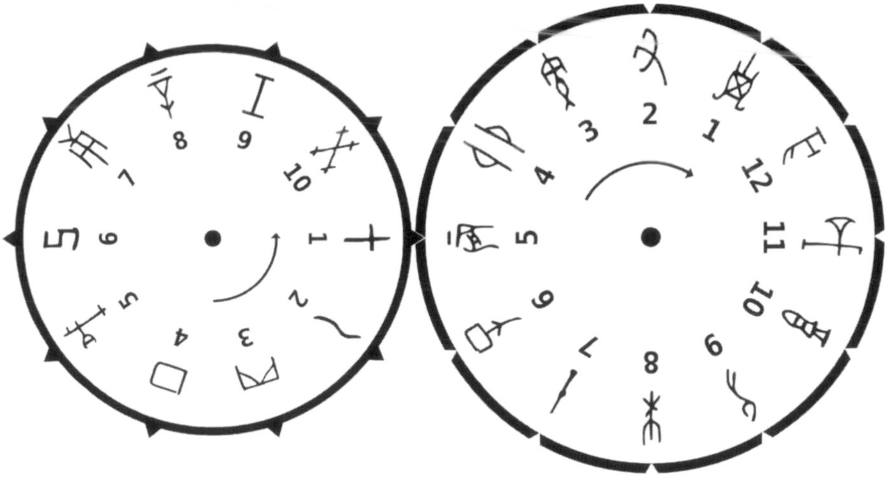

FIGURE 1. The 60-cycle envisaged as a pair of toothed wheels representing the 10-cycle and the 12-cycle. Even-numbered positions never engage with odd-numbered positions. Six turns of the 10-cycle correspond to five turns of the 12-cycle, after which the system has returned to its original state. The arrangement shown corresponds to Day 41/60.

The Shang king list

The Shang (ca. 1600–1050 BC)[8] king list, a sequence of more than thirty names over approximately twenty generations, is one of the earliest complex documents from East Asia that can be demonstrated to have been reliably preserved through textual transmission. A version of this list was available during the Western Han (206 BC – 25 AD), and is preserved in the *Shi Ji* (史記 Grand Scribe's Records).[9] This received version of the list is a very close match for the list that was reconstructed by twentieth-century scholarship from the sacrificial schedules reflected in divination records excavated at Anyang, location of the seat of the last seven generations of kings to appear in the list (table 3).[10] Besides the bare sequence of royal names, the transmitted list was evidently equipped with further ancillary information. It marked instances of fraternal succession, for example, and may have provided cues to some of the anecdotes that pad out the version of it that appears in the *Shi Ji*.

A remarkable feature of the king list, that the list itself does nothing to explain, is the fact that every king is named after a term in the 10-cycle.[12] No other list of rulers from early China has this property. Clearly, the Shang had an intimate relationship with the cyclical terms, beyond the fact that they were the first to write them down. From the early centuries AD, attempts have been made to explain the relationship between the use of the 10 cycle to write these royal names—the so-called 'temple names' (*miaohao* 廟號) or 'day-names' (riming 日名)—and its use to record dates. Early proposals included suggestions that the names reflected birth days, or that they referred in some way to objects representing the dead kings in the ancestral temple (*miao zhu* 廟主). The archaeological rediscovery of the Shang in the last century prompted a revival of interest in the question.[13]

Since the king list contains more than ten kings, some terms from the 10-cycle will

Generation	Succession	Name	Pinyin	Day-name	Son of	Wives' day-names
G1	K1	上甲	Shang (Higher) Jia	1		
G2	K2	報乙	Bao Yi	2	K1	
G3	K3	報丙	Bao Bing	3	K2	
G4	K4	報丁	Bao Ding	4	K3	
G5	K5	示壬	Shi Ren	9	K4	7
G6	K6	示癸	Shi Gui	10	K5	1
G7	K7	大乙	Da (Greater) Yi	2	K6	3
G8	K8	大丁	Da (Greater) Ding	4	K7	5
G9	K9	大甲	Da (Greater) Jia	1	K8	8
G8	K10	外丙	Wai (Outer) Bing	3	K7	
G10	K11	大庚	Da (Greater) Geng	7	K9	9
G11	K12	小甲	Xiao (Lesser) Jia	1	K11	
	K13	大戊	Da (Greater) Wu	5		9
	K14	雍己	Yong Ji	6		
G12	K15	中丁	Zhong (Middle) Ding	4	K13	6, 10
	K16	外壬	Wai (Outer) Ren	9		
	K17	戔甲	Jian Jia	1		
G13	K18	祖乙	Zu (Ancestor) Yi	2	K15	6, 7
G14	K19	祖辛	Zu (Ancestor) Xin	8	K18	1
	K20	羌甲	Qiang Jia	1		
G15	K21	祖丁	Zu (Ancestor) Ding	4	K19	6, 7
	K22	南庚	Nan Geng	7	K20	
G16	K23	陽甲	Yang Jia	1	K21	
	K24	盤庚	Pan Geng	7		
	K25	小辛	Xiao (Lesser) Xin	8		
	K26	小乙	Xiao (Lesser) Yi	2		7
Earliest divination records appear at Anyang						
G17	K27	武丁	Wu Ding	4	K26	8, 10, 5
G18	K28	祖己	Zu (Ancestor) Ji	6	K27	
	K29	祖庚	Zu (Ancestor) Geng	7		
	K30	祖甲	Zu (Ancestor) Jia	1		5
G19	K31	康丁	Kang Ding	4	K30	8
G20	K32	武乙	Wu Yi	2	K31	5, 10
G21	K33	文武丁	Wen Wu Ding	4	K32	
G22	K34	帝乙	Di Yi	2	K33	
G23	K35	帝辛	Di Xin	8	K34	

TABLE 3. The Shang King list (after Chang Yuzhi 1987, p. 134).[11]

Day-Names	Day 1	Day 2	Day 3	Day 4	Day 5	Day 6	Day 7	Day 8	Day 9	Day 10	Total
Count (entire list)	7	6	2	7	1	2	4	3	2	1	35
Count for Anyang Period (from K24)	1	3	0	3	0	1	2	2	0	0	12

TABLE 4. Frequency of day-names in Shang king list (from table 3).

inevitably occur in the names of multiple kings. Various disambiguating epithets are applied. For instance, the seven kings with day-name 1/10 are disambiguated as 'The Highest Day 1/10' (K1 in table 3), 'The Greater Day 1/10' (K9), 'The Lesser Day 1/10' (K12), 'Ancestor Day 1/10' (K30), and in the remaining three cases (K17, K20, K23) by more unusual prefixes of uncertain meaning.

Although all ten possible day-names occur in the list, their distribution appears neither uniform nor random. Some patterns in the sequence are more remarkable than others. Those that have previously attracted most notice are the following. The king list begins with six day-names in the ordered sequence 1–2–3–4–9–10 (K1–K6). After this opening sequence, kings named Day 4/10 tend to reappear with an interval of two generations, often separated by kings named Day 1/10 or Day 2/10. No fraternal or filial successor shares a day-name with his immediate predecessor. Some day-names are considerably more frequent than others (table 4).

No fully satisfactory account has been provided for any of these patterns, and how terms from the 10-cycle were assigned to individuals is not perfectly understood. They do, however, make it unlikely that the day-names relate (in any straightforward, un-manipulated manner) to a uniformly distributed random variable such as date of birth or death. Earlier proposals along those lines can be ruled out. Nevertheless, a great deal more information about Shang day-names and the early calendrical functioning of the three cycles can be recovered from archaeological evidence in the form of contemporary divination records and bronze inscriptions.

Late Shang divination records

Textual remains from the Late Shang period (ca. 1300–1050 BC) are overwhelmingly dominated, numerically speaking, by records of divination. Almost all of these records incorporate a cyclical date of some kind. These divination records were incised onto the bony parts of dead animals—most often turtle shells and scapulae of large mammals—that were themselves the instruments used in the pyro-osteomantic divination that the records served to document.[14] Although divination records are by far the most commonly attested textual genre at this stage, it is not obvious whether this points to a central role for divination record-keeping in incipient Chinese literacy, or to an accident of archaeological preservation and discovery.[15]

Pyro-osteomancy had been in widespread use throughout northern China from the latter half of the third millennium BC,[16] but without leaving any evidence of written documentation or its direct precursors. Over the course of the second millennium, this form of divination appears to have been practiced with growing frequency, reaching a peak of intensity at large, late second-millennium sites associated with the Shang royal lineage. It is during the reign of the Shang king Wu Ding (K27, ca. 1250–1200 BC), and during the high-point in the elite patronage of pyro-osteomancy, that evidence of its written documentation first appears. Over the course of the twentieth century, many tens of thousands of such records were recovered from the large complex of archaeological sites near Anyang, in northern China's Henan Province. Ongoing excavations continue to produce further examples.

To date, only one other site contemporary with Anyang has provided unproblematic evidence of the written documentation of divination. At the site of Daxinzhuang in Shandong, 250 km east of Anyang, in addition to approximately 1,000 fragments of bones and shells used in divination, a single example inscribed with multiple records has also been found.[17]

At Anyang, divinations were performed and recorded on a daily basis by multiple teams of specialists on behalf of Wu Ding and succeeding kings of the Shang dynasty, and for certain members of their immediate family. These teams of specialists are distinguishable from one another by the scribal hands that kept the records, the named diviners mentioned in the records, and the differing localities within the moated enclosure at the centre of the Shang-period complex at Anyang where the remains of their activities have been found.[18] The diviners and their patrons were preoccupied with the health and well-being of the Shang royal family, social and political interaction, the weather, success in hunting, the exchange of goods, and with the frequent sacrificial rituals towards dead royal kin that were the focus of religious activity at Anyang.

The majority of records specify the date of the divination using cyclical dates, but only exceptionally with supporting notations of the month or year.[19] The forms that cyclical dates take in the divination records are most easily explained by example. Consider the inscriptions on HD17 (figure 2).[20] This is one of approximately 500 inscribed divinatory plastrons and fragments that were found together in a single pit at Anyang in 1991.[21] The plastrons and the nearly 2,500 divination records inscribed onto them represent the output of a team of diviners working for a patron who was almost certainly a son of the reigning Shang king Wu Ding (K27). The patron is referred to in the records as *zi* 子, literally 'the child', to be understood as something like 'the prince'. Plastron HD17 appears to have been used many times for divination, and two of those occasions have been recorded in inscriptions on its surface. One of these reads:

(1) 甲辰，歲祖甲一牢，子祝。
Day 41/60, perform a *sui*-sacrifice to Male Ancestor Day 1/10 with one *lao*-ox, and with the Child invocating. (HD17)

The form of the sexagenary date notation used in divination records like these, consisting of a 10-cycle term (in this instance *jia* 甲 'day 1/10') followed by a 12-cycle term (*chen* 辰 'day 5/12'), is identical to that used in all later periods. The details of the *sui*-sacrifice, the *lao*-ox and the 'invocation' need not concern us here, and are in any case only imperfectly understood. The established understanding is that inscriptions like these record a proposition about an action to be performed that required validation or testing through divination. In this case, and in countless others like it, the proposition is that a particular

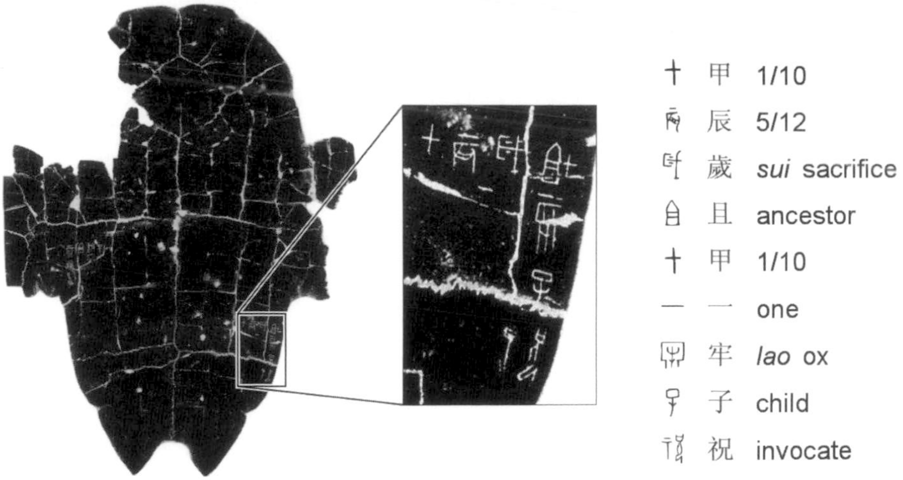

FIGURE 2: Plastron (HD17, ca. 1200 B.C.) bearing divination records with 60-cycle date notations. After: Zhongguo Shehuikexueyuan Kaogu Yanjiusuo (ed.), *Yinxu Huayuanzhuang dong di jiagu*. (Kunming: Yunnan Renmin Chubanshe, 2003), p. 102.

dead relative of the patron receive a particular kind of sacrifice on a particular day. Typically, the cyclical date that opens an Anyang divination record is explicitly marked as the date of the divination rather than of the proposed action, which may be some time later. In example (1), however, it is not made explicit whether the day 41/60 is the date of the divination or the sacrifice, but it is likely to be the date of both.

The recipient of the proposed sacrifice in (1) above is referred to by a combination of a kinship term and a term from the 10-cycle, in this case *zu* 祖 'male relative of grandparental or higher generation' and *jia* 甲 'day 1/10'. This combination of kinship term and 10-cycle term is the standard form for day-names for referring to dead relatives in all Shang-period texts.[22] The kinship term is determined by a combination of the sex of the sacrificial recipient and his or her generation relative to the divinatory patron proposing to perform the sacrifice (table 5). Although we are used to referring loosely to the Shang elite's ritualized relationship with their dead relatives as 'ancestor worship', it is worth noting that kin receiving sacrifice are by no means all 'ancestors' in the strict sense, since they include brothers, paternal uncles, paternal great-uncles, etc., and their wives. It should also be noted that, certainly for the royal lineage and perhaps for other Shang families too, several of the kinship terms refer to broader categories than their conventional English translations suggest. 'Father', for instance, can refer to paternal uncles as well as fathers, and the category 'Brother' probably includes half-brothers by different mothers, and cousins.

Sacrificial recipients with the same kinship term are distinguished from one another by the term from the 10-cycle which follows it. Unlike the kinship term, which varies depending on the relationship to the divinatory patron who is to perform the sacrifice, the term from the 10-cycle is fixed for any given recipient, no matter who is divining about the sacrifice. The Anyang period king Wu Ding (K27), for example, would be referred to

Generations older than ego		Male		Female
2 or more	*zu* 祖	Paternal (great etc.) grandfather, and patrilineal great uncles.	*bi* 妣	Paternal grandmother and other wives of *zu*.
1	*fu* 父	Father and paternal uncles.	*mu* 母	Mother and wives of *fu*.
0	*xiong* 兄	Elder brothers (and cousins?)	——	
-1	*zi* 子	Sons (and nephews?)	——	

TABLE 5. Common kinship terms in Shang day-names.

as 'Father Ding' (i.e. Father Day 4/10) by kin of his children's generation, and as 'Ancestor Ding' (i.e. Ancestor Day 4/10) by younger generations.

The regular recipients of sacrifice mentioned in the Anyang divination records are for the most part precisely those individuals who appear in the Shang king list of the *Shi Ji*. Matching up the two sets of day-names was one of the foundational achievements of early scholarship on the Anyang inscriptions.[23] The divination records also refer frequently to sacrifice directed towards wives of members of the royal patriline, who are missing entirely from the received king list. Additional less frequently-occurring male day-names that cannot be matched with the king list are probably those of royal brothers who did not succeed to the kingship. Since almost all our examples of recorded divinations were produced under the patronage of a single family, and since that family targeted its sacrifices towards its own kin, the divination records provide no dependable examples of day-names belonging to individuals far removed from their patrilineal line of descent.[24] This restriction is compensated for by the evidence from bronze inscriptions reviewed below.

To return to example (1), it is not simply a coincidence that the date of the record, day 41/60, and the name of the sacrificial recipient both comprise the same term from the 10-cycle. A second record on the same plastron reads:

(2) 乙巳，歲祖乙一牢，𡆥祝。
Day 42/60, perform a *sui*-sacrifice to Male Ancestor Day 2/10 with one *lao*-ox, and with [unknown name] invocating. (HD17)

Day 42 (2/10 and 6/12), a day later than the date in (1), corresponds to the second day in the 10-cycle. The sacrificial recipient's day-name is Day 2/10. This well-known pattern, in which the day of a proposed sacrifice according to the 10-cycle corresponds with its recipient's day-name, does not hold in all cases. Nevertheless, the association is a strong one. Table 6 shows the frequency across the HD corpus with which the two sacrificial recipients from examples (1) and (2) occur in records dated with different 10-cycle terms. The majority of records have dates that correspond with the day-name of the sacrificial recipient they mention. The most common exceptions have dates one day earlier than the day-name of the recipient. These for the most part reflect divinations carried out a day before the sacrifice they are intended to validate.[25]

There is, then, a strong interrelationship between the notation of days using the Shang 60-cycle and the sacrificial performances of Shang religion. The evidence just reviewed

	Divination record dates										
Recorded Day (n/10)	1	2	3	4	5	6	7	8	9	10	Total records
Ancestor Day 1/10 (祖甲)	49	4	2	4	2	1	2	1	1	10	76
Ancestor Day 2/10 (祖乙)	17	53	2	7	2	1	2	3	0	3	90

TABLE 6. Dates of HD divination records concerning sacrifice to Ancestors Day 1/10 and Day 2/10.

suggests that the day-names are primarily indicators of the day on which an individual routinely received sacrifice.

A final point about the Shang-period use of cyclical terms that can usefully be made here is that, in the various applications to which they are put, the 10-cycle appears dominant. The 12-cycle plays a more ancillary role, serving merely to disambiguate the consecutive passages of the 10-cycle. For example, although dates in divination records are typically expressed with the 60-cycle as in (1) and (2) above, using a compound of terms from the 10-cycle and the 12-cycle, there are nevertheless many examples of the systematic use of the 10-cycle alone, to record days modulo 10.[26] The use of the 12-cycle alone, on the other hand, is rare enough to appear anomalous when it does occur.[27] Furthermore, the 'day-names' of sacrificial recipients draw only on the 10-cycle and never on terms from the 12-cycle.[28]

The primacy of the 10-cycle is also clear from the fact that scribes responsible for maintaining divination records conceived of the 60-cycle as comprising six ten-day weeks (*xun* 旬, etymologically 'cycle; round') each corresponding to a single passage of the 10-cycle. (These will simply be referred to as 'weeks' henceforth). This is reflected in both the format of the date tables used for training scribes (described above),[29] and also in the practice of 'divining for the week ahead' (*bu xun* 卜旬). Records of 'divining for the week ahead' document a series of divinations at ten-day intervals, each on the last day of a *xun*-week (i.e. on a day 10/10), sometimes accompanied by additional statements of events that transpired during the week. Scribal conventions also mark a distinction between future dates that lie within the current week, and dates that lie beyond its end. Although one could imagine the 12-cycle similarly, as a concurrent twelve-day week, there is little sign that it was thought of that way by the Anyang scribes, who seem to have had no term parallel with *xun* to refer to it.

'Day-names' on Late Shang bronzes

The day-names for recipients of sacrifice that occur in the divination records from Anyang belong overwhelmingly to dead members of the royal family—the Shang kings and their wives—going back many generations and into the first half of the second millennium BC. However, the use of day-names for deceased kin was not confined to the Shang kings at Anyang, but was shared by the Shang-influenced elite of a much broader region of North China during the latter part of the Anyang period and the immediately subsequent centuries. This is clear from numerous short inscriptions on bronze objects, most often ritual food or drinking vessels, that feature exactly the same compounds of kinship term and day-name as those used by the Shang kings. The consensus is that bronze vessels of this kind were employed in ritual feasts offered to deceased kin, procedures similar to the

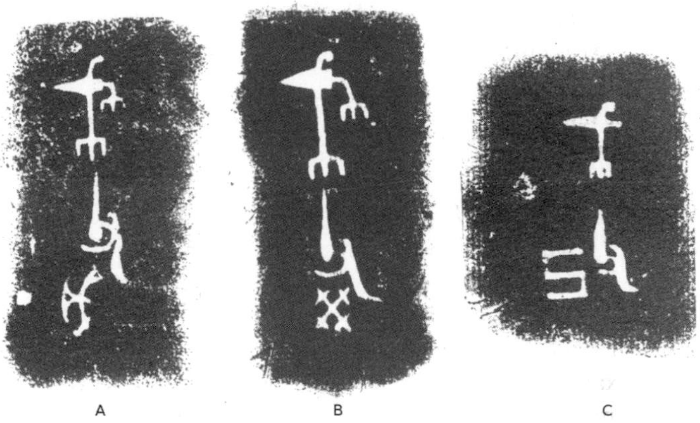

Figure 5: Day-name inscriptions on bronzes from Gaojiapu, each with the "dagger-axe" pictogram. A: Tomb M1, "Father Day 5/10". B: Tomb M3, "Father Day 10/10". C: Tomb M4, "Father Day 6/10". After: Shaanxisheng Kaogu Yanjiusuo, Gaojiapu Ge guo mu (Xi'an: San Qin Chubanshe, 1995), pp. 23, 63 & 75.

sacrifices that the Anyang royal diviners frequently validated through divination. A day-name that appears on one of these bronze vessels is assumed to indicate the dead relative to whom the object was dedicated.

A second category of Late Shang bronze inscription is made up of the so-called 'clan signs' or 'lineage emblems' (*zuhui* 族徽).[30] These can occur either independently or together with day-names on the same bronze (as in figure 3). In contrast to the day-names, the clan signs are typically composed of more obviously pictographic elements only loosely related to the script proper. The tendency for the same clan-sign to occur repeatedly in a single cemetery is the main reason why these are understood to indicate affiliation with descent groups of some nature.[31]

A third category of inscriptional content specifies the name of what might be called the maker or donor, or perhaps commissioner, of the bronze. Again, content of this kind can occur either with or without the other categories just mentioned. Inscriptions that go beyond these three simple categories are exceptionally rare during the Anyang period.

Inscriptions of these kinds on bronzes are, like the divination records, unknown prior to the Anyang period. Among the earlier examples of inscribed bronzes from Anyang are those from the only intact tomb of a member of the (nuclear) royal family to have been excavated, that of Fu Hao 婦好 ('Wife Hao'). She was one of the spouses of Wu Ding (K27) and was buried with over 1,600 kg of bronze objects. She was also probably the mother of the patron of the HD divination records mentioned above.[32] The name 'Fu Hao' appears frequently, referring to a living individual, in divination records from the time of Wu Ding. Its appearance on many of the bronzes from the tomb, presumably cast and used during her lifetime, is the primary grounds for the identification of the tomb occupant. A second group of bronzes from the same tomb included two massive (120 kg each) quadripod vessels inscribed with the day-name 'Mother Day 8/10' (母辛).[33] Divination records make it clear that one of the wives of Wu Ding received sacrifice after her death under the day-name Day 8/10. The inscriptions from the tomb invite the conclusion that this day-name and 'Fu Hao' refer to the same individual. Fu Hao's day-name would then be one the very few that are known to occur in both divination records and bronze inscriptions. The identification is also significant in showing that the dedicatee of ritual bronzes buried in a tomb, and the referent of day-names inscribed upon them, can be the tomb occupant herself, as well as her deceased kin. Since day-names seem to have been exclusively posthumous appellations, it is likely that those bronzes from Fu Hao's tomb that bear her day-name were specially cast by one or more of her children in the interval between her death and her burial.

By the end of the Anyang period, a comparable use of day-names on ritual bronzes found buried in tombs had become widespread throughout northern China, from the Wei river valley in modern Shaanxi in the west, to the East Coast province of Shandong, an east-west range of over 1,000 km. Simple bronze inscriptions are the only known regularly-occurring examples of the Shang writing system outside Anyang. Their geographic distribution implies a widespread familiarity among northern Chinese elites with the 10-cycle and an apparently consistent understanding of its religious applications, but not necessarily with any more complex Shang calendrical schemes.

Many sites could be selected to illustrate the deployment of Shang-style day-names and clan-signs in mortuary contexts outside Anyang, and thus to demonstrate the geographically distributed nature of the day-name tradition towards the end of the second millennium.[34] Here we examine briefly the inscriptions from the cemetery at Gaojiapu, located 540 km away from Anyang, in Jingyang County, Shaanxi.[35] The four elite burials (M1–M4) that were excavated at the cemetery all date to around 1000 BC, at the very end of the Shang occupation of Anyang or during the early reigns of the Western Zhou (ca. 1050–771 BC).[36] Between them, these four tombs contained 140 kg of bronze ritual objects, and extensive evidence for their use in ritual feasting on the occasion of the burial. Many of the tripod and quadripod vessels contained deer, sheep or ox bones, or the evaporated crust of cereal porridge. The remains of hemp binding around the handles suggested to the excavators that the vessels had been positioned in the tomb while still hot.

Twenty-seven of the bronze objects from the tombs bore inscriptions, including a number of clan signs and day-names. The presence of the 'dagger-axe' (*ge* 戈) pictogram in eight of the inscriptions, distributed across all four of the tombs, led the excavators and subsequent commentators to conclude that the four tomb occupants were members of a descent group that took the 'dagger-axe' as its identifying emblem. The following day-names occur (figure 3):

> Tomb 1 – Fathers Day 5/10 and Day 6/10,
> Tomb 2 – Fathers Day 4/10 and Day 8/10,
> Tomb 3 – Fathers Day 4/10 and Day 10/10,
> Tomb 4 – Ancestor Day 10/10, and Fathers Day 4/10, Day 5/10, Day 6/10 and Day 10/10.

If we can assume that something similar to the practices and terminology of the Shang royal family are at work here also, the bronzes dedicated to 'Fathers' can be taken to include vessels cast and used by the tomb occupant, dedicated to his fathers and paternal uncles. There are probably also bronzes cast by mourners a generation below the occupant and dedicated to the occupant himself, in the same manner as the Mother Day 8/10 bronzes from Fu Hao's tomb.

Unfortunately, little can be said about the relationships of the four tomb occupants to one another, and therefore to each others' inscriptional dedicatees, beyond some possibilities suggested by certain features of the bronzes and their inscriptions. For example an identical inscription mentioning both the day-name of the dedicatee (Father Day 4/10) and the personal name of the maker of the vessel occurs on two similar quadripod vessels from Tombs 3 and 4. Among the less convoluted explanations that could be imagined, is that the maker of the two vessels was the occupant of one of the tombs, and his Father Day 4/10 the occupant of the other. The two vessels could in that case have been cast at the same time, prior to the burial of Father Day 4/10. One was used in his interment ceremony and buried within the tomb, and the second retained for honouring the deceased in above-ground rituals, until it accompanied its maker into the second tomb.

When considering the appearance towards the end of the second millennium BC of geographically dispersed evidence for the 10-cycle, and of its Shang-style ritual use and written notation, a central question is whether this was due to routine and direct interaction with Anyang or whether the users of the 10-cycle were drawing on more ancient shared traditions. Several lines of argument converge on the likelihood that the adoption across much of North China of the 10-cycle and the uses we have been describing was a relatively rapid process under the influence of royal Shang models.

As we have noted, little evidence for literacy or its immediate precursors has been found in contexts earlier than Anyang,[37] nor does any category of text more complex than the simplest bronze inscriptions occur with any frequency at locations outside Anyang until after the fall of the Shang. The Shang script itself has traits that imply it is a recent innovation. The first excursion of the writing system beyond the focal point of its application in the ritual life of the Shang kings may well have been to disperse a system of nomenclature for deceased relatives among neighbouring elites. Certainly, no regionalisms have been detected among bronze inscriptions of the kind we have been considering: the forms of the day-names show no sign of local variation. Clan signs also recur at widely dispersed locations. The 'dagger-axe' clan sign, for example, which has its most concentrated presence with eight exemplars in the cemetery at Gaojiapu discussed above, also occurs at 27 other localities, including Anyang, spread across eight provinces during the Late Shang and Western Zhou periods, implying considerable mobility of the inscribed objects and their owners.[38]

The large numbers of bronzes with Shang-style day-names (1,610 according to a recent count)[39] makes it possible to generate informative summary statistics that would not be possible with the much more limited data from the Shang king list. These reveal striking patterns in the use of day-names that also suggest that these appellations for dead kin were employed inter-regionally in a remarkably consistent (and probably Anyang-centric) fashion. Several studies have found that every even-numbered day-name is far more popular than any odd-numbered day-name (figure 4),[40] although the odd-numbered names also occur frequently. The pattern is clearly visible for the male kinship terms (86% of 1,321 day-names are even), and probably holds also for the much less well-attested female ones (84% of 57 female day-names are even). Like the previously-mentioned patterns within the king-list, but with far greater statistical force, this tendency demonstrates that the assignment of day-names is not a simple reflection of any evenly-distributed variable such as date of birth or death, as K. C. Chang was the first to remark.[41]

A less salient trend is the contrasting distribution of male and female day-names. From the bronze inscription data, the male day-names appear to be weighted towards the earlier days in the 10-day week: 48% are days 2/10 and 4/10, rather than the 40% expected from

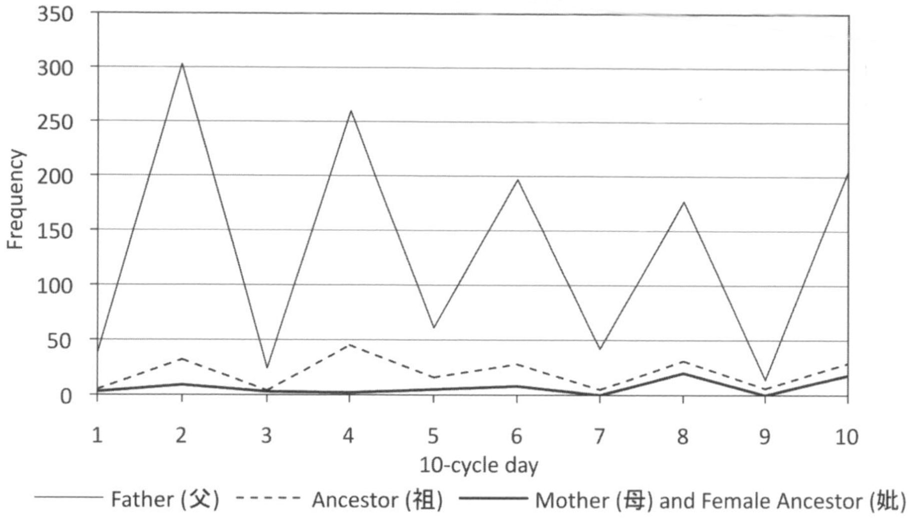

Figure 4. Frequency of 10-cycle day-names in bronze inscriptions. Chart redrawn from data in Yan Zhibin & Hong Mei (2008), p. 185.

an even distribution. Names of female kin are weighted towards the later days: days 8/10 and 10/10 make up 67% of the total (compared with the expected 40%).

Fu Hao, or posthumously Mother Day 8/10, is one of the very few possessors of a bronze-inscribed day-name whose spouse we can identify in the Anyang divination records. As mentioned previously, her husband can be identified as Wu Ding, posthumously named Day 4/10. We thus have a couple, of which the male has a day-name earlier in the week than his wife. Including Fu Hao, the day-names of twenty-two wives of Shang kings are known from the sacrifice divinations from Anyang. Nineteen of these are day-names later in the week than those of their husbands, and only three are exceptions to this tendency (K5, K6 & K19, see table 3).[42] Among the known royal wives, the three exceptions are additionally distinctive in that they are the only ones with husbands whose day-names occur in the last three days of the week, and they include the only two instances of wives with day-names at the very beginning of the week. Moreover, as mentioned previously, there are no instances of royal wives with the same day-names as their husbands.

Thus, the procedure for assigning day-names seems to have treated a Shang king and his wives as a unit, endeavouring to accommodate them on separate days within a single week with males ordered before females. When for whatever reason a male was assigned a more unusual day-name late in the week, there would be a likelihood that his spouse would 'roll over' to a similarly unusual (for a woman) day-name at the beginning of the following week. Similar procedural constraints are likely to have been behind the patterning of the bronze-inscription day-names noted above.

The counts of inscribed bronzes mentioned above, and their wide region of distribution, are striking. However, it is important to remind ourselves that the institution of the day-name can only be firmly associated with a very small portion of the late second-millennium population. It was only a very small proportion of individuals that had bronzes buried with them, and only a small proportion of those bronzes that had day-names inscribed onto them. For example, of the 939 Late Shang burials, predominantly of humble status, that were excavated from the 'western zone' cemetery at Anyang, only 61 tombs contained bronze ritual vessels, and only 14 day-names occur among the inscriptions.[43] Elite tombs can also sometimes surprise with an absence of day-name inscriptions. Tomb M160 from the Guojiazhuang cemetery at Anyang, although not furnished with quite the richness of Fu Hao's tomb, was nevertheless far more lavishly filled than the tombs from Gaojiapu discussed above, and contained 250 kg of bronze objects.[44] Forty-one of the ritual bronzes from the tomb are inscribed, in almost all cases with variants of a single emblem, presumably identifying the occupant or his kin group. The absence of any day-names implies that, if the ritual food and wine vessels were dedicated to dead kin in the usual manner, a rather different labelling convention was being followed from that of either the Gaojiapu tombs or that of Fu Hao.

The Procedure for Assigning Shang Day-Names: A Review of Candidate Hypotheses

Having surveyed the two major sources of contemporary evidence concerning the Shang use of day-names, we are now in a position to review attempts to elucidate the institution that lay behind it. Besides general plausibility within the cultural context, candidate hypotheses have to fulfil two criteria in order to be viable: they must explain, or at least comfortably accommodate, the distributional patterns described above, and they must account for the evidently calendrical nature of the day-name institution, that is, they must explain why the names given to dead kin are also names for days in the 10-cycle.[45]

Chang Kwang-chih, initially focusing only on the apparent regularities within the Shang king list, proposed a highly elaborate and unusual system of royal succession.[46] The Shang kings, according to Chang, were all members of a single clan. They were, however, divided into 'ten exogamous descent groups', with the same names as the ten days of the week. Successive Shang kings were alternately taken from these patrilineal descent groups, from some more frequently than others, but with the rule that no group could provide two successive kings. Successors were picked by a 'council of elders', and the ten groups bound together by cross-cousin marriage, so that kings would be maternal uncles of their successors.

Despite its evident shortcomings, Chang's proposal did much to stimulate renewed interest in the question, and continues to inspire kinship-based solutions of the day-names problem. Chang was also the first to produce statistical summaries of day-names in bronze inscriptions of the kind that we reviewed above. Nevertheless, the hypothesis is in conflict with too many independent lines of evidence to be in any way tenable. It requires that the all the assertions of paternity and fraternity in the received king list be rejected—neither the received king list nor contemporary texts give any sense that the kingship is alternating between different descent groups. It does nothing to explain why clans should be named after days of the week or why even-numbered clans should appear very much more often in bronze inscriptions than odd-numbered ones. The idea of rulership alternating by consensus between lineages is perhaps conceivable, but what version of this alternation could be imagined to apply to all the other elite lineages that used day-names?[47] Since membership of a descent group is determined by birth, it is odd that the names of Chang's ten groups are only ever used to refer to dead recipients of sacrifice. Finally, the patterns of male vs. female day-names become puzzling under Chang's interpretation—why do the descent groups that produce the most named males produce the fewest females?

Similar kinship-based models inspired by Chang's are vulnerable to the same objections. Zhang Fuxiang's proposal that day-names are matrilineal names is perhaps sociologically more credible, but again fails to account either for the patterns in the use of names or for the fundamentally calendrical nature of the institution.[48]

Ma Chengyuan, drawing attention to the principle of kings having day-names earlier in the week than their wives, proposed that divination was used to assign males a day-name as a 'courtesy name' (*zi* 字) at their coming-of-age 'capping ceremony' (guan li 冠禮), and to females at their betrothal.[49] The evidence of a central role for divination is appealing and will be considered in detail below. However, the evidence Ma offered in support of an association with the capping ceremony is exceedingly weak. Ma understood the capping ceremony primarily from compendia of ritual prescriptions that took their current form a millennium after the appearance of the 10-cycle and day-names.[50] Although similarities between prescriptions of the ritual compendia and attested Shang practice are in some spheres remarkable (we will examine some subsequently), continuity between the two must be demonstrated rather than assumed. The practice of choosing a 'courtesy name' at the coming-of-age is firmly established for the Eastern Zhou period (770–256 BC) upper classes, but this was a name for use by one's peers outside the family, not a posthumous name used by kin. Ma collected an interesting list from Eastern Zhou literary texts of names of living individuals that include 10-cycle terms, but this can readily be explained as a product of the ongoing interest in their calendrical or magical associations. Perhaps most puzzling in Ma's approach is the idea that the Shang would have attempted to distinguish themselves from one another socially using courtesy-names drawn from a repertoire of just ten possibilities.

A more promising account for Shang day-name usage can be arrived at by considering the interaction of three different aspects of Shang religious practice that have each been the subject of intensive discussion in the Chinese-language literature: funeral divination, funeral scheduling and an evolving calendrical structure that I will refer to as the 'Cyclical Sacrificial Roster' (CSR). The complexities of the CSR will be dealt with in the following section. Here we examine the evidence for funeral scheduling and the divinatory determination of day-names and funeral days.

The accidents of preservation and discovery have preserved for us a detailed divinatory record of the funeral of precisely one individual at Anyang, a royal wife, probably the wife of Zu Geng (祖庚, K29).[51] She has the title 'Lesser Queen' (*xiao hou* 小后), but since no phonological value has been identified for her personal name we will have to refer to her as 'Lesser Queen X'. There are at least eighteen divination bones or fragments thereof that mention this woman in the context of her funeral arrangements or her posthumous receipt of sacrifice.[52] Most of the divinations were performed by diviners Chu 出, Xiong 兄 and Da 大, three colleagues from a divination workshop. The inscriptions produced by this workshop are classified as the 'Chu Group' (*Chu zu* 出組) of divination records, named after the first of the diviners.[53] Since many of the records specify the month as well as a cyclical day, what might be called the 'microchronology' of this set of inscriptions is relatively clear.

In the eighth month of an unknown year, probably during the reign of Zu Geng, a routine 'divination for the week ahead' (*bu xun*) was performed on day 20/60. The record, which was copied onto two bones (HJ04962, HJ04963), is badly damaged. Enough remains to see that a 'verification' (*yan ci* 驗辭, a statement of 'what really happened' after the divination was performed) was added. It mentioned that on the subsequent day

26/60 an uncertain event involving Lesser Queen X took place. The following week her funeral was being planned, and so it is likely that the event was, or somehow involved, her death.

On day 33/60, in what must surely be the same eighth month, a divination was carried out by Diviner Chu testing the proposition,

(3) 作小后X日，惠癸。
In making a day for Lesser Queen X, it should be day 10/10.

The proposition appears on three separate bones (HJ23712–HJ23714). This divination seems to be the one that determined Queen X's posthumous day-name, the popular female name of Day 10/10. The following day, day 34/60, sees a flurry of divinatory activity related to the funeral process, and also to the selection of a new queen.[54] Subsequently, in the tenth month, and on days 50/60 and 20/60 in months unknown, we find divinations concerning sacrifice to Minor Queen X of sheep, oxen and humans. Note that the cyclical days for the sacrifices are both day 10/10, and thus match the previously determined day-name.[55]

Having reviewed late second millennium evidence that establishes a relationship between divination, funerals and day-name determination, we can now examine later literature for comparative examples and signs of cultural continuity. Two sources have been found to be especially relevant. The first are the ritual texts, the *Zhou Li* 周禮, *Yi Li* 儀禮 and *Li Ji* 禮記, which probably reached their present form during the last centuries of the first millennium BC but nevertheless contain material reflecting institutions and practices of varying dates across the first millennium.[56] The second is the so-called *Springs and Autumns* (*Chun Qiu* 春秋) chronicle of the state of Lu 魯, which documents a selection of significant events, including deaths and funerals, over the span from 722 to 481 BC. The chronicle preserves chronological information with considerable accuracy, and of a kind that could not readily be constructed retrospectively but which would have required contemporary record-keeping (the solar eclipse records in the text will be discussed subsequently).[57]

Inoue Satoshi was the first to link the prescriptions of the ritual compendia and the funeral dates in the Springs and Autumns with the evidence for Shang practice, in particular the day-name frequency data collected by K.C. Chang.[58] Inoue's treatment of the testimony in received textual sources has been extended considerably by Yu Wanli in a recent article on names and appellations during the Shang and Zhou periods.[59] To these should be added an important paper by Liu Xu that provides a complete tabulation and analysis of the funeral dates in the Springs and Autumns.[60]

Inoue's contribution was to recognize that the Shang bias in favour of even-numbered day-names is matched by an even more absolute bias in favour of even-numbered days for funerals recorded in the Springs and Autumns. This accords with prescriptions in the ritual texts and their early commentaries that funeral events take place on even-numbered days (so-called 'soft days' *rou ri* 柔日) to be determined by divination. Inoue concluded that the day-name was simply the day of interment (*zang ri* 葬日) determined according to such a procedure.

Yu Wanli makes the important observation that the interment itself was not the only stage of the funeral process that required scheduling. Other post-burial ritual performances specified by the ritual texts include a repeated procedure (*yu* 虞) for 'settling' the interred, and another (*fu* 祔) after the 'termination of wailing' (卒哭) for accommodating the deceased together with other kin as a recipient of regularized sacrifice in the lineage temple. The ritual texts and their commentaries make similar prescriptions about these later funerary activities taking place on even-numbered days, though not on the same 10-cycle day as the burial. Yu makes the specific claim that the Shang day-names reflect the 10-cycle day of the *fu* procedure, when the deceased was installed in the lineage temple. The (even) number of days between the burial and the *fu* procedure is, according to Yu's reconstruction, a function of the social rank of the deceased, while the day of burial is determined by divination.

Yu's scheme is appealing as a sketch of how the Shang day-names might be linked to divination, burial and the initiation of sacrificial routine. However, it also stretches the methodology of comparing the ritual texts with the second millennium evidence beyond plausible limits, resulting in a misleadingly precise conclusion—the identity of the Shang day-name with the day of the *fu* procedure. The terminology of the ritual texts is largely alien to the Shang period inscriptions. There is no sign from the divination records that *fu* or *yu* procedures were distinguished by the Shang, still less that they were scheduled according to Yu's reconstruction. The terminology and scheduling of Minor Queen X's funeral arrangements for example, to the extent that they can be made out, appear to be entirely different. The terminology of 'hard' (odd-numbered) and 'soft' (even-numbered) days is similarly a product of late first-millennium BC, and not inherited from the Shang.

Although there is continuity between the second and first millennia in the use of the 10-cycle to schedule elite funerals, there are clear differences also. The data from the Springs and Autumns presented by Liu Xu is particularly valuable in this respect. Liu tabulates all 35 records of burials (*zang*) that specified the 60-cycle date on which the event was scheduled to take place.[61] All are burials of the highest ranking aristocrats, that is, rulers of states and their wives. Of these 35 burials, only one is scheduled on a 'hard' or odd-numbered day.[62] This is clearly distinct from the Shang day-names, where odd-numbered day-names, though the minority, are nevertheless common in both the bronze inscriptions and the king list. The relative frequency of the five 'soft days' also differs from the Shang model: days later in the week are distinctly more frequent than earlier days (figure 5), despite the great majority of the deceased being male.

In summary, there is good evidence that divination played a role in the assignment of Shang day-names after death, and in funerary arrangements more generally. Divination can accommodate the right mix of deterministic and aleatoric procedural constraints (as well as human manipulation) of the kind that might have produced the statistical patterns discussed above. The favouring by elites of the first-millennium of even-numbered days for burials, determined by divination, likely represents inheritance with modification of aspects of Shang funerary procedures and their symbolic imprint on the system of cyclical days. Second- and first-millennium elites were both commemorated ritually in lineage temples, and the Shang day-names reflected the day of the 10-cycle on which that commemoration typically occurred. However, there is no grounds for thinking that the day-name was set by an event in the Shang funerary schedule, either the burial or any other, that can be simply identified with procedures known from later texts.

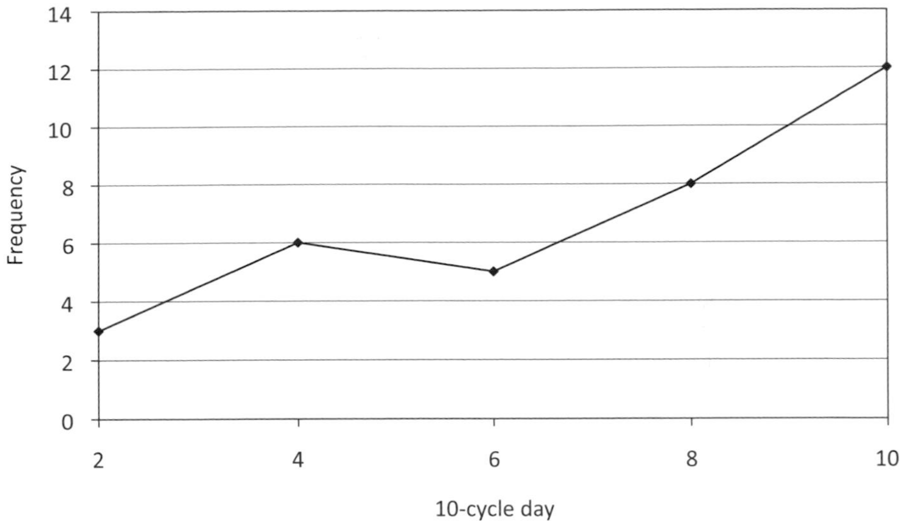

Figure 5. Distribution of 34 even-numbered funeral days in the Springs and Autumns. Chart prepared from data in Liu Xu (1994), table 3, p. 195.

The Cyclical Sacrificial Roster

What I will refer to here as the 'Cyclical Sacrifical Roster' (CSR, *zhou ji zhidu* 周祭制度) is a complex structure based, ultimately, on the 10-cycle, that was used to schedule ritual procedures performed on behalf of the current king, and directed at his dead predecessors and their wives. It illustrates how the wish to schedule the royal family's commemoration of dead kin drove the evolution of mechanisms capable of tracking events and processes over long periods of time. Indeed, the written documentation that sustained the CSR may have provided important systematic data to stimulate interest in predictive, as opposed to observational, timekeeping.

The existence of the CSR has been known about since Dong Zuobin's pioneering attempt in the 1940s to reconstruct it on the basis of Anyang divination records. Reconstructions based on his work continue to be refined and applied to chronological questions, specifically to the absolute dating of the reigns of the last few Shang kings. The demonstration that the *Shi Ji* king list was substantially accurate, and corrections of its errors of detail, were dependent on the reconstruction of the CSR. Problems and uncertainties remain in aspects of the reconstruction, but the system of the CSR is understood in great detail. What follows is a necessarily highly compressed summary, focusing on the results of reconstruction efforts and only alluding to the elaborate argumentation that lies behind them.[63]

We noted previously, in discussing citations (1) and (2) above, the tendency, visible in the earliest records from Anyang, for kin to receive sacrifice on their name-days. A second tendency is for kings to receive sacrifices in the order of their succession. The CSR seems

S1	S2	S3	S4	S5
翌	祭	𧶠	劦	彡

TABLE 7. The five procedures of the Cyclical Sacrificial Roster.

to have emerged through a progressively stricter application of these two principles to a king list that grew with the death of each king.

Five kinds of sacrifice are regulated according to the CSR. Table 7 shows conventional transcriptions of the graphs used in the divination records to write the sacrificial procedures.[64] Since in several cases we have no readily typeable transcription or romanization for their names, I will simply refer to them as S1 through S5. During the periods when the CSR can be shown to be in operation, it is not the case that all sacrifices are scheduled according to the CSR. Even sacrifices S1–S5, or those to kings and their wives that feature in the roster, can be scheduled outside as well as within the scheme of the CSR. Only sacrifices of type S1–S5 that can be shown to be scheduled according to the complex arrangement based on day-name and order of succession to be described below are considered instances of the CSR in operation.

The CSR is most completely understood from 365 inscriptions in the so-called Huang Group of divination records, which date to the last three reigns at Anyang (K33–K35, ca. 1100–1050 BC). The Chu Group (which includes the divinations about Minor Queen X discussed above), includes 140 further examples dating to the reign of Zu Jia (K30, ca. 1150 BC). A continuous evolutionary history can probably be presumed for the CSR outside the testimony of these chronologically disjoint groups, but insufficient inscriptions from the interim are available to reconstruct it to any degree. As we will see, the CSR was still evolving during the period of the Chu Group inscriptions, but had reached a stable state before the time of the Huang Group records.

The CSR provides a schedule according to which all five of the sacrificial procedures (S1–S5) could be applied, one after the other, to an uninterrupted sequence of kings in the king list, in order of royal succession, and to their wives. Shang Jia (K1), the first Shang ancestor to have a day-name, begins the sequence. The list of kings appearing in the roster had not yet reached its greatest extent during the period of the Chu Group records. In the Chu Group records, it terminated with Zu Geng (K29), referred to (from the perspective of his younger brother, Zu Jia, K30) as 'Elder Brother Day 7/10'. From the later Huang Group records, it can be seen that the list was subsequently extended to include Zu Jia (K30) and Kang Ding (K31), but no further. K32–34 were not incorporated into the CSR by their successors.[65]

Table 8 shows the schedule according to which the CSR sacrifices were performed to each of the kings and their wives. The same schedule was followed for each of the procedures S1–S5, but staggered at intervals as described below. The schedule was spread over nine weeks during the period of the Chu Group records, and over ten for the Huang Group.

The following principles can be seen to apply:

1. Kings and wives receive sacrifice on their personal name-days (cf. table 3).
2. No two kings occupy the same slot, nor do any two wives (with one exception

	Day 1	Day 2	Day 3	Day 4	Day 5	Day 6	Day 7	Day 8	Day 9	Day 10
Week 1	K1	K2	K3	K4					K5	K6
Week 2		K7		K8			K5:7			
Week 3	K9 K6:1		K10 K7:3		K8:5		K11	K9:8	K11:9	
Week 4	K12				K13	K14			K13:9	
Week 5				K15		K15:6			K16	K15:10
Week 6	K17	K18				K18:6	K18:7	K19		
Week 7	K20 K19:1			K21		K21:6	K22 K21:7			
Week 8	K23						K24	K25		
Week 9		K26		K27		K28	K29 K26:7	K27:8 (Fu Hao)		K27:10
Chu Group CSR ends here										
Week 10	K30			K31	K27:5 K30:5			K31:8		

TABLE 8. CSR schedule of sacrifices to 31 kings and 20 wives (after Chang Yuzhi 1987, p.110). Kings are indicated by their K-numbers from table 3. Wives are indicated by their husband's K-number, followed by the number of their own day-name. Thus Fu Hao appears as K27:8, since she is wife of K27 (Wu Ding) and named 'Day 8/10'.

mentioned below), though a king and another's wife may occupy a single slot.

3. Kings are in order of their succession.
4. Wives fill the first available slot after their husbands, and after all wives of earlier kings have been accommodated. Notice, for example, how this last rule pushes wives K6:1, K7:3 and K8:5 into a later week than might otherwise be expected, due to the precedence of K5:7.
5. Only wives of kings on the main line of descent are represented in the CSR. Remember that because of instances of fraternal succession (table 3), some kings are not strict ancestors of their successors. Those kings are present in the CSR but their wives are not.

The exception to rule 2 is in Week 10 (Huang Group only), where the two wives K27:5 and K30:5 occupy the same slot on day 5/10. K27:5 could not have been placed in the open slot in the previous week because of the precedence of K26:7. K30:5 would thus be expected to occupy a slot in a subsequent Week 11. A Week 11 could also have accommodated Kings K32 and K33. However, although the CSR was extended by a week after the period of the Chu Group inscriptions, it was not extended again to include additional weeks. This is so even during the reigns of K34 and K35, who might be expected to have done so, and who did in fact offer non-CSR rituals to those of their predecessors whom such an extension could have accommodated. The probable rationale for this will

<table>
<tr><th></th><th>S1</th><th>S2</th><th>S3</th><th>S4</th><th>S5</th></tr>
<tr><td>Week 1</td><td>Presentation of S1 Roster</td><td colspan="4"></td></tr>
<tr><td>Weeks 2–11</td><td>S1 Sacrifices</td><td colspan="4"></td></tr>
<tr><td>Week 12</td><td></td><td>Presentation of S2 Roster</td><td colspan="3"></td></tr>
<tr><td>Week 13</td><td></td><td rowspan="3">S2 Sacrifices</td><td>Presentation of S3 Roster</td><td colspan="2"></td></tr>
<tr><td>Week 14</td><td></td><td rowspan="3">S3 Sacrifices</td><td>Presentation of S4 Roster</td><td></td></tr>
<tr><td>Weeks 15–22</td><td></td><td rowspan="3">S4 Sacrifices</td><td></td></tr>
<tr><td>Week 23</td><td colspan="2"></td><td></td></tr>
<tr><td>Week 24</td><td colspan="3"></td><td></td></tr>
<tr><td>Week 25</td><td colspan="4"></td><td>Presentation of S5 Roster</td></tr>
<tr><td>Weeks 26-35</td><td colspan="4"></td><td>S5 Sacrifices</td></tr>
<tr><td>Week 36</td><td colspan="5">Rest Week</td></tr>
</table>

TABLE 9. The 36-week CSR during the period of the Huang Group (after Chang Yuzhi 1987, pp. 191–200).

be considered below, but one consequence of the reluctance to extend the schedule was the cramming of the two 'Day 5/10' wives into the same slot in Week 10.[66]

Prior to the performances of a round of sacrifices according to the scheme of table 8, a week was given over to a procedure known in the divination records as the *gong dian* 工典. The precise meaning of this term is obscure, but the second word almost certainly refers to a written document of some kind. It will be translated here as 'Presentation of the Roster'. Including this 'Presentation of the Roster', a single round of any one of the five sacrificial procedures S1-S5 thus took eleven ten-day weeks. If performed head to tail, the five procedures would have taken 550 days to complete. However, reconstructions of the CSR have shown that sacrifices S2–S4 were performed staggered by a week, and also that a 'rest week' with no CSR-related activities completed the sequence (table 9) before the entire cycle was begun again.[67]

This brings the total time required for a complete round of the Huang Group CSR (five sacrifices, S1–S5, applied to 31 kings, K1–K31, and their wives) to 36 10-day weeks or 360 days, approximating the length of the solar year.[68] In addition, three sets of divination inscriptions individually attest to the insertion of an additional 'rest week', either after the 'Presentation of the Roster' for S1 (i.e. after the 1st week) or after the 'Presentation of the Roster' for S2 (after the 12th week). Either of these insertions would bring the period of the CSR to 370 days, a move probably intended to keep the running average of the period of successive CSR rounds close to a solar year.[69] The realization that the round of sacrifices could be used to approximate a solar year provides a reason for the apparent reluctance to extend the schedule of table 8 into an eleventh week. That would have brought the period of the entire cycle to a total of 390 days—too long to be a creditable approximation for the solar year—if the terminating rest-week and staggered arrangement of S2–S4 were to be retained. Any further extensions to include the last generations of Anyang kings would, if the basic shape of the CSR were to be conserved, have removed the period even farther beyond a year.

Maintaining and executing a complex scheduling apparatus like the CSR would presumably have required an explicit visual schema of some kind, the Shang equivalent of our tables 8 and 9, especially during episodes of the concurrent performance of S2–S4, when sacrifices to multiple kings and multiple wives might fall on the same day. The terminology of the 'Presentations of the Rosters' seems to refer to something of this nature. However, it is important to realize that no such complete document or table has been found, and we can only imagine what its visual and information-bearing characteristics might have been. Instead, the reconstruction of the CSR is dependent on local snapshots of its global structure provided by the records of divinations that were routinely performed to validate its progress or reassure its royal patrons that it was functioning correctly.

These CSR divinations follow a number of different formats. Some were performed at the initiation of the five sub-sequences, S1–S5. Others were 'divinations for the week ahead' (*bu xun*), done on the final day of a week to validate the sacrifices scheduled for the coming week. Others reference the sacrifices to be performed on a specific day. Because divination scapulae and plastrons were typically used multiple times, they often bear sequential records that can be used to track the progress of the CSR over several weeks. It is by chaining together these sets of sequential records that the global structure of the CSR has been pieced together.

Contemporary with the CSR of the Huang Group records, characterized by its potential for a controlled alignment with the solar year, there appears for the first time evidence for an interest in maintaining counts of years. Earlier inscriptions sometimes record a count of months within a year (as with the Lesser Queen X records discussed above), presumably counting lunations from some observed or stipulated beginning of the year, the nature of which remains obscure.[70] The early inscriptions refer to years only relatively, however, as for example in divinations about the prospects of a forthcoming agricultural year.[71] No counts of reign years are attested. This changes by the period of the Huang Group records, when the date of divinations begins to be recorded not just with 60-cycle dates, and sometimes lunation counts, but with reign years also. The notation of years is applied to CSR divination records, to hunting and military campaign divinations, and also to a small number of longer bronze inscriptions that begin to appear during this period.[72]

The decisive role that the existence of the 360- to 370-day CSR is likely to have played in inspiring this innovation is suggested by two things. First of all, the term used for 'year' in these notations (*si* 祀) is a word that in other contemporary and later contexts means something like 'sacrificial ritual' or 'religious service'. A 'year' was thus, etymologically at least, a ritual cycle. Secondly, the current position within the CSR (i.e. the current sacrifice S1–S5, or the current recipient from table 8) was used as a way of specifying dates of events that were not directly connected with the performance of the CSR itself.[73] Consider the following two dates excerpted from Shang bronze inscriptions:

(4) 甲子... 在十月又二，遘祖甲劦日，唯王廿祀。
Day 1/60 … in the 12th lunation, coinciding with the S4 sacrifice to Zu Jia (K30), being the 20th year (i.e. si 'sacrifice') of the [reigning] king.[74]

(5) 隹王六祀，彡日，才四月。
It is the [reigning] king's sixth year (i.e. si 'sacrifice'), an S5 day, in the 4th lunation.[75]

In both of these cases, the inscription on the bronze serves to commemorate its own manufacture consequent to a royal gift, an event not directly related to the status of the CSR which is used to mark the date. Note also that in (4) the position in the CSR is specified almost unambiguously, the only uncertainty being whether one of the additional 'rest weeks' discussed above has been inserted into the cycle. If no insertion has been made, the position in the cycle is the first day of Week 24 (i.e. Week 10 of S4), and the 60-cycle dates for all other events in that round of the CSR can be determined from the basis of the 60-cycle date given in the inscription (day 1/60).

It will be clear from the preceding presentation that complex dates of this kind, because they combine years, lunations and a ritual sequence with the rigid counts of the 60-cycle, hold out the promise of an absolute chronology for the period of the Huang Group records (reigns K33–35). This was one of the goals of Dong Zuobin's pioneering but now superseded reconstruction of the CSR in the 1940s. It remains a focus of contemporary studies, including those within the institutional framework of the Xia-Shang-Zhou Chronology Project.[76]

The basic procedure for deriving such an absolute chronology is clear. Relationships between dates put constraints on where within a lunation a particular 60-cycle date may fall, enabling one to determine a set (hopefully very small) of possible 60-cycle days for the new moon that began that lunation. Using tables of calculated new-moon dates, one may then derive a list of years in which the 60-cycle date of a new moon (in an appropriate season) belonged to that set. Although the procedure is clear, the assumptions that are required to carry it out are complex. To illustrate, I will summarize a recent argument used by Xu Fengxian to determine possible absolute dates for the reign of Di Xin (K35). Rather than attempting to assess the validity of the argument in its entirety, I will simply emphasize her explicit and implicit assumptions as they occur.[77]

Xu identifies 15 dated objects from the reign of Di Xin bearing notations of years (*si*), months, 60-cycle dates, and references to the current state of the CSR. These include a mixture of bronze inscriptions, divination records and an inscribed tiger bone (a hunting trophy). The first assumption, naturally, is that the reconstruction of the CSR that is being used, the philological treatment of the inscriptions, and the attribution of these objects to the reign of Di Xin, are all correct. A second is that the texts themselves contain no scribal errors affecting the dates. A third assumption concerns the minimum and maximum number of days in a month.[78] Under those assumptions, Xu claims that the data from these 15 objects is sufficient to derive the following constraint:

Day 53/60 (bing chen 丙辰*) in the first month of the second year of the reign (K35) must be either the first or the last day of that month.*[79]

To move from numbered months to astronomical new moons requires an additional decision about the nature of the Shang month. Xu assumes that the first day of the month will always be either the date of conjunction of the sun and moon (*shuo* 朔), or the first visibility of the new moon (*fei* 朏) which she takes to be one or two days after conjunction.[80] This gives six possible 60-cycle dates for the conjunction near the beginning of the first month of the second year of K35. Knowing the season in which the month fell, or equivalently, knowing the approximate point in the solar year from which the Shang counted their months, narrows down the number of possible years to which the date might correspond.

Xu takes the position, based on what appears to be rather modest evidence, that the first month of the year corresponded to the lunation in which the winter solstice fell (*jian zi* 建子), or the following lunation (*jian chou* 建丑), or the one after that (*jian yin* 建寅).[81] Xu's final explicit assumption, that the first year of the reign of Di Xin fell in the range 1100–1050 BC, depends on proposed dates for the Zhou conquest (set at 1046 BC by the Chronology Project to which her work is a contribution). With these limits, she finds fifteen possible correspondences of the day 53/60, falling in eight different years.[82]

One other assumption that is made in this argument, which remains unspoken, is that of unbroken continuity of the 60-cycle with later periods, when its correspondence with Julian days can be explicitly determined.[83] Although there is no positive reason to think that such a disruption to the 60-cycle ever took place, the issue of continuity in its use will be considered in the following section.

In considering reconstructions of the CSR and its probable role as a frame of reference for time-keeping, there is one additional aspect that should be mentioned, and which suggests (to this author at least) that some substantial unresolved problems remain in our understanding of the institution. We have discussed three separate phenomena that could all in some sense be taken to represent the beginning of the Shang year: the first numbered month of the year (when the year-count in *si* is incremented), the beginning of a new CSR round,[84] and some fixed season (or observable point such as a solstice) in the solar year. Given that periodically inserting intercalary months, and the additional 'rest week' in the CSR, are presumed to have been done with the aim of keeping both the first month and the ritual cycle aligned with the seasons, it is puzzling to find that current reconstructions imply that no such alignment was successfully maintained.

In Chang Yuzhi's reconstruction of the CSR for one reign, the beginning of the CSR (the 'Presentation of the Roster' for S1) drifts from a position at the end of the seventh month in the first year (*si*), to the beginning of the tenth month by the tenth year of the reign. This is substantially due to the fact that she reconstructs no intercalary months for this interval.[85] Her reconstructions for other reigns find the beginning of the CSR variously in the third, fourth or sixth months.[86]

Xu Fengxian takes a somewhat different approach to the reconstruction, correcting at least one error in Chang's analysis. Nevertheless, she concludes that a similar phenomenon is taking place: during the reign of Di Yi (K34), either the beginning of the CSR, or the first month, or both, were drifting rapidly against the backdrop of the solar year.[87]

Having described the functioning of the CSR, we are now in a position to make some concluding remarks about the question that we left behind in the previous section—the assignment of day-names and their patterning. We have already established that divination is likely to have played a role in the determination of the particular day from the 10-cycle with which a relative would be posthumously labeled. We have seen that one of the central roles of the day-name was to set the 10-cycle day on which the dead individual would routinely receive sacrifice. We also considered the possibility that funeral scheduling—the interment itself, or subsequent rituals serving to incorporate the deceased into the regular round of sacrifices—may have been reflected in the choice of day-name.

The positioning of kings within the CSR suggests a further rationale that may have informed the choice of day-name. Consider once again table 8 and notice that, apart from the exceptional (and wife-free) Week 1, a single week typically accommodates two to three kings, rising to four in the busiest Week 9. It seems likely that this represented a ritually pleasing and administratively tractable spacing of sacrificial events, compact but not crowded. Certainly, any assignment of the same day-name to successive kings (something which never occurs in the king list) would have resulted in a sparse ritual program for the week separating them in the CSR. Although the CSR is only clearly attested from the reign of K30, long after most of the day-names in the king list had been determined, it is nevertheless probable that it represents an evolved form of earlier patterns of sacrificial scheduling.

Continuity and Change After the Zhou Conquest

The production of divination records at Anyang, and all other significant elite activities at the site, terminated with the Zhou conquest (ca. 1050 BC).[88] From that date, all textual production shifted abruptly from a focus on the activities of the Shang kings and their family members, to a new preoccupation with events and perspectives centred on the Zhou court. The site at Anyang was largely abandoned and a new, eastern capital for the Zhou was founded at Cheng Zhou 成周 (now Luoyang), approximately 250 km to the southwest.

Many Shang cultural institutions were left to continue their gradual evolutionary development across the rupture of regime change. The writing system in particular, and the language it was used to write, continued into the first millennium, initially without dramatic change. So too did the technologies required to produce bronzes and ritual objects in other media. Continuity of this kind likely represents continuity in patronage of those families of technical specialists who had been employed at Anyang. Both contemporary evidence and later literary accounts can be used to support a picture of the redeployment of expertise from Anyang to Cheng Zhou, and to other major centres of the Western Zhou (ca. 1050–771 BC) state.

The Western Zhou calendar, too, for the most part retained the fundamental properties that it had had during the last reigns at Anyang. A count of years, presumed to be approximations of solar years, was maintained for each king's reign. The term for the count of reign years inherited from Anyang, *si* 祀 '[round of] sacrifice', probably a terminological by-product of the mature CSR as we have seen, was gradually over the course of the Western Zhou displaced by *nian* 年, a term meaning 'harvest' in the Shang inscriptions but stripped of that sense in its use in the Western Zhou and later calendars. Lunations were counted for each year, from a point within the year that was probably routinely determined by seasonal observation of uncertain accuracy, rather than by dependable long-term calendrical calculation. The location of this start of the year, from which the months were numbered, is conjectured to have been close to the winter solstice, on the assumption of continuity with the later royal Zhou calendar reflected in the *Springs and Autumns* chronicle (722–481 BC). The existence of an early Western Zhou bronze dated by inscription to a '14th month' certainly implies that determinations of the start of the year and the placement of intercalary months were at times haphazard.[89] The 60-cycle continued its role as the only means of maintaining a count of days.[90]

For the Western Zhou period, there is no conclusive means of demonstrating that the 60-cycle was uninterrupted, either in its progress from the earlier Shang period, or onwards to later periods when the mapping of Julian days to 60-cycle days can be performed with complete confidence. Conceivably, the 60-cycle could have been reset in an assertive act of calendrical reform. However, no trace of such a move is to be found in any text, and scholarly doubts about the continuity of the 60-cycle are seldom raised.[91]

An argument for unbroken continuity might emphasize the functions and significance of the 10-cycle beyond the sphere of the calendars maintained under the direct control of the Zhou court and their Shang predecessors. We noted previously the geographically dispersed occurrences of bronzes bearing day-name dedications, notationally indistinguishable from contemporary models at Anyang, which suggest that elite groups across much of North China were, before the end of the second millennium, already synchronized with respect to the 10-cycle, and carrying out ancestral rituals scheduled with reference to it. Although the royal Zhou lineage seems to have shown no interest in constructing anything similar to the CSR, and employed a different terminology for referring to dead ancestors, many families living under and participating in the Zhou regime continued to employ the day-name system in commemorative bronze inscriptions.[92]

The best-known such family deposited a spectacular hoard of bronzes, many with lengthy inscriptions, at a location near the modern village of Zhuang-Bai in Fufeng County, Shaanxi, which was excavated in 1976.[93] The bronzes were cast on behalf of multiple generations of the same patriline, and span the stylistic range of the Western Zhou period. Four generations of the partriline are referred to in the inscriptions using posthumous day-names (Day 2/10, Day 8/10, Day 2/10, Day 4/10).[94] A number of features of the bronzes and their inscriptions invite the conclusion that this lineage transferred its loyalty, and its literate and administrative expertise, from the Shang to the Zhou around the time of the Conquest. Other Western Zhou bronzes that employ day-names in their inscriptions have similarly been associated with families of pre-Conquest Shang affiliations.[95] Whether or not the use by certain elite families of day-names in the Shang manner should be understood in terms of a persisting and distinctive Shang identity, it certainly implies that any resetting of the 10-cycle would have had consequences beyond the royal calendar and considerable cultural inertia to overcome.

The use of day-names declined noticeably, however, over the course of the Western Zhou, and they were extinct before the middle of the first millennium.[96] This decline in the earlier religious or ritual significance of the cyclical terms seems to have made possible a projection onto them of modified significations, often of a magical nature, and a redeployment of the cyclical terms for a much more diverse set of uses than previously. For unknown reasons, day 24/60 (*ding hai* 丁亥) becomes overwhelmingly popular as the date for a bronze inscription. The tendency towards the use of this 'auspicious day' is already apparent toward the end of the Western Zhou, and during the Eastern Zhou period (770–256 BC) a majority of inscriptions with 60-cycle dates bear this particular date.[97] Whether days 24/60 were in fact given over to the casting of bronze vessels, or whether the date is merely a conventionalized fiction is impossible to determine. The patterning of funeral days in the *Springs and Autumns*, discussed above, is another phenomenon that seems to reflect distantly the Shang application of cyclical dates for scheduling significant events, but stripped of the original specificities of their ancestral cult.

A proliferation of calendars, in simultaneous use by the multiple independent, literate states that asserted themselves during the Eastern Zhou period, was probably another stimulus to experimentation and speculation regarding the 10- and 12-cycles and their possible human and cosmological correlates. However, perhaps precisely because of the difficulties of inter-state timekeeping using multiple calendars, the 60-cycle count of days was the one constant feature amongst the competing counts of reign-years and lunations. The period of the *Springs and Autumns* annals (722–481 BC) is the first time that dates kept using the 60-cycle can be mapped to Julian days beyond any doubt.

The *Springs and Autumns* contains 37 accounts of solar eclipses during its 240-year span, all but three of which are recorded with a 60-cycle day, as well as a month and year according the calendar of the state of Lu.[98] Although the nature of the Lu month (the schedule of intercalary months, the pattern of alternation of long months with short, and the positioning of the first month of the year) is still not entirely agreed upon, the seasons in which the numbered months occur and the absolute years of the successive reigns are known. This makes possible a demonstration that 31 of the eclipse records accurately document real eclipses. Three of them, moreover, are accurate records of near-totality.[99] The argument for this conclusion is normally presented with 60-cycle continuity as an assumption. However, the density of the recorded observations of solar eclipses also means that the argument can be turned around to demonstrate that only one possible mapping from Julian days to the 60-cycle is compatible with the records.[100]

The final great diversification in the applications of the 60-cycle and its sub-cycles took place during the Warring States period (mid 5th century – 221 BC), as a reflection of what Donald Harper has referred to as "the idea that all phenomena and human activity were linked in microcosmic synchronicity", a dominant thread in the intellectual history of the late Warring States period.[101] We have already reviewed the earlier history of the use of 60-cycle days as 'lucky days', significant for the scheduling of significant social or religious events. This practice continued in a much more elaborated fashion during the Warring States and into the Qin (221–206 BC) and early Western Han (206 BC – 25 AD). 'Day books' (*ri shu* 日書) consisting of tables categorizing cyclical days according to their fitness for a variety of activities, including religious procedures, divination, child birth, illness, marriage, journeys and building projects have been recovered from a number of late 3rd century and early 2nd century tombs, the most complex and intensively studied of which are those from Shuihudi tomb 11, sealed ca. 217 BC.[102]

A more innovative departure is the application of the 12-cycle to a division of the constellations (*xing xiu* 星宿), and to the periods of time marked by the passage of heavenly bodies through those divisions. The earliest representation of these constellations occurs in the form of a lacquer-painted diagram on a clothes chest from the late 5th century tomb of Zeng Hou Yi 曾侯乙 .[103] The names of the 28 constellations are distributed in a ring, around a depiction of the Big Dipper at the centre. The process that led to the partition of these 28 constellations into twelve clusters and their correlation with the terms of the 12-cycle is not fully clear. However, it was probably inspired by the observation of two phenomena that have periods of approximately 12 when expressed in appropriate units. The first is the orbit of Jupiter, with a period of just under twelve years (11.86 years). The second is the solar year, taking somewhat more than twelve lunar months. The approximate coincidences of these two periods with the number of terms in the 12-cycle, the only duodecimal cycle available from earlier Chinese textual history, presumably motivated the adaption of the 12-cycle to this innovative use. The fact that both the orbit of Jupiter and the solar year can be tracked by observing the positions of the respective heavenly bodies against the backdrop of the *xing xiu*, provided a common rationale for the grouping of those constellations into twelve clusters. The orbit of Jupiter was presumably of interest from a purely astronomical or astrological point of view. Keeping the lunar calendar aligned with the solar year, on the other hand, was a priority for administrative timekeeping and state calendars.

The first extant text explicitly to fix the twelve months of the year to the position of the sun among the constellations is the *Yue Ling* (月令 'Monthly Ordinances') compiled in the 3rd century BC.[104] The correlation with the 12-cycle is made explicit in a number of other visual and textual representations from the 3rd and 2nd centuries BC. The earliest of these may be an astrological instrument (*shipan* 式盤) from Wangjiatai tomb 15, in Jiangling, Hubei, dated to the mid-3rd century, although only a brief verbal description has been published.[105] The instrument consists of a wooden board indicating the Five Phases, the 'months' (whether numbered, or indicated by the 12-cycle, or both, is not clear from the description), and the *xing xiu*. The 12-cycle and the numbered months are clearly present on a more complex version of the same piece of equipment from the tomb of Xiahou Zao 夏侯竈 in Fuyang, Anhui (165 BC).[106] Like the clothes chest from the tomb of Zeng Hou Yi, mentioned above, this instrument also bears a depiction of the Big Dipper. Observation of the orientation of the Dipper provided an alternative and equivalent means of tracking the progress of the solar year, and the twelve orientations of the Dipper were similarly mapped to the terms of the 12-cycle. The Huai Nan Zi 淮南子 (c. 139 BC) is the earliest received text to document the seasonal orientations of the Dipper and their mapping to the terms of the 12-cycle.[107]

Although the movement of Jupiter through twelve divisions is likely to have motivated the adoption of the 12-cycle as a way of counting years, its long-term use as a year-count is handicapped by an accruing discrepancy: after 84.7 years, Jupiter is precisely one term ahead in the cycle.[108] This discrepancy may already have been noted by the 3rd–2nd century BC, and prompted the decoupling of the 12-cycle year count from the observed motion of Jupiter.[109] Interestingly, an additional set of names for the years of the Jovian cycle also appears around this time. Although written using Chinese graphs, these polysyllabic names are etymologically opaque in Chinese and invite the suspicion that the technical vocabulary of some unidentified language was drawn upon, and rendered using Chinese phonetic transcription.[110]

For a cyclical year-count with a longer period, a natural move was to extend the 12-cycle count just described by combining it with the 10-cycle in precisely the same manner that had been used since the second millennium to count days. The earliest example of such a usage is an annotation on a diagram of the 60-cycle appearing among the silk manuscripts from Mawangdui tomb 3, sealed in 168 BC. An annotation marking the first year of the reign of Qin Shi Huang 秦始皇 (246 BC) is applied to the diagram next to the position of the 60-cycle term 52/60 (*yimao* 乙卯). Two later reign years are similarly marked on the diagram.[111] The correspondence between 60-cycle terms and years seen in the document from Mawangdui is identical to that in subsequent uninterrupted continuity throughout Chinese history, employed in parallel with counts of reign-years and entirely divorced from any synchronization with the orbit of Jupiter.

Notes

1. During the Han period (206 BC – 220 AD) and subsequently, the terms of the 10-cycle were known as the ten 'stems' (*gan* 干, or 'heavenly stems' *tian gan* 天干) and those of the 12-cycle as the twelve 'branches' (*zhi* 支, or 'earthly branches' *di zhi* 地支). The terms used to refer to the cycles at the time of their first appearance are unknown.
2. A number of influential general books on Chinese culture state that the 12-cycle at the time of its appearance was associated with the moon or counting months (e.g. de Bary (1999), p. 351 and Wilkinson (2000), p.177). I cannot find a basis for this claim in the specialist literature. Its first attested use as an indicator of a twelve-fold division of the solar year was not until the 2nd century BC.
3. A variety of spatial arrangements used during different historical periods are surveyed in Kalinowski (2007).
4. Kalinowski (2007) p. 158, fig. 3; Smith (2010).
5. Bartle (1978).
6. For proposals of a Babylonian origin for the 12-cycle, originally published in 1931, see Guo Moruo (1982). For suggestions of trans-Pacific connections, see Whittaker (1991). For possible Austronesian linguistic connections, see Norman (1985). Pulleyblank (1991; 1995) proposed that the cyclical signs corresponded to the 22 simple consonants he reconstructed for Old Chinese. None of these proposals has met with any general acceptance. There is an obvious connection between the 10-cycle and myths about ten suns (Allan 1991 ch. 2), although the literary texts in which the mythical accounts are preserved long post-date the first attestation of the 10-cycle. More recently, Pankenier (2010) has suggested connections between the origins of the cycles and specific early practices of astronomical observation.
7. The graph used to write 6/12 was redeployed to write 1/12 around the middle of the first millennium BC, hence the apparent mismatch between ancient and modern graph forms in table 1.
8. Dates are given according to those in Xia Shang Zhou Duandai Gongcheng Zhuanjia Zu (2000). Since all Shang dates are approximate or tentative, I will consistently round Shang dates to the nearest 50 years.
9. A recent English translation is provided by Nienhauser (1994), "The Yin, Basic Annals 3", pp. 41–54.
10. See the extensively annotated tables in Keightley (1985), pp. 185–187, 204–209.
11. Note that the succession is probably the sequence of appointed heirs, some of whom (e.g. K28) may not have inherited the kingship. The record of fraternal vs. filial succession ('Generation' and 'Son of' columns) is substantially dependent on the received *Shi Ji* rather than excavated sources. The royal wives on the other hand are known only from the texts excavated at Anyang.
12. This is to ignore the sequence of proto-ancestors that, in the *Shi Ji*, precedes the sequence of kings with day-names.
13. Yu Wanli (2006), pp. 38–39, provides a concise review of ancient and modern attempts to explain the Shang kings' day-names.
14. The best overview of the Shang divination records in English remains Keightley (1985), supplemented by Keightley (1997; 2000). For an up-to-date and comprehensive Chinese summary, see Wang Yuxin and Yang Shengnan (1999).
15. Bagley (2004) has argued that the divination records are a highly unrepresentative sample of Shang literacy, with more representative textual genres having been lost with the decay of the wood or bamboo on which they were written.
16. Flad (2008), p. 408.
17. Li Min (2008), pp. 156–221.
18. A detailed typological study of the Ayang divination records is provided by Li and Peng (1996), whose classificatory scheme is followed in this chapter.
19. One major class of exceptions is connected with the Cyclical Sacrificial Roster, described subsequently.
20. Abbreviations for published sources of inscriptions are given at the head of the list of references.
21. The primary publication for the HD inscriptions is Zhongguo Shehuikexueyuan Kaogu Yanjiusuo

(2003). HD numbers are given according to that publication. The most important study and authoritative edition of the texts is Yao Xuan (2006). For an English overview of the HD inscriptions, see Smith (2008), ch. 3, pp. 174–302.

22. In a minority of cases, more frequently on bronze inscriptions than in divination records, the word *ri* 日 'sun; day' is inserted between the kinship term and the day-name. This makes it especially clear that day-names for kin are derivative of names of the days of the week. See, for example, the three dagger-axes (*ge* 戈) inscribed with multiple day-names discussed by Ma Chengyuan (2002).
23. The identifications were first made by Wang Guowei in 1917 (Wang Guowei 1959, pp. 409–450; Wang Yuxin and Yang Shengnan 1999, p. 337).
24. The situation is only made moderately more complicated by the 'non-royal divination records' (*fei wang buci* 非王卜辭). These groups of inscriptions, contemporary with the reign of Wu Ding (K27), each use a distinct set of day-names that only partially aligns with those used by the king's diviners. However, it is likely that the divinatory patrons were close relatives of the Shang kings (Li Xueqin and Peng Yushang 1996, pp. 313–327).
25. Sometimes the record makes this explicit, as with a record dated Day 30/60 (i.e. a day 10/10) on HD426. The proposition reads, "Tomorrow, day 1/10, *sui*-sacrifice to Male Ancestor Day 1/10 ... at sunrise." Perhaps divination a day in advance was required to allow for preparations for a sacrifice early the next day.
26. Chang Yuzhi (1998), pp. 89–93, counts 268 examples of plastrons or scapulae on which dates recorded modulo 10 appear. Note, however, that in all the cases that she transcribes, the divination itself is dated modulo 60. The modulo 10 dates occur within the divinatory propositions and can be assumed to be within 10 days of the divination date. They are thus still unambiguous modulo 60. The HD corpus, published subsequent to Chang's survey, is distinctive in its frequent use of 10-cycle dates for dating the divination records themselves, as an alternative to the more usual 60-cycle dates, which are nevertheless also common with HD. The choice of one convention over the other within the HD corpus is correlated with the writing style of the scribes that produced the inscriptions (Smith 2008, pp. 246–253).
27. Chang Yuzhi (1998), pp. 93–95, counts nine examples and Gan Lu (2002) lists only 14 more from the entire available corpus.
28. The only exception is the distant and shadowy proto-ancestor Wang Hai 王亥, whose name appears to include the 12-cycle term Day 12/12 (Zhang Guangzhi 1983).
29. Smith (2010), pp. 181–189, figs. 6.1, 6.2, 6.3; Pankenier (2010), fig. 2.3, table 2.1.
30. He Jingcheng (2009); Barnard (1986).
31. During the Western Zhou period (ca. 1050–771 BC), there are demonstrable instances of the heritability of clan signs within patrilines. The best example is provided by the inscriptions from the Zhuang-Bai hoard, discussed subsequently.
32. For the excavation report, see Zhongguo Shehuikexueyuan Kaogu Yanjiusuo (1980); for a study of the inscriptions, see Cao Dingyun (1993); for the relationship with the HD patron, see Yao Xuan (2006); for scholarship in English, see the papers collected in Chang (1986), pp. 65–140.
33. Zhongguo Shehuikexueyuan Kaogu Yanjiusuo (1980), pp. 34–38, col. pl. 1; Cao Dingyun (1993), pp. 105–124.
34. Yan Zhinbin and Hong Mei (2008), p. 179, report 1,275 inscribed Shang-period bronzes from known locations, of which 867 are from Anyang. Figures provided by Venture (2002), p. 390, annexe iii, show that almost all these examples come from the five Central Plains provinces through which the Yellow River flows: Shaanxi, Shanxi, Henan, Hebei and Shandong.
35. Shaaxisheng Kaogu Yanjiusuo (1995).
36. Shaaxisheng Kaogu Yanjiusuo (1995), pp. 121–129.
37. The best candidates for written signs related to but earlier than the Anyang script are those found at the Middle Shang site of Xiaoshuangqiao (ca. 1450–1400 BC), brush written in red pigment on pottery vessels (Song Guoding 2003).
38. He Jingcheng (2009), pp. 113–123.
39. Yan Zhibin and Hong Mei (2008), pp. 184–185. The authors state that this is a count for 'Shang

period bronzes', implying that it excludes the many early Western Zhou bronzes with Shang-style day-names.

40. Chang (1978); Yan Zhibin and Hong Mei (2008), p. 185; Ma Chengyuan (2002), p. 199. All data used here are from Yan Zhibin and Hong Mei (2008).
41. Chang (1978), p. 17.
42. Ji Dewei [Keightley] (1989); Ma Chengyuan (2002), pp. 198–199. There are a number of minor points of disagreement in the scholarship matching royal wives' day-names to those of the kings. The 'Wives' day-names' column in my table 1 is based on the most sophisticated and comprehensive presentation, that of Chang Yuzhi (1987), pp. 113–138. For a comparison of the alternatives, see Wang Yuxin and Yang Shengnan (1999), p. 444, table 17.
43. Zhongguo Shehuikexueyuan Kaogu Yanjiusuo Anyang Gongzuodui (1979).
44. Zhongguo Shehuikexueyuan Kaogu Yanjiusuo (1998).
45. Here I selectively review only those proposals that, whether still viable or not, have contributed significantly to the current understanding of the functioning of the 10-cycle within attested Shang practice.
46. Chang (1978); Zhang Guangzhi (1983).
47. Zhu Fenghan (1990) has shown that the clan signs or lineage emblems on Shang bronzes are essentially free to co-occur with any day-name.
48. Zhang Fuxiang (2005).
49. Ma Chengyuan (2002).
50. For concise overviews of these anthologies of ritual usage, see their respective entries ("Li chi" & "I li") in Loewe (1993), pp. 234–243, 293–297.
51. For aspects of her status as a Shang queen and the identification of her husband, see Guo Xudong (2009).
52. HJ04962–3, HJ17097–8, HJ22559, HJ23708–19, HJ24951.
53. More precisely, in the scheme of Li Xueqin and Peng Yushang (1996), pp. 128–132, the inscriptions are assigned to Chu Group I Subgroup 2, dated to "the reign of Zu Geng [K29] or the very end of the reign of Wu Ding [27]."
54. The details are not entirely clear, but the graph identified as *yun* 蘊 'enclose; pile up' presumably refers to either the interment or the encoffining. Guo Xudong (2009) understands some of the day 34/60 divinations (HJ23715–6), to be attempts to predict the day of death of the queen. But if the microchronology presented above is correct, she was already dead by the time these divinations were performed. The diviner was certainly trying to determine a date of some kind—day 4/10 is the proposal—but I suspect that it was a component of the funeral schedule.
55. This identification of day-name determination by divination was first proposed by Li Xueqin (1957), p. 123. A second example proposed in the same article, possibly divining the day-name for the recently deceased king Kang Ding (K31) has also been supported by subsequent scholarship (Peng Yushang 1999, p.8; Wang Yuxin and Yang Shengnan 1999, pp. 600-601; Ji Dewei [David N. Keightley] 1989, p.21). For a competing proposal that the divination concerns the day of the funeral, rather than the day-name, see Cao Dingyun and Liu Yiman (2004).
56. Loewe (1993), "Chou li" pp. 24–32; "I li", pp. 234–243; "Li chi", pp. 293–297.
57. Loewe (1993), "Ch'un ch'iu", pp. 67–76.
58. Inoue (1990).
59. Yu Wanli (2006), pp. 38–46.
60. Liu Xu (1994).
61. Liu Xu (1994), p. 195, table 3. Note that two of the 35 examples are imported from the *Zuo Zhuan* 左傳, a text distinct from though related to the *Springs and Autumns.*
62. In addition to the one exception, two more of the 35 interments are not completed on schedule, however, and are recorded as being delayed a day by rain, pushing them onto 'hard' odd-numbered days.
63. The best recent study is that of Chang Yuzhi (1987), on which the summary provided here is based. For a briefer overview, see Wang Yuxin and Yang Shengnan (1999), pp. 603–627. Xu Fengxian (2006) is an important recent attempt to build an absolute chronology on the basis of the reconstructed CSR.

The only English-language study is that of P'an Wu-su (1976).

64. I will refer to these procedures as 'sacrifices' for convenience, and because that is the translation most readily suggested by the term used in Chinese scholarship (*ji* 祭). It should be noted, though, that not enough is known about the procedures of the CSR to be sure that this is an accurate term. 'Ritual service' or 'ritual procedure' might be more precise.
65. On this point, Chang Yuzhi (1987), pp. 126–133, departs from the conclusions of some of her predecessors.
66. It will also be noticed that K27:5 falls outside the scope of the Chu Group schedule, whereas her husband Wu Ding (K27) falls within it. Perhaps K27:5 was still alive when the Chu Group divinations and their corresponding rituals were being performed in the reign of K30.
67. The rest weeks and their positioning are another point where Chang Yuzhi's reconstruction is at variance with some earlier versions (Chang Yuzhi 1987, pp. 213–216).
68. Chang Yuzhi (1987), p. 199, proposes that the period of the less well-attested Chu Group CSR was 32 weeks, as one would expect it to be if one week of sacrifices were removed from the S1 schedule, from the concurrent S2–S4 set, and from S5.
69. Chang Yuzhi (1987), pp. 199–200; Xu Fengxian (2006), p. 33.
70. Chang Yuzhi (1998), pp. 383–422.
71. Chang Yuzhi (1998), pp. 341–352.
72. Chang Yuzhi (1998), pp. 352–366.
73. Keightley (1985), pp. 115–116, nn. 99, 102 and 107.
74. Qin Luan *fang ding* 寝孿方鼎 (Zou Heng et al. 2000, vol. 3, p. 348). The year notation in this inscription is controversial. See Xu Fengxian (2006), pp. 146–155, for a review of the debate that concludes that the date indicated is in fact the first, not the twentieth, year of a reign.
75. Xiao Chen Yi *jia* 小臣邑斝, JC09249.
76. Xu Fengxian (2006).
77. Xu Fengxian (2006), ch. 3, pp. 45–83.
78. For example, at Xu Fengxian (2006), p. 55, last full para, Xu states that in a month with only two days 1/10, the second must be the 20th day of the month. This is true only under the assumption that no 28-day months occur, where the second day 1/10 could fall on either the 19th or the 20th day. Given the evidence gathered by Chang Yuzhi (1998), pp. 267–299, regarding the irregular nature of the Shang month, the assumption does not seem entirely safe.
79. Xu Fengxian (2006), p. 57.
80. It is thought that two successive Shang months were typically 59 days in length. However, instances of two short months (each 29 days or less) in succession, as well as of two long months (each 30 days or more), are known to occur in the divination records. There are also six known instances of months of at least 31 days, and one of a month with fewer than 29 days (Chang Yuzhi 1998, pp. 275–281; Xu Fengxian 2006, pp. 43–44). It seems likely that the start of a Shang month was routinely determined by sight of the new moon.
81. Xu Fengxian (2006), pp. 65–66. Attempts have been made to determine the season of the first month of the Shang year by examining the correlations of numbered months with meteorological or agricultural divinations (Xu Fengxian 2006, pp. 41–42; Chang Yuzhi 1998, pp. 383–422). Results of such studies have placed the first month everywhere from late spring to mid winter. They offer no support for Xu's assumption, but since they are based largely on early (reign of Wu Ding, K27) divination records, their relevance is uncertain. More relevant is the dramatic change in the position of the first month of the year that reconstructions of the CSR for the preceding reign (K34) seem to suggest.
82. Xu Fengxian (2006), p. 67, table 3–2.
83. Keightley (1977), p. 271, n. 8, gives the formula for converting to the 60-cycle as "dividing the Julian Day number by 60 and adding 50 or subtracting 10 from the remainder".
84. The 'Presentation of the Roster' for S1, according to Chang Yuzhi (1987), pp. 186–191.
85. Chang Yuzhi (1987), pp. 256–259. The absence of intercalary months would imply that it is primarily the numbered months that are moving relative to the seasons, rather than the CSR. She reconstructs

four long CSR rounds of 370 days, and six of 360 days during this span. As Xu Fengxian (2006), pp. 39–40, points out, there is at least one certain (and uncharacteristic) error in Chang's reconstruction, namely her assumption that over this long period of ten years, every month would contain three days 1/10 (*jia* 甲). In the long run, approximately one in twenty months will have only two days 1/10.

86. Chang Yuzhi (1987), pp. 263–298.
87. Chang Yuzhi (1987), pp. 263–298.
88. For the conquest and its background, see Loewe and Shaughnessy (1999), pp. 307–313, 385–389.
89. Li Boqian (2001); Shang Tongliu and Sun Qingwei (2001), p. 9.
90. See Shaughnessy (1991), pp. 134–155, for a concise overview of the the Western Zhou calendar.
91. The only expression of skepticism regarding the continuity of the 60-cycle that I am aware of in Chinese-language scholarship is by Li Xueqin (1957), p. 122. Shaughnessy (1991), pp. 135–136, and Keightley (1977), p. 267, simply note the nature of the assumption being made.
92. A small number of important exceptions to the general rule that Shang-style day-names were not used for members of the royal Zhou lineage and their close relatives are discussed by Zhang Maorong (2009).
93. Yin Shengping (1992); von Falkenhausen (2006), pp. 29–73; Shaughnessy (1991), pp. 1–4, 183–192.
94. An additional day-name (Day 4/10) appears on two of the earliest bronzes. However, other than their presence in the hoard, there is nothing to tie the objects or their inscriptions to the same lineage.
95. Shaughnessy (1991), pp. 209–210. See also von Falkenhausen (2006), pp. 169–203, for a more wide-ranging review of archaeological evidence for distinctively Shang cultural traits persisting after the Conquest.
96. This is not to say that personal names of various kinds do not sometimes incorporate terms from the 10- or 12-cycle. See the examples collected by Ma Chengyuan (2002). However, these are names used by living individuals, without any kinship prefixes.
97. Huang Ranwei (1995), pp. 96–107.
98. For a recent reconstruction of the Lu calendar, see Gassman (2002).
99. Stephenson and Yao (1992); Guan Liyan (1998; 2000).
100. Note that a similar approach is not possible for the small number of lunar eclipse records that have been identified in Anyang divination records. The chronological arguments of Chang Yuzhi (1998), pp. 20–65, and Zhang (2002) that involve these lunar eclipse records are dependent on 60-cycle continuity as an assumption. If correct, they do not help to support that assumption.
101. Harper (1999), p. 831.
102. Loewe (1994); Kalinowski (1986; 2008).
103. Harper (1999), pp. 833–836, fig. 12.1.
104. Kalinowski (1996), p. 71. Versions of the text of the *Yue Ling* are preserved in a number of received texts, including the *Lüshi Chunqiu*, compiled in 239 BC For a translation, see Knoblock and Riegel (2000), pp. 59–273.
105. Jingzhou Diqu Bowuguan (1995); Harper (1999), p. 841.
106. Described and illustrated in Harper (1999), pp. 836–840, fig. 12.5. See also Kalinowski (1996), pp. 71–72.
107. For a translation of this section of the Huai Nan Zi, see Major (1993), pp. 88–92. For the correspondence between the months and path of the sun along the ecliptic in the same text, see pp. 127–128.
108. Zhongguo Tianwenxue Shi Zhengli Yanjiu Xiaozu (1981), p. 115.
109. As Kalinowski (1998) notes, the details of this shift from an astrologically-inspired Jovian year count to a simple count of solar years using the 12-cycle are far from clear. The situation is made additionally complex in the period under discussion by the positing of an entirely imaginary heavenly entity (*taiyin* 太陰, *taisui* 太歲 or *suiyin* 歲陰) rotating through the twelve stations in the opposite direction to Jupiter but with a similar 12-year period (Zhongguo Tianwenxue Shi Zhengli Yanjiu Xiaozu 1981, pp. 114–116; Kalinowski 1998, pp. 148–154).
110. Isolated instances of the use of these names are found in 3rd century BC texts, and a systematic listing

appears twice in the Huai Nan Zi in association with the astrological schemes relating to the Jovian cycle (Major 1993, pp. 118–126, 136–139).

111. Kalinowski (1998), pp. 135–148, fig. 3.

References

HD: Zhongguo Shehuikexueyuan Kaogu Yanjiusuo 中國社會科學院考古研究所, 2003, *Yinxu Huayuanzhuang dong di jiagu* 殷虛花園莊東地甲骨 (Kunming: Yunnan Renmin Chubanshe 雲南人民出版社).

HJ: Guo Moruo 郭沫若 (ed.), 1978-1983, *Jiaguwen heji* 甲骨文合集 (13 vols.) (Beijing: Zhonghua Shuju 中華書局).

JC: Zhongguo Shehuikexueyuan Kaogu Yanjiusuo 中國社會科學院考古研究 (ed.), 1984-. *Yin Zhou jinwen jicheng* 殷周金文集成 (18 vols.) (Beijing: Zhonghua Shuju 中華書局).

Allan, S., 1991, *The Shape of the Turtle: Myth, Art, and Cosmos in Early China* (Albany, NY: State University of New York Press).

Bagley, R., 2004, "Anyang Writing and the Origins of the Chinese Writing System", in S. Houston (ed.), *The First Writing: Script Invention as History and Process* (Cambridge UK: Cambridge University Press) 190–249.

Barnard, N., 1986, "A New Approach to the Study of Clan-sign Inscriptions of Shang", in K. Chang (ed.) *Studies of Shang Archaeology: Selected Papers from the International Conference on Shang Civilization* (New Haven: Yale University Press), 141–206.

Bartle, P. F. W., 1978, "Forty Days: The Akan Calendar", *Africa: Journal of the International African Institute* 48(1), 80–84.

de Bary, W., 1999, *Sources of Chinese Tradition: From Earliest Times to 1600*, vol. 1 (New York: Columbia University Press, 2nd ed.).

Cao Dingyun 曹定雲, 1993, *Yinxu Fu Hao mu mingwen yanjiu* 殷墟婦好墓銘文研究 (Taibei: Wenjin Chubanshe 文津出版社).

——, and Liu Yiman 劉一曼, 2004, "Yinren bu zang yu bi 'fu ri' 殷人卜葬與避'復日'", in Wang Yuxin 王宇信 et al. (eds.), *2004 nian Anyang Yin Shang wen ming guo ji xue shu yan tao hui lun wen ji* 2004年安陽殷商文明國際學述研討會論文集 (Beijing: Shehui kexue wenxian chubanshe 社會科學文獻出版社), 294-298.

Chang, K. (ed.), 1986, *Studies of Shang Archaeology: Selected Papers from the International Conference on Shang Civilization* (New Haven: Yale University Press).

——, 1978, "T'ien kan: a Key to the History of the Shang", in D. Roy & T. Tsien, (eds.), *Ancient China: Studies in Early Civilization* (Hong Kong: Chinese University Press), 13–42.

Chang Yuzhi 常玉芝, 1987, *Shangdai zhouji zhidu* 商代周祭制度 (Beijing: Zhongguo Shehui Kexue Chubanshe 中國社會科學出版社).

——, 1998, *Yin Shang lifa yanjiu* 殷商歷法研究 (Changchun: Jilin Wenshi Chubanshe 吉林文史出版社).

Falkenhausen, L., 2006, *Chinese Society in the Age of Confucius (1000-250 BC): the Archaeological Evidence* (Los Angeles: Cotsen Institute of Archaeology, University of California).

Flad, R., 2008, "Divination and Power: a Multiregional View of the Development of Oracle Bone Divination in Early China", *Current Anthropology* 49(3), 403–437.

Gan Lu 甘露, 2002, "Jiaguwen dizhi jiri bu li 甲骨文地支紀日補例", Yindu xuekan 殷都學刊 2, 5–7.

Gassmann, R., 2002, *Antikchinesisches Kalenderwesen: die Rekonstruktion der chunqiu-zeitlichen Kalender des Fürstentums Lu und der Zhou-Könige* (Bern: Lang).

Guan Liyan 關立言, 1998, "Chunqiu rishi sanshiqi shi kao 春秋日食三十七事考", *Shixue Yuekan* 史學月刊 2, 95-103.

——, 2000, "Chunqiu rishi kao bu yi 春秋日食考補遺", *Kaifeng Daxue Xuebao* 開封大學學報 14(1), 62-74.

Guo Moruo 郭沫若, 1982, "Shi zhi gan 釋支干", in *Guo Moruo quanji, kaogu bian, di yi juan* 郭沫若全集一考古編一第一卷 (Beijing: Kexue Chubanshe 科學出版社), 155–340.

Guo Xudong 郭旭東, 2009, "Yinxu buci suo jian Shangdai pinli wanghou zhidu kao 殷虛卜辭所見商代品立王后制度考", *Wen shi zhe* 文史哲 1, 121–129.

He Jingcheng 何景成, 2009, *Shang Zhou qingtongqi zushi mingwen yanjiu* 商周青銅器族氏銘文研究 (Jinan: Qi Lu Shushe 齊魯書社).

Huang Ranwei 黃然偉, 1995, *Yin Zhou shiliao lunji* 殷周史料論集 (Hong Kong: Sanlian Shudian 三聯書店).

Inoue Satoshi 井上聰, 1990, "Shangdai miaohao xin lun 商代廟號新論", *Kaogu yu wenwu* 考古與文物 2, 54–60.

Ji Dewei 吉德煒 [David N. Keightley], 1989, "Zhongguo gudai de jiri yu miaohao 中國古代的吉日與廟號", in Hu Houxuan 胡厚宣 (ed.), *Yin xu bo wu yuan yuan kan* (*chuang kan hao*) 殷墟博物苑苑刊(創刊號) (Beijing: Zhongguo Shehui Kexue Chubanshe 中國社會科學出版社), 31–70.

Jingzhou Diqu Bowuguan 荊州地區博物館, 1995, "Jiangling Wangjiatai 15 hao Qin mu 江陵王家台15號秦墓", Wenwu 文物 1, 37–43.

Kalinowski, M., 1986, "Les traités de Shuihudi et l'hémérologie chinoise à la fin des Royaumes-Combattants", *T'oung Pao* 72, 175–228.

——, 1996, "The Use of the Twenty-eight Xiu as a Day-count in Early China", *Chinese Science* 13, 55–81.

——, 1998, "The Xingde 刑德 Texts from Mawangdui", *Early China* 23–24, 125–202.

——, 2007, "Time, Space and Orientation: Figurative Representations of the Sexagenary Cycle in Ancient and Medieval China", in F. Bray (ed.), *Graphics and Text in the Production of Technical Knowledge in China: The Warp and the Weft* (Leiden: Brill), 137–168.

——, 2008, "Les livres des jours (rishu) des Qin et des Han: la logique éditoriale du recueil A de Shuihudi (217 avant notre ère)", *T'oung Pao* 94, 1–48.

Keightley, D. N., 1977, "On the Misuse of Ancient Chinese Inscriptions: an Astronomical Fantasy", *Histroy of Science* 15, 267–272.

——, 1985, *Sources of Shang History: the Oracle-bone Inscriptions of Bronze Age China* (Berkeley, CA: University of California Press, 2nd edn.).

——, 1997, "Shang Oracle-bone Inscriptions", in E. Shaughnessy (ed.), *New Sources of Early Chinese History: An Introduction to the Reading of Inscriptions and Manuscripts* (Berkeley: Society for the study of Early China and the Institute of East Asian Studies, University of California Berkeley), 15–55.

——, 2000, *The Ancestral Landscape: Time, Space, and Community in Late Shang China, ca. 1200-1045 B.C.* (Berkeley: University of California, Berkeley, Center for Chinese Studies).

Knoblock, J., and Riegel, J., 2000, *The Annals of Lü Buwei: a Complete Translation and Study* (Stanford CA: Stanford University Press).

Li Boqian 李伯谦, 2001, "Shu Ze fang ding mingwen kaoshi 叔夨方鼎銘文考釋", Wenwu 文物 8, 39–41.

Li Min, 2008, *Conquest, Concord, and Consumption: Becoming Shang in Eastern China* (PhD dissertation, University of Michigan).

Liu Xu 劉緒, 1994, "Chunqiu shiqi sangzang zhidu zhong de zang yue yu zang ri 春秋時期喪葬制度的葬月與葬日", in Beijing Daxue Kaoguxi 北京大學考古系 (ed.), *Kaoguxue yanjiu* (*er*) 考古學研究(二) (Beijing: Beijing Daxue Chubanshe 北京大學出版社), 189–200.

Li Xueqin 李學勤, 1957, "Ping Chen Mengjia Yinxu buci zongshu 評陳夢家《殷虛卜辭綜述》", *Kaogu xuebao* 考古學報 3, 119-130.

——, and Peng Yushang 彭裕商, 1996, *Yinxu jiagu fenqi yanjiu* 殷虛甲骨分期研究 (Shanghai: Shanghai Guji Chubanshe 上海古籍出版社).

Loewe, M., 1993, *Early Chinese Texts: A Bibliographical Guide* (Berkeley, CA: Society for the Study of Early China; Institute of East Asian Studies University of California Berkeley).

——, 1994, "The Almanacs (Jih-shu) from Shui-hu-ti: a Preliminary Survey", in *Divination, Mythology and Monarchy in Han China* (Cambridge & New York, NY: Cambridge University Press), 214–235.

——, and Shaughnessy, E. L., 1999, *The Cambridge History of Ancient China: from the Origins of Civilization to 221 B.C.* (Cambridge: Cambridge University Press).

Harper, D., 1999, "Warring States Natural Philospohy and Occult Thought", in M. Loewe and E. L. Shaughnessy (eds.), *The Cambridge History of Ancient China : from the Origins of Civilization to 221 B.C.* (Cambridge UK & New York: Cambridge University Press), 813–884.

Ma Chengyuan 馬承源, 2002, "Guanyu Shang Zhou guizu shiyong rigan chengwei wenti de tantao 關於商周貴族使用日干稱謂問提的探討" in *Zhongguo qingtongqi yanjiu* 中國青銅器研究 (Shanghai: Shanghai Guji Chubanshe 上海古籍出版社), 187–200.

Major, J., 1993, *Heaven and Earth in Early Han Thought: Chapters Three, Four and Five of the Huainanzi* (Albany: State University of New York Press).

Nienhauser, W. H., 1994, *The Grand Scribe's Records Volume I: the Basic Annals of Pre-Han China* (Bloomington–Indianopolis: Indiana University Press).

Norman, J., 1985, "A Note on the Origins of the Chinese Duodenary Cycle", in G. Thurgood et al. (ed.) *Linguistics of the Sino-Tibetan Area* (Canberra: Australian National University), 85–89.

Pankenier, D., 2010, "Getting 'Right' with Heaven and the Origin of Writing in China", in D. P. Branner and Li Feng (eds.), *Writing and Literacy in Early China* (Seattle: University of Washington Press), in press.

P'an Wu-su, 1976, *Religion and Chronology in Shang China: the Scheduled Ancestor Rituals and the Chronology of the Late Shang Period* (PhD dissertation, University of Pennsylvania).

Peng Yushang 彭裕商, 1999, "Shifa tanyuan 諡法探源", *Zhongguo Shi Yanjiu* 中國史研究 1, 3–11.

Pulleyblank, E. G., 1991, "The Ganzhi as Phonograms and their Application to the Calendar", *Early China* 16, 39–80.

——, 1995, "The Ganzhi as Phonograms", *Early China News* 8, 29–30.

Shaaxisheng Kaogu Yanjiusuo 陝西省考古研究所, 1995, Gaojiapu Ge guo mu 高家堡戈國墓 (Xi'an: San Qin Chubanshe 三秦出版社).

Shang Tongliu 商彤流, and Sun Qingwei 孫慶偉, 2001, "Tianma-Qucun yizhi Beizhao Jin Hou mudi di liu ci fajue 天馬—曲村遺址北趙晉侯墓地第六次發掘", *Wenwu* 文物 8, 4–21.

Shaughnessy, E., 1991, *Sources of Western Zhou History: Inscribed Bronze Vessels* (Berkeley: University of California Press).

Smith, A.D., 2008, *Writing at Anyang: the Role of the Divination Record in the Emergence of Chinese Literacy* (PhD dissertation, UCLA).

——, 2010, "The Evidence for Scribal Training at Anyang", in D. P. Branner and Li Feng (eds.), *Writing and Literacy in Early China* (Seattle: University of Washington Press), in press.

Song Guoding 宋國定, 2003, "Zhengzhou Xiaoshuangqiao yizhi chutu taoqi shang de zhushu 鄭州小雙橋遺址出土陶器上的朱書", *Wenwu* 文物 5, 35–44.

Stephenson, F. R., andYau, K. K. C., 1992, "Astronomical Records in the Ch'un-Ch'iu Chronicle", *Journal for the History of Astronomy* 23, 31–51.

Venture, O., 2002, *Étude d'un emploi rituel de l'écrit dans la Chine archaïque (XIIIe-VIIIe siècle avant notre ère): réflexion sur les matériaux épigraphiques des Shang et des Zhou occidentaux* (PhD dissertation: Université Paris 7).

Wang Guowei 王國維, 1959, *Guan Tang ji lin* 觀堂集林 (Beijing: Zhonghua Shuju 中華書局).

Wang Yuxin 王宇信, and Yang Shengnan 楊升南 (eds.), 1999, *Jiaguxue yibai nian* 甲骨學一百年 (Beijing: Shehui Kexue Wenxian Chubanshe 社會科學文獻出版社).

Whittaker, G., 1991, *Calendar and Script in Protohistorical China and Mesoamerica: A Comparative Study of Day Names and their Signs* (Bonn: Holos).

Wilkinson, E., 2000, *Chinese History: A Manual* (Cambridge, MA: Harvard University Asia Center, rev. & enl.).

Xia Shang Zhou Duandai Gongcheng Zhuanjia Zu 夏商周段代工程傳家組 (ed.), 2000, *Xia Shang Zhou Duandai Gongcheng 1996-2000 nian jieduan chengguo baogao: jian ben* 夏商周段代工程1996—2000年階段成果報告—簡本 (Beijing: Shijie Tushu Chuban Gongsi Beijing Gongsi 世界圖書出版公司北京公司).

Xu Fengxian 徐鳳先, 2006, *Shang mo zhou ji sipu heli yanjiu* 商末周祭祀譜合歷研究 (Beijing: Shijie Tushu Chuban Gongsi Beijing Gongsi 世界圖書出版公司北京公司).

Yan Zhibin 嚴志斌, and Hong Mei 洪梅, 2008, *Yinxu qingtongqi* 殷墟青銅器 (Shanghai: Shanghai Daxue Chubanshe 上海大學出版社).

Yao Xuan 姚萱, 2006, *Yinxu Huayuanzhuang dong di jiagu buci de chubu yanjiu* 殷墟花園莊東地甲骨卜辭的初步研究 (Beijing: Xianzhuang Shuju 線裝書局).

Yin Shengping 尹盛平 (ed.), 1992, *Xi Zhou Wei shi jiazu qingtongqiqun yanjiu* 西周微氏家族青銅器群研究 (Beijing: Wenwu Chubanshe 文物出版社).

Yu Wanli 虞萬里, 2006, "Shang Zhou chengwei yu Zhongguo gudai biwei qiyuan 商周稱謂與中國古代避諱起源", in Qian Hang 錢杭 (ed.), *Chuantong Zhongguo yanjiu jikan* 傳統中國研究集刊 (Shanghai: Shanghai Shehuikexueyuan 上海社會科學院). http://www.historicalchina.net/admin/WebEdit/UploadFile/NameWL.pdf (last accessed: 5th April 2010).

Zhang Fuxiang 張富祥, 2005, "Shang wang minghao yu shanggu riming zhi yanjiu 商王名號與上古日名制研究", *Lishi Yaniu* 歷史研究 2, 3–27.

Zhang Guangzhi 張光直, 1983, "Tan Wang Hai yu Yi Yin de jiri bing zai lun Yinshang wangzhi 談王亥與伊尹的祭日並再論殷商王制", in *Zhongguo qingtong shidai* 中國青銅世代 (Taipei: Lianjing Chuban Shiye Gongsi 聯經出版事業公司), 197–222.

Zhang Maorong 張懋鎔, 2009, "Zai lun 'Zhou ren bu yong ri ming shuo' 再論'周人不用日名說'", *Wen bo* 文博 3, 27–29.

Zhang, P., 2002, "Determining Xia-Shang-Zhou Chronology through Astronomical Records in Historical Texts", *Journal of East Asian Archaeology* 4(1–4), 347–357.

Zhongguo Shehuikexueyuan Kaogu Yanjiusuo Anyang Gonzuodui 中國社會科學院考古研究所安陽工作隊, 1979, "1969–1977 nian Yinxu xiqu muzang fajue baogao 1969–1977年殷虛西區墓葬發掘報告", *Kaogu Xuebao* 考古學報 1, 27–146.

Zhongguo Shehuikexueyuan Kaogu Yanjiusuo 中國社會科學院考古研究所, 1998. *Anyang Yinxu Guojiazhuang Shangdai muzang: 1982 nian ~ 1992 nian kaogu fajue baogao* 安陽殷墟郭家莊商代墓葬：1982年～1992年考古發掘报告 (Beijing: Zhongguo Da Baike Quanshu Chubanshe 中國大百科全書出版社).

——, 1980, *Yinxu Fu Hao mu* 殷虛婦好墓 (Beijing: Wenwu Chubanshe 文物出版社).

——, 2003, *Yinxu Huayuanzhuang dong di jiagu* 殷虛花園莊東地甲骨 (Kunming: Yunnan Renmin Chubanshe 雲南人民出版社).

Zhongguo Tianwenxue Shi Zhengli Yanjiu Xiaozu 《中國天文學史》整理研究小組, 1981, *Zhongguo tianwenxue shi* 中國天文學史 (Beijing: Kexue Chubanshe 科學出版社).

Zhu Fenghan 朱鳳瀚, 1990, "Jinwen riming tongji yu Shangdai wanqi Shangren riming zhi 金文日名統計與商代晚期商人日名制", *Zhongyuan Wenwu* 中原文物 3, 72–77.

Zou Heng 鄒衡, Beijing Daxue Kaoguxuexi Shang Zhou zu 北京大學考古學系商周組, and Shanxisheng Kaogu Yanjiusuo 山西省考古研究所 (eds.), 2000, *Tianma-Qucun (1980–1989)* 天馬——曲村(1980–1989) (Beijing: Kexue Chubanshe 科學出版社).

Mathematical Astronomy and the Chinese Calendar

N. Sivin

One of the main rituals of state in China over the past two thousand years was the emperor's 'granting the seasons'—issuing an almanac for the new year that included a civil calendar, predictions of important astronomical phenomena, and indications of lucky and unlucky days for the activities of daily life. An official history of 1345 explains the almanac's importance:

> In antiquity, when monarchs put the realm in order, they gave priority to mathematical harmonics and mathematical astronomy. When scholars sought to comprehend the relations of heaven and man, they did not need to go beyond harmonics and astronomy. Mathematical astronomy begins with numbers, and numbers begin with harmonic relationships. Thus when harmonics and astronomy have been correctly understood, the cold and hot [seasons] are correctly demarcated; the fruits of agriculture come to maturity; the affairs of the people attain the right sequence; every kind of activity reaches fruition:[1] the roots of a myriad matters are founded on this.[2]

Put more prosaically, every dynasty depended for legitimacy on the idea that a stable state had to be consonant with the dynamic patterns of the cosmos. The emperor maintained this relationship primarily by correctly performing state rituals. Carrying them out at the right time in the right way and accompanying them with the right music were essential, as the author insists, to public order.

Astronomical Ritual

The ritual of 'granting the seasons' was an essential part of the imperial new year ceremony, and of the rites for a new emperor's accession to the throne. When a Manchu became emperor in 1644, Jesuit missionaries produced the almanac, and its ephemeris was largely European in its computational techniques. Nevertheless, the Court for State Ceremonial closely based the ritual on that of the dynasty the Manchus had just vanquished.

Very early in the morning, the civil and military officials, robed for imperial audience and hierarchically arrayed, waited for the new emperor to take the throne, after which the elaborate ceremony of Presenting the Almanac (*jin li* 進曆) began. The officials of the Directorate of Astronomy first presented the almanacs containing the 'Monthly Ordinances' (*yueh ling* 月令; see below) for imperial perusal, then the almanac for the Empress Dowager, then the almanacs for the imperial princes, and finally the almanac for 1645 generated by the Temporal Pattern system(*Shixian li* 時憲曆). The emperor consummated the ritual by decreeing that it be promulgated throughout the realm.[3]

The 'Monthly Ordinances' which appear in several early classics set out rites that the emperor and certain of his high officials performed each lunar month—supposedly in high antiquity—to align the operations of the state with the cycles of the seasons. The officials first presented a set of almanacs that contained them and related documents, prepared for the emperor himself, then a series with hemerological notes intended individually for other members of the imperial family, and finally the version meant for the hundreds of millions of imperial subjects.

A look at a much earlier ritual, performed five times a year, reveals why the monthly ordinances were important:

> According to the Han ritual [late third century BC through the early third century AD], every year the Grand Astrologer submitted [to the throne] the almanac for the [coming] year. It was the custom to read aloud the ordinances for the five seasonal divisions of the year[4] before the beginning of each one. For this ceremony the emperor wore the colour that corresponded to the season. He ascended to his throne. The Director of the Imperial Secretariat and those who ranked below him took their places on the mat. A Secretarial Court Gentleman placed the ordinances on a desk and respectfully carried it in. After he took his place and read it out completely, a cup of wine was granted to everyone.[5]

In addition to the twelve months, the monthly ordinances also referred to certain points that began the seasons (the solstices and equinoxes, in the Chinese view, fell at their midpoints). Here is a brief excerpt from the detailed ordinances for the first month.

> This month is that of "Enthronement of Spring". Three days before Enthronement of Spring, the Grand Astrologer reports it to the Son of Heaven: "Such-and-such a day will be the Enthronement of Spring. The preponderant power [among the five phases, *wuxing* 五行] will become that of the phase Wood." The Son of Heaven then undertakes a ritual of self-purification. On the day of Enthronement of Spring, the Son of Heaven personally leads the Three Dukes, Nine Chamberlains, feudal lords, and Grand Masters to welcome spring in the eastern suburbs. When they return, he rewards the Dukes, Chamberlains, feudal lords, and Grand Masters in audience. He commands them to make known the moral authority of his government, propagate his ordinances of instruction, execute celebratory commemorations, and bestow favours so that they reach his innumerable subjects.... In this month
>
> It is not appropriate to assemble military forces,
> For when they are assembled, natural calamities are certain to occur.
> When armed forces are not to be raised,
> It is not appropriate for us to originate warfare.
> Do not transgress the Dao of Heaven;
> Do not contravene the pattern of order in Earth;
> Do not disrupt the guiding principles of men.[6]

Thus we can see that, in addition to guiding the agricultural and other activities of the entire realm, the almanac was the basis of ceremonies within the court that were essential to the emperor's own paramount task: ritually bringing the state into harmony with the macrocosm, and asserting the government's ability to do so. That harmony was dynamic, and needed correct timing. As the empire's territory grew larger and climatically more diverse, the almanac's claim to prescribe accurate dates for the tasks of farming lost its validity. We can appreciate that the lasting authority of the ephemeris was based on its use in the court, and on the state's symbolic claim to control time as well as space.

Historians of astronomy generally ignore the continuity of astronomy, astrology and divination, but this makes a balanced picture of Chinese sky knowledge impossible—as impossible as understanding the career of, say, Kepler, while assuming that he did not take his work on horoscopes seriously. Through history ordinary educated Chinese normally had more than a little knowledge of mathematical astronomy, astrology, and non-astrological divination, which in their eyes were closely connected.[7] The term *yinyang* 陰陽 referred, among other things, to the simultaneous practice of all three, or to anyone who was expert in them. In 1644, when the Manchu conquerors gave the Jesuit missionary Johann Adam Schall von Bell authority in the Directorate of Astronomy, he was expected not only to generate ephemerides and interpret celestial omens, but to determine propitious days for imperial ceremonies—and promptly obliged.[8]

Astronomy and the Calendar

The word *li*, conventionally translated 'calendar', has several meanings, often confused. One is the art of computing the times or locations of certain future or past phenomena in the sky. That sense corresponds to what historians have called 'mathematical astronomy', and I so translate it here. Speaking of mathematical astronomy as 'calendrical science' obscures the similarity between the Chinese technical literature, Islamic tractates—most historians of Muslim astronomy translate *zij* 'table', although they are actually handbooks like the Chinese ones—and Western practical treatises from Ptolemy's *Handy Tables* to Peuerbach.

A second sense is a step-by-step sequence of computations to generate an ephemeris for the next year. The lunisolar calendar was based on actual predictions of lunar conjunctions (the beginnings of months) and winter solstices (to which the solar new year was keyed). It was usual from AD 85 on to include predictions of eclipses and certain planetary events as well. That set of procedures I call an 'astronomical system'.

A project designed to produce a new computational system that would generate more accurate ephemerides is an 'astronomical reform (*kai li* 改曆)'. Some historians have called it a 'calendar reform', but that is misleading. What *kai li* reforms is not a calendar but an astronomical system. The notion of a calendar reform in European history differs fundamentally from the Chinese practice. The term normally refers to the changes that Pope Gregory XIII made in 1582 to the Catholic church's ecclesiastical calendar, to replace both the Julian calendar used since 46 BC and the various local lunisolar calendars of the sixteenth century. The goal of the Gregorian reform was to end the prediction of solstices and lunations as elements of calendars. Its product was not an ephemeris, but the purely solar calendar that most of the world now uses for secular purposes. It is based simply on counting off in a fixed order months of 28 to 31 days and years of 365 or 366 days. The Gregorian calendar reform, in other words, was a decisive rejection of astronomical reforms.[9]

A third *li* is the physical embodiment of the astronomical system, namely a computational treatise. The treatises that have survived because they were included in the official histories of Chinese dynasties are abridgments, not the complete originals.

The fourth *li* is the products of computational treatises, namely ephemerides published in almanacs. Historians usually refer to official almanacs simply as calendars, but this ignores most of their content. Almanacs predicted regular events such as the new moons that began each lunar month, and irregular ones such as eclipses. Their rich hemerological data allowed users to anticipate propitious and unpropitious days for most of their activities—beginning a journey, planting crops, sponsoring a ritual, and so on. On the one hand, the almanac was a basic tool of governance and, on the other, its predictions and indications embodied governmental order and control. The government prepared certain versions meant for official use, and others for public distribution. For instance, non-quota tax income for the year 1328 included receipts from the sale of 3,123,195 almanacs, of which 5257 were Muslim.[10] By this time private publishers had begun reproducing them (but not contributing taxes).

To avoid confusion, I use 'calendar' only to mean the ephemeris, the calendrical component of an almanac.[11] Of the four senses of *li*, the least consequential and most routine work of the imperial astronomical bureau was making calendars. This was done by low-ranking computists who needed only basic arithmetical skills, following step-by-step instructions in the current astronomical treatise. It provided tables that made more complicated operations unnecessary. Like other astronomical functionaries, the computists were usually hereditary appointees. The calendar was, in other words, the routine bureaucratic product of an official astronomical system.

Chinese Calendars

Producing a correct calendar was essential to dynastic legitimacy. Failures of prognostication were warnings from Heaven that the reigning dynasty, neglecting its duties, was liable to lose the mandate to rule. When Heaven, duly exasperated, transferred the mandate to another family, a change of dynasty quickly resulted. A new ruler thus routinely explained the victory of his regime as not a triumph of force but an accomplished destiny, justified by concern for the sufferings of the people under his degenerate predecessor.[12]

That made predicting phenomena accurately a matter of what today we call national security. In most periods, the state massively subsidized celestial observation and computation. An astronomical bureau staffed by a hundred career civil servants, more or less, was not unusual. Because a rebel whose functionaries could improve on official predictions was a considerable threat, in a few eras astronomical work by people outside the bureaucracy was a serious legal offense.

The calendars of imperial China (from 221 BC to AD 1911) had a great deal in common with the religious and secular lunisolar calendars that coexisted with the Julian calendar in various European countries before the Gregorian reform (1582), and very little with calendars that followed it. Traditional lunisolar calendars were ephemerides, sets of predictions for the coming year. They defined astronomically the new year, the beginning of the month, and other events in ways that varied from one civilization to the next.

The earliest standard in China counted the year from the winter solstice, and the month from the conjunction of moon and sun (an invisible event). Thus, originally, the first day of the first month in the civil calendar was the new moon of the month that contained the winter solstice. Early rulers who claimed the aegis of a new cosmic order shifted the beginning of the calendar year to the new moon of the second month after the solstice. There it remained for two thousand years. Even today that is the date of the popular 'Chinese New Year'. Astronomers, to simplify their computations, used what they called the 'astronomical new year (*tianzheng* 天正)', in which the first month remained the one that contained the solstice.

Widely distributed in almanacs, the annual calendar remained tied to phenomena. The beginning of the year was defined, directly or indirectly, by the solstitial shadow, the longest that a gnomon cast at noon over the year. The month began on the night when no moon was visible because it rose and set with the sun.[13] The very visible full moon fell halfway through the month. The ephemeris, as I have noted, predicted eclipses and various planetary phenomena.

It was only when the nationalist government replaced the empire, at the beginning of 1912, that China adopted the Gregorian calendar. It became simply a matter of counting fixed sequences of days, and no longer corresponded to anything happening in the sky. Changes in education and social customs came so slowly that people in the countryside still thought in terms of the lunisolar calendar until late in the 20th century. The government of the People's Republic in 1949 began the year with the so-called solar new year. It officially renamed the lunar new year the 'Spring Festival', but most people, including government employees, still celebrate it more elaborately, and for a longer time, than the solar new year. The latter follows closely upon the solstice, but the beginning of a new day-counting cycle, not a solar phenomenon, determines its date.[14]

In early China, the need of governments to produce an authoritative almanac meant frequent pressure for improvement. That in turn meant maintaining an elaborate and expensive astronomical bureau. Two thousand years ago, the basic calendrical problems—the mean length of a lunar month and a tropical year—were solved adequately to meet practical needs.

But no calendar can be purely calendrical, since both the month and the year must contain an integral number of days. The length of a mean lunar month is 29.53 days, but a calendar day must be either 29 or 30 days long. Alternating months of 29 and 30 days to give an average length of 29½ days is not good enough. Furthermore, 12 months that alternated lengths of 29 and 30 days added up to only 354 or 355 days. 13 months included 383 or 384 days, which is too long. It was therefore necessary, first, to work out some scheme of alternating long and short months to give the correct long-term average of days per month. Second, it was essential to add a thirteenth (or intercalary) month every so often to adjust the long-term average of days in a year.

The Chinese method at first depended on what used to be called the cycle of Meton: adding at more or less equal intervals 7 extra (intercalary) months every 19 years. That made the average tropical year 12 7/19 months long. Every so often two sequential months 30 days long brought the long-term average up to the length of a mean synodic month. That value by 104 BC was taken to be 29.5309 days (modern value 29.53059). The mean tropical year of 12 7/19 such months was thus 365.2500 days long (modern value 365.2422). Astronomers soon improved that average by slightly modifying the length of the intercalary cycle. As they learned to compute true years and months, from 657 on, they discarded such cycles.

But the calendar and divination portions of the almanac were the least problematic.[15] The problems of the month and year were easily solved. Divination was simply a matter of interpreting archival records of omens and their aftermaths by methods that did not need frequent revision. It was not at all simple to perfect methods for calculating ephemerides. Chinese astronomical techniques were numerical (that is, algebraic). Because long before eclipses could be predicted people had considered them ominous—threats to dynastic legitimacy—over the centuries great effort went into their prognostication. It was not difficult to predict when a solar or lunar eclipse will be visible from somewhere on the earth; certain counting cycles are fairly reliable.[16] But using numerical techniques to predict accurately where on earth solar eclipses will be visible is much harder than using the geometric methods the Greeks favored. The problem, after all, amounts to solving the intersection of a small moving cone of shadow with the spherical earth. Predicting planetary positions and phenomena were also difficult, and fitful effort went into improvement, but the political centrality of eclipses kept planets on the sideline.

Replacement of Astronomical Systems

The result of the continuing pressure for improvement was generally the complete replacement of the official computational system by a new one rather than piecemeal improvement. Over the two millennia of imperial China, roughly two hundred integral systems were proposed or used. We have at least basic data on about half of these. Roughly fifty were adopted by the government for periods ranging from a few months to more than three hundred years. The table in the Appendix lists some of the most important.

The process by which one system replaced another was supposed to be simple: an order in the name of the emperor called for a new system, and the experts in the astronomical bureau did whatever was necessary to provide one, and ensured by testing that it was better than the current system. This was, to be sure, the most frequent scenario, except that the testing more often than not was cursory. What actually happened varied greatly in other ways, for instance[17]

1. the officials responsible for the work failed to do it, so that the new system was no improvement. Here is a well-known example from the polymath Shen Gua 沈括 (or Kuo, 1031–1095):[18]

> In [1072–1074], when I was performing additional duty as Director of the Astrological Service, [my protégé] Wei Pu 衛朴 was preparing an astronomical reform. He had worked out correct solar and lunar techniques, but [in the observatory] there was no register of planetary observations that he could use to verify his methods for the five planets. Previous generations, when making a new astronomical system, mostly just adjusted the constants in an old system without ever doing observational studies of celestial positions. The method [Wei found it necessary to use] was every night to observe the positions to a ten-thousandth of a degree of the moon and the five planets at dusk, dawn, and midnight, and to set up a register in which to record them.[19] Out of five full years, if he did not count cloudy nights and times when the luminaries would be visible only during daylight, he could have gotten three years' records of actual motions. Then he could have analyzed them mathematically. …
>
> At the time, the astronomical officials in the Astrological Service were all hereditary appointees. They were [experts] in name only, living well off their salaries although not one of them knew astronomy. Offended that Wei's skills surpassed theirs, they all hindered him, repeatedly bringing serious charges against him. Although from first to last they were unable to shake Wei, to this very day his register of observations remains unfinished. In the planetary technique of his Oblatory Epoch system (*Feng yuan li* 奉元曆), he was able only to modify the constants of the old systems and correct some seriously deficient portions of them, no more than five or six parts out of ten. Now or in the past there has never been [a command of] astronomical techniques [to compare

with] Wei's. How sad that because a bunch of calendar-makers (*qun liren* 群曆人) stymied him, he was unable to fully develop his art!

2. an administrative official (or, much more rarely, a commoner) expert in astronomy criticized the current system and proposed enhancements. After high officials verified their value, they accepted his suggestions. If necessary, he was given an astronomical appointment and put in charge of a reform.[20]

One of many famous examples is He Chengtian 何承天 (370–447). He began his career as a military official. After more than a dozen posts under two dynasties as a local magistrate, an Erudite in the National University, and a palace editor, he was assigned to compile the archival history of his dynasty (*guoshi* 國史). The emperor regularly consulted him on historical questions, which bulked large in policy-making.

He Chengtian learned astronomy in his youth from a maternal uncle who worked out his own astronomical system, and spent 30 years collecting observational data to improve it. As a result, He spent 40 years of his spare time in the same pursuit. When he sent his Epochal Excellence system to the ruler he was over 70 years old. Since the system was complete and testing revealed its superiority, there was no need to involve the technical bureaucracy.

It was He who first worked out methods for true rather than mean solar positions, apparent lunisolar conjunctions, the Annual Difference (an important quantity that corresponds to the European precession of the equinoxes),[21] and exact positions of the sun determined by the locations of lunar eclipses. He also made improvements in instruments and discussed the cosmology behind his system.

3. a new system organized by imperial favourites commanded exceptional resources that enabled exceptional innovation. This was the genesis of the most sophisticated and longest lived of China's systems, the Season-granting system (*Shoushi li* 授時曆).

Khubilai (born 1215, reigned 1260–1294) was one of several Mongol khans engaged in the world conquest begun by their grandfather Chinggis (reigned 1206–1227). Long before his own future role became clear, he began gathering about him a small group of Chinese advisors. The first was the Buddhist monk Liu Bingzhong 劉秉忠 (1216–1274), whom he chose because Liu's knowledge of '*yinyang*' was convincing evidence of his wisdom. Khubilai was 27 at the time, and Liu 26. Liu eventually became the most powerful Han Chinese in the Mongol empire, and remained for the rest of his life the Khan's closest councilor. Liu gradually introduced into Khubilai's circle a number of other Chinese chosen for their expertise in astronomy, astrology, and divination. As Khubilai undertook the conquest of north and then of south China, each of the group gradually became an important official, building within the Mongol imperium a Chinese-style administration that the Khan's new subjects could accept.

Liu persuaded Khubilai ca. 1251 that an astronomical reform was a key step in building that government. As the conquest of the south continued, he made detailed plans for the new system, and planned to take personal responsibility for it. His death in 1274 brought that project to a close but, in 1276, when the Southern Song dynasty surrendered, the Mongol emperor authorized and gave priority to the reform.

The people he chose to run it were seven of the officials who belonged to his inner circle. By the time Wang Xun 王恂 (1235–1281), whom Khubilai put in charge, was 30, he had played a large part in designing an administration as well as a set of imperial rituals. Guo Shoujing 郭守敬 (1231–1316) was an accomplished hydraulic engineer, director of a bureau in the Ministry of Works—and an all-round expert in astronomy, especially in instrumentation. The group also included Xu Heng 許衡 (1209–1281), the leading Neo-Confucian teacher in north China, and the Minister of Revenue, Zhang Wenqian 張文謙 (1217–1283). All seven were also experts in mathematical astronomy.

The expectant emperor gave them unlimited support from the beginning of the project in 1276 to its completion in 1280. There were already both Muslim and Han Chinese astronomical bureaus in the new capital, although there is no evidence that they were doing, or were adequately equipped to do, essential work. In order to obviate obstruction of the kind that had made Wei Pu's work impossible, the reform group formed a new Astrological Commission; the two previous bureaus had no role in the project but providing a certain number of qualified personnel and training others. The reformers also built a new, completely equipped observatory, for which Guo invented a number of new instruments. The record does not show that they made any use of the two observatories that already existed. The Commission was also equipped with a number of carefully chosen career astronomers from the newly conquered south, who had experience in a reform. Its full staff comprised 66 civil-service officials, 11 clerks, and 44 students.

As often happened to projects that began dynasties, time pressure left reforms barely finished. Nevertheless, the Season-granting system, which began with a thorough investigation of all its predecessors, used a wide range of their best techniques and invented many new ones. Its staff also compiled a large archive of past observational records against which to test the new computational techniques. The new system was so strongly designed that it remained in official use from 1280 to 1644; it was superseded only when the political maneuvering of Jesuit astronomers from Europe, combined with the advantages of their geometric methods, enabled them to dominate the astronomical bureau of the new Qing dynasty.[22]

4. a new system, despite demonstrated technical accuracy, was rejected as a result of palace infighting. The most notorious instance had to do with the exceptionally innovative Great Enlightenment system (*Daming li* 大明曆) of Zu Chongzhi 祖沖之 (ca. 430–510), which he completed in 462, when he was in his early thirties. He used the timing of total lunar eclipses to determine the quantity corresponding to the magnitude of the precession of the equinoxes, and overcame the difficulty of timing the winter solstice (and year length as the interval between two solstices) by linear interpolation of gnomon shadow lengths measured at noon.

After Zu submitted his system, a high official, well-known litterateur, and imperial favorite, Dai Faxing 戴法興 (414–465) began a savage polemic that lasted for two years. Dai, who had little interest in, and less knowledge of, astronomy, argued principally that Zu lacked respect for precedent, and was attempting to replace the ancient practices on which sound astronomy depended. Dai argued, for instance, that use of an improved algorithm for periodically adding lunar months, the distinction between the nodical and anomalistic months, a more accurate sidereal period for Jupiter than 12 years, and what in modern terms amounts to the precession of the equinoxes, were all undesirable.[23] Zu ably and vigorously rebutted Dai's charges, but in 465 a new emperor found the conflict unseemly. He discharged Dai, who died that year, but refused to adopt the new system.

In 493 an heir apparent unsuccessfully proposed it be put into use. Only in 510, a decade after Zu's death, did his equally talented son manage to have a modified form of it tested against a competitive one, whereupon the Great Enlightenment system became official and remained in use until 589.

* * *

Because of the highly political nature of everything connected with imperial charisma, prediction did not steadily improve. Given the turbulence of governmental transitions, and the pressure for quick results, new systems were not always innovative. Systems that incorporated major advances were more than once rejected, and newly adopted ones were sometimes inferior to their predecessors. In the sustained polemics of which we have records, the issue was sometimes technical, sometimes ideological, and sometimes both. Over the past thousand years, it became the norm at the inception of a new dynasty (or, sometimes, at the accession of a new emperor) to adopt a new astronomical system that would signal a new order.[24]

Appendix: Important Astronomical Systems.

The following table lists 32 exceptional astronomical systems from the first century A.D. to the end of imperial China. There are records of roughly 200; some basic information survives for 98.[25] In the Dates column, inclusive dates are those of official use. Single dates mark either systems that did not achieve official status or official systems for which the final dates remain unknown. Many dates require further study. The form "200–250" means "from 200 to 250"; "200/250" means "at some unknown time between 200 and 250." The Dynasty column uses the abbreviations F. (former, *qian* 前), L. (later, *hou* 後), N. (northern, *bei* 北), E. (eastern, *dong* 東), S. (southern, *nan* 南), and W. (western, *hsi* 西). I add a plus sign when a system remained official past the end of a dynasty. Titles in the form "*n*th-year epoch" refer to the number of the epochal year in the cycle of 60 years. Although the Author column lists only the person conventionally credited with authorship, most systems were the products of collaboration. The Year column, for length of the mean tropical year, lists the fractional part of a day. The modern value is 365.2422 days. There is no need to list values for the mean synodic month, since by A.D. 237 that constant had reached the modern value (29.53059 days).

Dates	Dynasty	Title	Author	Year
1/5–85	F. Han	Triple Concordance, Santong 三統曆	Liu Xin 劉歆	.2502
85–206	L. Han	Quarter-remainder, Sifen 四分曆	Bian Xin 編訢	.2500
206–237	L. Han	Supernal Emblem, Qianxiang 乾象曆	Liu Hong 劉洪	.2562
237–443	Wei+	Luminous Inception, Jingchu 景初曆	Yang Wei 楊偉	.2469
443–463	Song+	Epochal Excellence,[26] Yuanjia 元嘉曆	He Chengtian 何承天	.2467
510–589	Liang	Great Enlightenment, Daming 大明曆	Zu Chongzhi 祖沖之	.2428
518?–589	N. Wei	Orthodox Glory, Zhengguang 正光曆	Zhang Longxiang 張龍祥	.2437
540–550	E. Wei	Ascendant Harmony, Xinghe 興和曆	Li Yexing 李業興	.2442
609	Sui+	Sovereign Pole, Huangji 皇極曆	Liu Zhuo 劉焯	.2445
609–619	Sui	Great Patrimony, Daye 大業曆	Zhang Zhouxuan 張胄玄	.2430
619–665	Tang	Fifteenth-year Epoch, Wuyin 戊寅曆	Fu Renjun 傅仁均	.2446
665–728	Tang	Chimera Virtue, Linde 麟德曆	Li Chunfeng 李淳風	.2448
728–758	Tang	Great Expansion, Dayan 大衍曆	Yixing 一行	.2444
763–785	Tang	Fivefold Era, Wuji 五紀曆	Guo Xianzhi 郭獻之	.2448
785–806	Tang	Constant Epoch, Chenyuan 貞元曆	Xu Chengsi 徐承嗣	.2447
822–893	Tang	Extending Enlightenment, Xuanming 宣明曆	Xu Ang 徐昂	.2446
893–956	Tang+	Reverence for the Arcana, Chongxuan 崇玄曆	Bian Gang 邊岡	.2445
963–981	Song	Response to Heaven, Yingtian 應天曆	Wang Chune 王處訥	.2445
981–1101	Song	Supernal Epoch, Qianyuan 乾元曆	Wu Zhaosu 吳昭素	.2449
1001–1024	Song	Matching Heaven, Yitian 儀天曆	Shi Xu 史序	.2446
1024–1064, 1070?–1074	Song	Reverence for Heaven, Chongtian 崇天曆	Song Xinggu 宋行古	.2446
1094–1103	Song	Contemplation of Heaven, Guantian 觀天曆	Huang Juqing 皇居卿	.2436

Dates	Dynasty	Title	Author	Year
1106–1135	Song	Era Epoch, Jiyuan 紀元曆	Yao Shunfu 姚舜輔	.2436
1182–1280	Chin+	Revised Great Enlightenment, Chongxiu daming 重修大明曆	Zhao Zhiwei 趙知微	.2436
1199–1207	Song	Concord with Heaven, Tongtian 統天曆	Yang Zhongfu 楊忠輔	.2425
1207–1251	Song	Spreading Joy, Kaixi 開禧曆	Bao Huanzhi 鮑澣之	.2430
ca. 1221	Yuan	Western Expedition Seventh-year Epoch, Xi zheng gengwu yuan 西征庚午元曆	Yelü Chucai 耶律楚材	.2436
1281–1384	Yuan	Season-Granting, Shoushi 授時曆	Wang Xun 王恂	.2425
1382	Ming	Muslim, Huihui 回回曆	Wu Bozong 吳伯宗	.2422
1384–1644	Ming	Great Concordance, Datong 大統	Liu Ji 劉基	.2425
1644–1742	Qing	Temporal Pattern, Shixian 時憲曆	J. A. Schall von Bell, S.J.	.2422
1742–1911	Qing	Fortieth-year, Guimao 癸卯曆	Ignatius Kögler, S.J.	.2423

Notes

1. Allusion to *Shang shu*, "*Gao yao mo*" 尚書皋陶謨.
2. *Song shi*, 67: 1491. This treatise combined records of mathematical music theory and astronomy in the official history of the Song dynasty (960–1279).
3. Huang (1990), p. 474, citing *Shizu zhang huangdi shilu* 世祖章皇帝實錄, j. 8, s.v. year 2, 9th month, sexagenary day 49 (22 October 1645).
4. They are listed in the text as Enthronement of Spring (late January), Enthronement of Summer (late April), Greater Heat (mid July), Enthronement of Autumn (late July), and Enthronement of Winter (late October).
5. *Jin shu* 晉書, 19: 587–588. Another source cites this as a monthly ritual; *Hou Han shu* 後漢書, Treatises (*zhi* 志), 4: 3101.
6. *Lü shi chunqiu* 呂氏春秋 , *chi* 紀, 1.1.1.15–27, translation modified from that in Knoblock and Riegel (2000), pp. 61–63.
7. This became less prevalent from about 1400 on—for reasons not yet understood—but by no means rare. Chinese historians before modern times grouped observational astronomy with astrology, not with computational astronomy.
8. Huang (1990). The standard reference work for bureaucratic titles fittingly translates varying titles of organizations and officials "astrological" as often as "astronomical" (Hucker 1985).
9. For details see Anonymous 1961, chapter 14B–14C.
10. *Yuan shi* 元史, 94: 2404.
11. On the types of almanacs, and the government's control of their circulation, see the important study in Dong Yuyu 董煜宇 (2007), and details in Dong (2004).

12. Such claims by new emperors or their spokesmen were innumerable; for a typical example in 1368 see *Ming Shi*, 2:20.
13. Jiang Ji 姜岌 (ca. 380) discovered that in the maximal phase of a lunar eclipse the conjunction is perceptible; Sivin (2009), p. 101.
14. For further details on the calendar, see Martzloff (2009) and Sivin (2009).
15. See the systematic analysis of the day and month cycles in Martzloff (2009).
16. See Sivin (1969), pp. 33–64.
17. For additional details on those named below, the best source is Chen (2003).
18. *Mengqi bitan*, item 148. For details, see Sivin (1975).
19. A ten-thousandth of a degree was not accuracy but (spurious) precision.
20. "Commoner (*buyi* 布衣, etc.)" a juridical status, referred to lack of official status.
21. On the Annual Difference see Sivin (2009), pp. 100–101. This book includes a detailed study of the Season-granting reform and full references.
22. Huang (1990).
23. On the Annual Difference, which the Chinese envisioned quite differently than Europeans, see Sivin (2009), pp. 99–101.
24. For examples of issues mentioned here, and a translation and study of the Season-granting system, see Sivin (2009).
25. See Sivin (2009), table 2.1, pp. 43–56.
26. This system remained in use in the Qi dynasty under the name Established Epoch (Jianyuan 建元).

References

Primary sources

Hou Han shu 後漢書 (History of the Later Han period). By Fan Ye 范曄, 445. Covers A.D. 25–220. This and other histories are cited from Zhonghua Book Co. *Ershisi shi* 二十四史.

Jin shu 晉書 (History of the Jin period). By Fang Xuanling 房玄齡, 646. Covers 265–419.

Lü shi chunqiu 呂氏春秋 (Annals of Mr. Lü). Compiled by Lü Buwei, completed by 235 B.C. In *Lü shi chunqiu jiao shi* 呂氏春秋校釋.

Mengqi bitan 夢溪筆談 (Brush talks from Dream Brook). By Shen Gua (or Kuo 沈括), by 1095. Hu Daojing 1960.

Ming shi 明史 (History of the Ming period). By Zhang Tingyu 張廷玉, 1739. Covers 1368–1644.

Shang shu 尚書 (Revered documents), also known as *Shu ching* 書經 (Classic of documents). Anonymous. Documents in the two versions range from 8th century B.C. or earlier to 4th century A.D. In Harvard-Yenching Sinological Index Series.

Song shi 宋史 (History of the Song period). By Toghto 脱脱, 1345. Covers 960–1279.

Yuan shi 元史 (History of the Yuan period). By Song Lian 宋濂, 1370. Covers 1206–1369.

Secondary sources

Anonymous, 1961, *Explanatory Supplement to the Astronomical Ephemeris and The American Ephemeris and Nautical Almanac* (London: Her Majesty's Stationery Office).

Chen Meidong 陈美东, 2003, *Zhongguo kexue jishu shi. Tianwenxue juan* 中国科学技术史．天文学卷 (History of Chinese science and technology. Astronomy) (Beijing: Kexue Chubanshe).

Dong Yuyu 董煜宇, 2004, *Beisong tianwen guanli yanjiu* 北宋天文管理研究 (A study of astronomical administration in the Northern Sung dynasty). Ph.D. dissertation, history of physics, Shanghai Jiaotong Daxue.

———, 2007, "Cong wenhua zhengti gainian shenshi Song dai de tianwenxue—yi Song dai de liri zhuanmai we gean 从文化整体概念审视宋代的天文学—以宋代的历日专卖为个案 (An examination of the astronomy of the Sung period using the concept of cultural manifold: the case of the Sung monopoly on the sale of almanacs)," in Sun Xiaochun 孙小淳 and Zeng Xiongsheng 曾雄生 (eds.), 2007, *Songdai guojia wenhua zhong de kexue* 宋代国家文化中的科学 (Science and the state in the Song period) (Beijing: Zhongguo kexue jishu Chubanshe), 50–63.

Hu Daojing 胡道静, 1956/1960, *Mengqi bitan jiao zheng* 夢溪筆談校證 (Critical annotated edition of Brush talks from Dream Brook). 1956. Revised edition under the title *Xin jiao zheng Mengqi bitan* 新校證夢溪筆談, 2 vols (Beijing: Zhonghau Shuju).

Huang Yinong 黃一農, 1990, "Tang Ruowang yu Qing chu Xi li zhi zhengtonghua 湯若望與清初西曆之正統化 (Johann Schall and the legitimation of the Western calendar at the beginning of the Qing period)", in *Xin bian Zhongguo kejishi. Yanjiang wen gao xuan ji* 新編中國科技史. 演講文稿選集 (New history of Chinese science and technology: Selected lecture notes), (Taipei: Yinhe Wenhua Shiye Gongsi 銀禾文化事業公司), II, 465–491.

Hucker, C. O., 1985, A Dictionary of Official Titles in Imperial China (Stanford: Stanford University Press).

Knoblock, J., and Riegel, J. (trans.), 2000, *The Annals of Lü Buwei* (Stanford: Stanford University Press). [Translation of *Lü shi chunqiu*]

Martzloff, J.-C., 2009, *Le calendrier chinois: Structure et calculs (104 av. J.-C.–1644). Indetermination céleste et réforme permanente. La construction chinoise officielle du temps quotidian discret à partir d'un temps mathématique caché, linéaire et continu.* Sciences, techniques et civilizations du moyen age a l'aube des lumieres 11 (Paris: Honoré Champion).

Sivin, N., 1969, *Cosmos and Computation in Early Chinese Mathematical Astronomy* (Leiden: E. J. Brill).

——, 1975/1995, "Shen Kua (1031-1095)", in *Dictionary of Scientific Biography* (New York: Charles Scribner's Sons), XII, 369-393. Reprinted as "Shen Kua: A Preliminary Assessment of his Scientific Thought and Achievements," *Sung Studies Newsletter* 13, 1977 (published 1978), 331–356. Revised version in N. Sivin, *Science in Ancient China. Researches and Reflections* (Aldershot, Hants: Variorum, 1995), chapter III.

——, 2009, *Granting the Seasons: The Chinese Astronomical Reform of 1280, With a Study of its Many Dimensions and a Translation of its Records* 授時曆叢考 (Secaucus, NJ: Springer).

Calendars in India

Kim Plofker and Toke L. Knudsen*

1. Introduction

The Indian calendar, like the traditional Chinese and Jewish calendars, but unlike the year-reckoning of the West and the Islamic world, has continuously preserved luni-solar synchronization, so that the start of a solar year always more or less coincides with the start of a lunar or synodic month. The year is defined with reference to sidereal positions as well as to purely solar phenomena like equinoxes and solstices, so the stars as well as the sun and moon play a role in determining the passage of time. What the calendar thereby gains in comprehensiveness it loses in simplicity. The complications are increased by the inclusion of various invented time units, such as the so-called *tithi* or 'lunar day' (one-thirtieth of a synodic month). Moreover, although most Indian calendars share the same basic features, there is no one universally accepted system that completely standardizes their details.

This calendar system appears to have developed out of the merging of three basic time-keeping practices separately quantified in India at least as early as the second millennium BC: namely, the division of the annual meteorological cycle into several seasons, the ritual observance of ceremonies tied to solstices and equinoxes, and the identification of changing phases and positions of the moon in the course of a month. Over time, this synthesis expanded to include other astronomical cycles as well as astrological concepts.

Our article traces the origins of the system in the earliest extant Sanskrit sources and follows its subsequent development in texts on mathematical astronomy in the Classical Sanskrit period (from the late first millennium BC onwards). We conclude with a discussion of some of the crucial issues in interpreting dates expressed in Indian calendars and their relationships with other Indian and non-Indian calendrical systems.

2. Calendar Computations in the Earliest Indian Sources

The earliest writings that we have from India are the Vedas. The Vedas are a large textual corpus composed in Sanskrit, constituting the oldest of the Hindu scriptures. There are four proper Vedas, known as *Saṃhitās*, namely the *Ṛg-veda*, the *Yajur-veda*, the *Sāma-veda*, and the *Atharva-veda*. The former three are traditionally connected with the performance of sacrifices, while the latter is a collection of apotropaic incantations. Of these four

* Sections 1, 3, and 4 were written by Plofker and sections 2 and 5 by Knudsen.

Saṃhitās, the *Ṛg-veda* is considered the oldest, based on internal and linguistic evidence. Later layers of what is known as the Vedic literature are the *Brāhmaṇas*, which expound the ritual meaning of the *Saṃhitās*, and the *Upaniṣads*, philosophical-mystical treatises. The relative dating of these texts is again mainly based on internal and linguistic evidence, and is well established. The absolute dating of these texts, however, is controversial.

The Vedas describe and lay out rules for various rituals and sacrifices, which are often required to take place at a particular time, such as at full moon, at new moon, at the solstice, or at the equinox. As such, some knowledge of the movement of the heavenly bodies, by which we can keep track of seasons and months, is necessary to carry out these rituals and sacrifices properly. In other words, calendrical knowledge is important to Vedic culture.

2.1 The Vedas

Considering the importance of calendrical knowledge to Vedic ritual, it is not surprising to find references to the year and seasons, as well as months, in the early parts of the *Ṛg-veda*. In these sections of the *Ṛg-veda*, month names are associated with particular seasonal characteristics. An example of the importance of the calendar in the Vedic texts is in the *Śatapatha-brāhmaṇa*, where the year is identified with Prajāpati, the creator god. A late section of the *Ṛg-veda* speaks of twelve months and then an additional one, i.e., what we call an intercalary month. The intercalary month is inserted to keep the year of twelve lunar months (a lunar month is the time from one conjunction of the sun and the moon to the next) in sync with the seasons of the solar year. At this period, therefore, attempts were made to operate a luni-solar calendar.

In order to do real quantitative astronomy, it is necessary to have a system in which positions in the sky can be indicated. In general, the position of a luminary or a planet is given with reference to the fixed stars or clusters of stars. In the *Ṛg-veda*, stars are mentioned, and in later texts, constellations, called *nakṣatras*, are given. The *nakṣatras* are 27 or 28 divisions of the sky into constellations, each identified by a particular star of the *nakṣatra* in question. As such, the *nakṣatras* are equivalent to the lunar mansions of the Islamic and Chinese traditions. According to Yano, the Indian and Chinese systems are independent, and the Islamic system is derived from the Indian one.[1] However, the origin of the system in India is not clear.

Some sources, like the *Atharva-veda* (19.7.2–5), give 28 *nakṣatras*, while others, like the *Yajur-veda* (*Taittirīya-saṃhitā* 4.4.10.1–3), give 27 *nakṣatras*; the Classical tradition of Indian astronomy operates with 27 *nakṣatras*. The location of each *nakṣatra* can be identified in the Classical tradition, but it is not clear that such identifications are relevant to similar identifications in the earlier texts. The motion of the moon through the *nakṣatras* is important for the timing of sacrifices. For example, a sacrifice might be required to take place when the moon is in a certain *nakṣatra*. Why the *nakṣatras* are important for the Vedic sacrifices is not fully understood.

In addition to month names associated with seasons, the Vedas also have names for months that are also related to *nakṣatra* names, i.e., the time of year when the moon is in a particular *nakṣatra*. Unfortunately, the details of these Vedic calendars cannot be worked out from the brief and inconsistent descriptions in the texts.

2.2 The *Jyotiṣa-vedāṅga*

While the Vedic texts contain poetic descriptions of the heavens, observational records are rare and there is no mathematical formulation of the changes in the heavens and their periodic nature. The first explicit description of astronomical and calendrical knowledge in ancient India is not found in the Vedas themselves but in a text belonging to the ancillary branch of the Vedas dealing with the timing of the Vedic rituals, entitled the *Jyotiṣa-vedāṅga*. This *Jyotiṣa-vedāṅga* is the link between the vague astronomical and calendrical material of the Vedas and later astronomy of India.

There are two recensions of the *Jyotiṣa-vedāṅga*. A shorter recension of 36 verses is associated with the *Ṛg-veda*, and is attributed to a Lagadha, or a Śūci presenting the teachings of Lagadha, but nothing further is known about him. Then there is a longer recension of 44 verses associated with the *Yajur-veda*. The former belongs to the fifth century BC, the latter to a somewhat later period, as noted by Pingree.[2] Many of the verses are common to both recensions.

Both recensions consist of unclear formulas and are thus not a real exposition of astronomy and calendrics. They both open by identifying the year with the deity Prajāpati. The *Ṛg-veda* recension of the *Jyotiṣa-vedāṅga* further states that the Vedas came about for the sake of sacrificial rituals and that the proper performance of such rituals depends on time; therefore, knowledge of the science of time (i.e., astronomy and calendrics) is a key factor in the performance of rituals.

As noted, the *Jyotiṣa-vedāṅga* is the earliest calendrical text from India. It is meant to be a calendrical aid (in fact, all of the main components of the Indian calendar are found in the *Jyotiṣa-vedāṅga*)[3] in fixing the dates and times of the various sacrifices prescribed in the Vedic corpus. As such, it is silent on the planets. The calendar described in the text is based on a five-year cycle, featuring two intercalary months in each cycle; in the *Jyotiṣa-vedāṅga*, a year is 366 days.

Unfortunately, there are many things that we do not know about the *Jyotiṣa-vedāṅga*, including its age. The text contains a statement to the effect that the winter solstice is at the beginning of the *nakṣatra* Śraviṣṭhā, corresponding, in later Indian astronomical texts, to the neighborhood of β Delphini, which would provide an astrochronological dating of about 1200 BC; other interpretations push this date even further back in time. However, it is not known where the boundaries of the *nakṣatras* were back then, nor are we sure of how various celestial phenomena, including solstices and equinoxes, were identified, and we cannot be sure of the parameters, if any, that were established at the time. Therefore it is impossible to give a precise date of the *Jyotiṣa-vedāṅga*.

A related question is where the *Jyotiṣa-vedāṅga* was composed. Since the text gives a ratio of 3:2 for the longest day to the shortest night, a latitude of about 33–35 degrees is implied, but this is north of most of the subcontinent of India. It has been suggested that the *Jyotiṣa-vedāṅga* has a Mesopotamian origin, from which the Indians borrowed it; the ratio of the longest day to the shortest night fits well in Mesopotamia. Other suggestions are the far northwest of India or in the Ganges River basin.[4]

So, while we cannot be sure of the dating of the *Jyotiṣa-vedāṅga*, nor whether its calendrical material is borrowed from a foreign culture, it is still in this text that we find the earliest explicit exposition of the science of astronomy and calendrics.

2.3 The calendar of the Jyotiṣa-vedāṅga

As noted, the purpose of the *Jyotiṣa-vedāṅga* is to define a calendar for the purpose of fixing the time for various sacrifices. As we have seen, the calendar of the *Jyotiṣa-vedāṅga* utilizes a five-year cycle with two intercalary months being added to each cycle. The text discusses the beginning of the cycle (when the sun and the moon are in conjunction in a particular *nakṣatra*), the change in the length of the day during the passing seasons, and measuring time during the day. As noted above, the year is taken to be 366 days long; in addition, we have that 1 year = 366 days = 6 seasons = 12 solar months; 1 civil month = 30 days; and 5 years = 60 solar months = 61 civil months = 62 synodic months = 67 sidereal months. From this it follows that 1 synodic month is about 29.515 days, a value that, as noted by Yano,[5] is not very accurate (the modern value is about 29.530589 days).

The text takes into account the change of the length of daytime and nighttime during the year. A day and night is divided into thirty units, called *muhūrtas* (each about equal to 48 of our minutes). It is further divided into sixty units called *ghaṭikās*. The total change in daytime length over half a year is six *muhūrtas*. In other words, on the summer solstice day, the day will last 18 *muhūrtas* and on the winter solstice day 12 *muhūrtas* (counting from sunrise to sunset). This gives the ratio 3:2 mentioned earlier, and the information on daytime, while not directly related to a calendar, therefore has bearing on the age of the text.

The text also tells us how to find where in the cycle of the moon the current equinox falls. This is given in terms of *tithis*, or lunar days, which were discussed earlier. In addition, the text gives more rules concerning this luni-solar calendar. Furthermore, it links *nakṣatras* with deities.

2.4 Astrochronology

As was mentioned above, while there is an established relative chronology for the Vedic corpus, the absolute chronology is controversial. One of the ways that scholars have sought to establish absolute dates for strata of the Vedas, as well for later Sanskrit literature, is through astrochronology. The approach here is to find statements in the texts that can be interpreted astronomically to yield a date.

For example, a passage in the *Śatapatha-brāhmaṇa* (2.1.2.3–4) can be interpreted to mean that the Pleiades rise exactly at the east point of the horizon, and such an intepretation implies that the vernal equinox was located in the Pleiades when the statement was composed. This would date the passage to 2950 BC.[6] Other similar passages in various Vedic and later texts have been used to date them.

There are, however, numerous problems with such interpretations. For one, we cannot be certain that the passages in question are to be taken as precise statements. The passage from the *Śatapatha-brāhmaṇa* mentioned above, for example, could alternatively simply mean that the Pleiades always rise in the eastern direction, in which case no date can be inferred from it. In other words, when taken at face value, such statements do not yield any reliable dates. Among other problems are that we do not know the boundaries of the *nakṣatras* in the Vedic period. These problems show themselves in the inconsistencies between the various dates given for Vedic texts. For example, the *Ṛg-veda*, which is universally agreed upon as being older than the *Śatapatha-brāhmaṇa* (based on linguistic and other arguments), can be astrochronologically dated to about 3300 BC, while astrochronological interpretations can be used to date the *Śatapatha-brāhmaṇa* to about 4000 BC. Another passage in the *Śatapatha-brāhmaṇa* yields an astrochronological dating of 3000 BC.[7]

Another calendrical issue is the dating of the so-called *Mahā-bhārata* war. The *Mahā-bhārata* is a famous and voluminous Indian epic, the central theme of which is a large battle between two factions of the same clan. Traditionally, the battle is believed to have occurred at the beginning of a particular era, dated by Indian astronomers to ca. 18 February 3102 BC, at which time a particular alignment of the heavenly bodies is said to have occurred. Attempts have been made to identify this alignment, as well as to date the battle based on other passages, with bearing on astronomy, found in the text. However, these approaches suffer from the same defects as was the case with similar passages from the Vedas; the date of the battle, if the battle indeed has a historical reality, cannot be pinpointed from these passages.

The passages in the texts, taken at face value, appear to have been for people who already knew the system, not by any means a systematic exposition of it. As such, it is no wonder that we cannot fix dates with any certainty using such astrochronological arguments.

3. Development of the Classical Calendar

In the course of several centuries following the codification of the calendar in the *Jyotiṣa-vedāṅga*, Indian astronomers refined the intercalation scheme and the metrology of time and celestial coordinates to produce the sophisticated calendar systems still in use in various Indian contexts. The rough five-year *yuga* intercalation cycle was replaced by more complicated period relations synchronizing months and years more precisely, and additional time units such as the seven-day week and the solar month were included in the system, along with standardized epoch dates identifying various commonly recognized eras.

Most of these incremental developments are not recorded in surviving texts, but the general outline of their accretion can be traced. Recall that the *Jyotiṣa-vedāṅga* calendar of the Late Vedic period was based on a *yuga* cycle of five 366-day solar years containing 62 lunar months (twelve regular months in each of the five years plus two intercalary months). The year, starting from the new moon corresponding to the winter solstice, is subdivided by the equinoxes and solstices, and the day is divided into thirty *muhūrtas* or sixty *ghaṭikās*, while the lunar month has thirty equal subdivisions called *tithis*. The positions of the sun and moon are measured in units called *nakṣatras* or arcs equal to 1/27 of the moon's circuit in the sky. The *nakṣatras* are demarcated by 27 recognized constellations, and the twelve lunar months are named after the constellations in which their full moons appear. The calculations prescribed in the text allow the user to keep track of the passage of these various units of time, and in particular, to figure out how many intercalary months have passed up to a given time in the *yuga*.

The earliest Indian inscriptions, from the reign of the Emperor Aśoka in the third century BC, do not mention intercalation and employ somewhat different time measures for the dates they refer to (including regnal years and times within specified months when the moon occupies a particular *nakṣatra*). This suggests that the civil calendar may have been adjusted on an *ad hoc* basis by administrative officials rather than in accordance with any regular cycle.[8] However, the *Artha-śāstra*, a comprehensive administrative manual probably also dating from the third century BC, prescribes the recording of dates by regnal year, month, half-month, and day (but does not specifically mention the *tithi*); standard accounting periods also include five-day and four-month intervals. The *Artha-śāstra* states that the fiscal year, which is twelve lunar months long, ends on the full moon of the month Āṣāḍha (near the summer solstice). The intercalary month, as in the *Jyotiṣa-vedāṅga*, is said to occur twice every five years, in the middle and at the end of the cycle.[9]

This rather rough but practical calendric system was later substantially modified, partly as a result of refinements and elaborations in Indian astronomical theory. Some of these modifications grew out of concepts borrowed from Hellenistic Greek astronomy and astrology, introduced by the Indo-Greeks (or 'Yavanas', a Sanskritization of 'Ionian') who settled in the north and west after the departure of Alexander, and the Indo-Scythians (or Śakas) who succeeded them. Before the middle of the first millennium AD, Indian astronomers had assimilated such concepts as the twelve signs of the zodiac, the seven days of the week and their association with the sun, moon, and the five star-planets, as well as the fundamentals of horoscopic astrology, base-60 units of arc and time measurement, and spherical coordinate systems for denoting celestial positions.[10] They combined these diverse elements into the standard structure of the Classical Indian calendar, whose astronomical and astrological rationales are described in the following sections.

3.1 Standardization of Various Calendar Eras

The most ancient calendar texts and recorded dates did not assume any fixed epoch for the reckoning of years. There were rules for computing the current year in a *yuga* or intercalation cycle, and administrative dates were identified with a regnal year of the reigning monarch, but continuous eras were not mentioned. By the mid-first millennium AD, however, when the earliest surviving comprehensive astronomical treatises were composed, several eras were used generally enough to be described as standard.[11] Years in a continuous era, as well as regnal years, might be computed either as 'current' (analogous to the Christian/Common Era, where, e.g., a date in the year 2010 indicates the two thousand and tenth year of the era), or as 'expired' (analogous to the usual Western convention for the age of individuals, where describing someone as, e.g., twenty years old means that the individual is in his or her twenty-first year). Users of all these eras generally placed the beginning of the calendar year at or near the start of a lunar month in the spring or autumn: that is, somewhere around an equinox, rather than at one of the solstices as in ancient times.

Śaka. The so-called Śaka era, associated with the Śaka dynasty of Ujjain known as the Western Kṣatrapas, begins in AD 78. How and when it became established as a continuous era is unclear, but its use (most commonly counting the years as expired) was widespread by at least the middle of the first millennium.[12] It has been suggested that its epoch may have been chosen for astronomical reasons rather than to mark some political event. Namely, near the vernal equinox of AD 78 there was a conjunction of the sun and moon with Jupiter; using that event as the era's epoch date would have conveniently synchronized the era with the Jupiter cycle (see below).[13]

Vikrama Saṃvat. The beginning of the Vikrama Saṃvat era, commonly called just Saṃvat or 'year', is dated to 58 BC. The era takes its name from a legendary King Vikramāditya who is said to have conquered the Śaka rulers of Ujjain at that time, although it appears actually to have originated with the reign of the Śaka king Azes I. Saṃvat years, like Śaka years, are typically counted as expired, and were employed most frequently in northern India, while Śaka dates were more common in the south.[14] However, there was a great deal of overlap between the two systems, and there are many examples of dates recorded in both eras simultaneously. The Śaka and Saṃvat eras were by far the most widely used eras in Indian records from early medieval up through modern times.

Kali. The legendary 'Kali Age' is the last and shortest of the four ages in Hindu mythology, a period of 420,000 years slightly reminiscent of the 'Iron Age' of Western classical myth. The Kali era, traditionally considered to have begun in 3102 BC as a consequence of the *Mahā-bhārata* war (see section 2.4), is chiefly a scientific convention used by astronomers rather than a standardized part of a civil calendar, somewhat like the modern Julian Date. However, Kali year-numbers (usually expired) do sometimes accompany dates in other eras in civil records. Astronomers of the early first millennium AD appear to have chosen the Kali epoch based on back-calculating the occurrence of an approximate conjunction of the sun, moon and planets when the sun was at the beginning of the zodiac in that year, a date corresponding to 18 February 3102 BC.[15]

3.2 Cyclical Eras

The Jupiter (Bārhaspatya) cycle. The dating convention associated with Jupiter ('Bṛhaspati') is not a continuous era but rather a cyclic sequence of sixty years, each with a distinctive name, recorded either instead of or in addition to a year-number in one of the non-cyclical eras. This cycle originated in the fact that the sidereal period of Jupiter is approximately twelve solar years, so sixty years corresponds to about five of Jupiter's revolutions through the sky. Since the years are conventionally referred to by name rather than by number, they are recorded as current years; for example, most of AD 2010 falls in the 24th year of the Jupiter cycle, named Vikṛta.[16]

The Saptarṣi era. This reckoning, named after the constellation known to us as the Big Dipper and in Sanskrit as the Saptarṣi or 'Seven Sages', is theoretically a cycle of 2700 years commencing in Kali 26 or 3076 BC, rather than a continuous era in its own right. However, it is typically computed as though it were counted continuously from Kali 26, and recorded in current years with the Saptarṣi millennium and century omitted. For example, AD 2010 mostly overlaps with Saptarṣi 5086, which would be denoted simply as Saptarṣi year 86.[17]

3.3 Astronomical Models for Calendar Computation

Classical Indian astronomy was influenced not only by the requirements of sacrificial ritual but also by some aspects of Greek astronomy. Its models assumed a vast sequence of time cycles (a lifetime of the universe, or *kalpa*) during which the stars, sun, moon and other planets along with their apogees and nodes periodically revolved around a central spherical earth.[18] Their motions were measured with respect to the same reference circles used in Hellenistic astronomy, namely, the celestial equator and ecliptic.

The passage of time was conventionally assumed to begin with all the celestial objects except the fixed stars conjoined at the zero-point of the ecliptic. The ecliptic was divided into twelve equal arcs corresponding to, and named after (see table 1 below), the Greek signs of the zodiac. However, its zero-point was defined sidereally, approximately at the star called Revatī (ζ Piscium), instead of exactly at the vernal equinox as in the case of the Greek ecliptic. Precession causes the location of the equinoxes and solstices to shift slowly along the ecliptic over time: consequently, in Indian calendrics the start of the astronomical solar year, when the sun returns to the sidereal zero-point, is gradually moving farther away from the vernal equinox at tropical longitude Aries 0°.[19]

Since the cycles of the solar year and the synodic (lunar) month are not perfectly synchronized, the sun's arrival at the ecliptic zero-point usually does not coincide with the syzygy that marks the beginning of a month. Depending on the particular variant of the calendar system in use, the calendar year might be officially considered to start at either of those times. So there would generally be a gap of some days between the beginning of the solar year and the beginning of the year of twelve lunar months, which would have to be calculated based on the period relations of the sun and moon. When the start of the year and the start of the first month got too far out of sync, an intercalary month would be added to re-synchronize them.

Moreover, neither the solar year nor the lunar month is perfectly synchronized with the rotation that produces the civil day, so the precise moment marking the astronomical start of the year might occur at any time during the current weekday. Days were generally considered to begin at local sunrise but in some calendar systems were reckoned from midnight instead, so if the start of a year fell between midnight and sunrise, there would be a discrepancy between different systems concerning which weekday it fell on.

Consequently, the calculation of calendar date information was crucially dependent on the details of the particular astronomical school followed by the calculator. Parameters such as the number of revolutions of the sun, moon or stars in a *kalpa* determined the length of the year and the month. The assumed sizes of their orbits, epicycles, and orbital inclinations affected the computation of their conjunctions. All these factors as well as the value assumed for the size of the earth could alter the reckoning of true local time, as did assumptions about which event properly marked the beginning of the year, the month or the day.[20] So astronomers in different schools who were technically working with the same calendar system might easily get different results when calculating the date or time of a particular occurrence in the calendar.

3.4 Astrology and the Calendar

Along with some models for spherical astronomy and the seven-day week, Hellenistic astral science also supplied astrological concepts that expanded the purpose of the ancient Indian calendar. The malevolence or beneficence of planetary influences upon individual time units such as days, months or *tithis* made it vitally important to keep track of where any given moment fell with respect to them. Given the complexity of the interrelated cycles of these time units and their constantly varying significance for good or bad fortune, it is no wonder that the production of a yearly calendar required the services of a professional astrologer.

4. Details of the Classical Calendar or *pañcāṅga*

The post-Vedic Indian calendar attained its established form (or forms, since there were many variations in the ways its chief characteristics were defined and combined in practice) in the early centuries AD. It synthesized the ancient ritual timekeeping, historical eras, astronomical models, and astrological purposes described above into a unified though complicated system. A complete calendar for a given year would list the sequence of all the days in the year, along with the specific times during each day marking the transitions of the other time units, and the occurrence of prescribed religious rites and festivals along with particularly auspicious or inauspicious celestial events such as eclipses.

4.1 Structure of the Calendar

The Classical calendar is called the *pañcāṅga* or 'five-part' (literally 'five-limbed'). This name refers to the five chief time units whose passage the calendar tracks:[21]

1. The *tithi*, which is slightly shorter than a day, is approximately one-thirtieth of a synodic month, or the time required for the moon to advance eastward of the sun in the sky by 12° of arc. When the moon has repeated this advance thirty times starting from conjunction or new moon, it has moved ahead of the sun by 360° or one full circle, and therefore has arrived back at the sun for the next conjunction in the following month. The *tithis* of each half-month are numbered from 1 to 15; *tithi* 1 is also called *pratipad* ('beginning'), while the *tithis* ending with new moon and full moon are called *amāvāsya* ('new moon') and *pūrṇimā* ('full moon') respectively.

2. The weekday (*vāra* or 'turn') is the civil day measured usually from one sunrise (but occasionally from midnight) to the next. Days of a month are numbered according to the number of the *tithi* in which the day-beginning falls. Since the *tithi* and the day are of different (and slightly varying) lengths, a particular *tithi* in a given month usually contains only one day-beginning, but sometimes contains two, or none. This means that occasionally a day-number might be omitted or repeated. The seven weekdays in Sanskrit, following Hellenistic sources, are named after the visible planets in the familiar order Sun, Moon, Mars, Mercury, Jupiter, Venus, and Saturn.

3. The *nakṣatra* is approximately 1/27 of a sidereal month, or the time required for the moon to advance 13° 20' (1/27 of a complete circle) eastward with respect to the fixed stars. This distance 13° 20' is the conventional length of each of the 27 lunar-path constellations or *nakṣatras*, hence the name. The individual time-unit *nakṣatras* bear the names of their corresponding constellations (listed in table 2).

4. The *yoga* is on average somewhat shorter than a *tithi*, and corresponds to the time required for the eastward advances of both moon and sun in the sky to add up (hence the name *yoga*, literally 'sum') to 13° 20'. The *yoga*-cycle is considered to reach its starting point when both bodies are at the initial point of the zodiac. Each of the 27 *yogas* in the cycle is individually named (see table 2).

5. The *karaṇa* is half a *tithi*, so there are sixty of them in each synodic month. The sixty *karaṇas* have eleven names (see table 2): four of them are assigned to four *karaṇas* in the interval containing new moon, and the remaining seven names cycle eight times through the sequence of 54 *karaṇas* beginning with the second *karaṇa* after new moon.

All the above units have astrological significance, and the last two have no other significance. (The *tithi* is extremely important astrologically but seems to have been originally developed to keep track of the phases of the moon.) In addition to these, the calendar also recognizes various larger time units:

- The solar year, beginning at the sun's annual arrival at the starting-point of the sidereal zodiac (that is, with the first solar month). The calendar year is usually held to begin at this moment or else with the first civil day of the lunar month containing this moment. (In some variants the calendar year begins instead in the autumn.)

- The half-year (*ayana* or 'going') from one solstice to the next. The so-called northern *ayana* begins at the winter solstice, when the sun's rising point on the eastern horizon starts shifting northward from day to day, and the southern *ayana* at the summer solstice, when the rising-point begins to shift southward instead.

- The season, a period of two months identified as a distinct meteorological season and named accordingly (see table 1).

- The solar month, demarcated by the sun's transition from one zodiacal sign in the sidereal zodiac to the next. Each month is named after its corresponding zodiacal sign (see table 1).

- The synodic (lunar) month, most commonly measured from one new moon to the next. In many calendar variants, the month extends instead from full moon to full moon. There are twelve individually named lunar months (see table 1), each of which typically contains the beginning of a corresponding solar month. However, since the average synodic month is shorter than the average solar month, this pattern slips over time. When the lunar and solar cycles get far enough out of phase (determined by calculations based on luni-solar period relations), an intercalary month is inserted in which no solar month begins. An intercalary month added after, say, month X has no name of its own but is simply called 'additional X'.

- The half-month (*pakṣa* or 'side') or period of fifteen *tithis* between new and full moon or vice versa. The so-called 'bright *pakṣa*' begins at new moon and the 'dark *pakṣa*' at full moon.

- The *ghaṭikā* or one-sixtieth of a day, which is further subdivided into smaller units, each of which is a sixtieth of the preceding. (The hour or *horā*, the 24th part of a day, was adopted from Hellenistic sources as an astrologically significant interval but was not typically used for timekeeping.)

Tables 1 and 2 list the names of the various time units in the abovementioned sequences. Table 1 shows the most commonly accepted correspondence between solar months, lunar or synodic months, and seasons, beginning with the sun's entrance into the zodiacal sign Meṣa (Aries) in the month Caitra, near the vernal equinox (although nowadays this year-beginning in the Indian calendar falls closer to mid-April than to the equinox itself).[22]

Signs/Solar Months		Lunar Months	Seasons	
Meṣa	(ram)	Caitra	Vasanta	(bright)
Vṛṣa	(bull)	Vaiśākha		
Mithuna	(couple)	Jyaiṣṭha	Grīṣma	(heat)
Karkaṭa	(crab)	Āṣāḍha		
Siṃha	(lion)	Śrāvaṇa	Varṣā	(rains)
Kanyā	(girl)	Bhādrapada		
Tulā	(balance)	Āśvina	Śarad	(ripening)
Vṛścika	(scorpion)	Kārttika		
Dhanus	(bow)	Mārgaśīrṣa	Hemanta	(winter)
Makara	(sea-monster)	Pauṣa		
Kumbha	(water-pot)	Māgha	Śiśira	(chilly)
Mīna	(fish)	Phālguna		

TABLE 1. Names of months and seasons.

Table 2 lists the names of the *nakṣatras* and *yogas* starting from the beginning of the Indian sidereal zodiac. (As explained in section 2.1, the lunar months originally took their names from the *nakṣatra* constellations occupied by the moon at particular times of the year; hence the close resemblance between month names and some of the *nakṣatra* names.) The eleven *karaṇa* names in the third column of table 2 are assigned to the sixty *karaṇas* beginning with the first *karaṇa* of the bright *pakṣa* of the lunar month, i.e., immediately after new moon. They have no relation to the position of the sun or moon in the zodiac, only to the moon's phase.[23]

4.2 Representing and Interpreting Dates

From about the middle of the first millennium AD onward, the standard way to express a date for record-keeping purposes (e.g., in the colophon of a manuscript or on a copper-plate deed) consisted of specifying the current *tithi* of either the bright or dark *pakṣa* of the current month and a year-number in one or more of the major eras, or perhaps in the Jupiter cycle.[24] Frequently scribes would include the corresponding weekday, and occasionally other information like the current *nakṣatra* or *yoga*, or the time of day in *ghaṭikās*. A scribe equipped with a current *pañcāṅga* and a water-clock or some other means of telling time during the day would find it quite straightforward to record any of these data.

Interpreting a recorded date without access to the particular *pañcāṅga* that the scribe was using, however, is far from straightforward. Any individual variant of the Indian calendar system is determined by a host of choices made by the astronomer who computes it. Are the years of an era considered to be current or expired? Did the year begin in the spring or the autumn? Do lunar months begin with new moon or full moon? Did the

Nakṣatras	Yogas	Karaṇas
Aśvinī	Viṣkambha	Kiṃstughna (1)
Bharaṇī	Prīti	Bava (2, 9, ..., 51)
Kṛttikā	Āyuṣmat	Balava (3, 10, ..., 52)
Rohiṇī	Saubhāgya	Kaulava (4, 11, ..., 53)
Mṛgaśiras	Śobhana	Taitila (5, 12, ..., 54)
Ārdrā	Atigaṇḍa	Gara (6, 13, ..., 55)
Punarvasu	Sukarman	Vaṇija (7, 14, ..., 56)
Puṣya	Dhṛti	Viṣṭi (8, 15, ..., 57)
Āśleṣā	Śūla	Śakuni (58)
Maghā	Gaṇḍa	Catuṣpada (59)
1st Phālgunī	Vṛddhi	Nāga (60)
2nd Phālgunī	Dhruva	
Hasta	Vyāghāṭa	
Citrā	Harṣaṇa	
Svāti	Vajra	
Viśākhā	Siddhi	
Anurādhā	Vyatipāta	
Jyeṣṭhā	Varīyas	
Mūla	Parigha	
1st Aṣāḍhā	Śiva	
2nd Aṣāḍhā	Siddha	
Śravaṇa	Sādhya	
Dhaniṣṭhā	Śubha	
Śatabhiṣaj	Śukla	
1st Bhadrapadā	Brahman	
2nd Bhadrapadā	Indra	
Revatī	Vaidhṛti	

Table 2. Names of *nakṣatras*, *yogas*, and *karaṇas*.

divergence between lunar and solar months require an intercalary month in this year? Which *tithis* correspond to one civil day, and which to two, or to none? What parameters were used to compute the local time? These and many other questions must be answered before we can know with certainty what date in a modern calendar is represented by a historical date in the Indian calendar. And since a researcher hardly ever knows exactly what astronomical calculations a particular recorded date was based on, date conversions can be quite conjectural.

For example, a certain manuscript colophon states that the copying was completed in Kāśī (Varanasi) on "Saṃvat 1815, in the month of Jyaiṣṭha, in the dark *pakṣa*, on the eighth [*tithi*], on the day of Mars [Tuesday]". A calendar conversion program, receiving this information along with the assumption that months begin at new moon, computes the given date as equivalent to 29 June in AD 1758, which unfortunately was a Thursday.[25] But if we assume instead that the lunar months begin at full moon, the equivalent modern date is calculated to be 30 May 1758, which indeed fell on a Tuesday, so we accept that as the date of the manuscript. Another colophon records the completion of the manuscript in the city of 'Suragiri' (possibly modern Girnar near Ahmedabad) in Śaka 1367, "in Vaiśākha, in the bright *pakṣa*, on the true tenth [*tithi*], on the day of Saturn [Saturday]". Here, the assumption that months begin at new moon does give us an equivalent modern calendar date on a Saturday, namely 17 April 1445 (Julian calendar).[26]

However, some recorded dates cannot be made to convert neatly for either possibility, as in the case of an inscription with an alleged date of Sunday *tithi* 11 of the dark *pakṣa* of Jyaiṣṭha in Saṃvat 1207, which equates to Wednesday 24 May or Tuesday 25 April of 1150 (Julian) depending on whether Jyaiṣṭha is held to commence at new moon or full moon. Moreover, interpreting the Saṃvat year-number as current rather than expired gives the possible equivalents as Saturday 4 June or Thursday 5 May in 1149. None of these attempts manages to extract from the given Indian calendar date a converted date that matches it at all points; a reconstruction with different astronomical parameters and assuming an autumn year-beginning is required to arrive at a converted date that actually falls on a Sunday, namely, 13 May 1151.[27] (And of course, that reconstruction also assumes that the scribe did not simply make a mistake in recording the weekday or *tithi* number, which might easily happen.)

Indian astronomers themselves were certainly well aware of the possibility of ambiguities and inconsistencies in dates computed in their highly complex calendar system. They acknowledged the possibility of having to make *ad hoc* adjustments to account for discrepancies. As the famous twelfth-century astronomer Bhāskara II serenely observed in his astronomy treatise:

> If the total of days [since the epoch must be] increased or decreased by one for the sake of [consistency with] the given weekday, then the *tithis* likewise [must be changed accordingly] ... If a true intercalary month that occurred was not included [in the computation], or if [it] was included but did not occur, then the current day is to be found by a wise [calculator] by means of the [computed number of] intercalary months plus or minus one, respectively.[28]

Modern researchers dealing with historical Indian calendar dates often need to be similarly flexible.

5. Calendrical Interactions

Within the Indian astronomical tradition itself there are a number of different schools. Each employs the same basic model, but the parameters differ. For example, two schools might have the moon make a different number of revolutions around the earth in a given span of time. This, in turn, means that other parameters, such as the length of a year, differ, as was described in section 3.3. The way to deal with this within the tradition itself was often by using so-called *bījas* . A *bīja* is a set of numbers to be applied to each luminary and planet to correct its position. Often the purpose of a given set of *bījas* is obscure, but some *bījas* are meant to correct positional data from the model of one school to that of another. Since positional data determine situations such as conjunctions of the sun and the moon, the sun's entry into a particular sign, and so on, there are small calendrical differences between the various schools. The *bījas* can thus also be employed to correlate calendars.[29]

When it comes to calendars that are not indigenous to India, calendars based on a model that differs from the one used in India, the situation is more complicated. The Islamic calendar, for example, does not start the year depending on the sun's position with respect to the fixed stars. Among the Islamic scholars, al-Bīrūnī (973–1048), who was the first Islamic scholar to study India, wrote about calendar conversions in his *Masudic Canon*.[30] In this treatise, al-Bīrūnī gives rules for converting between the calendars of India and those of the Islamic world.

The classical Indian calendar operates with a term known as the *ahargaṇa*. This is the number of days lapsed since a particular epoch (this could be the beginning of creation, or some other convenient date; see the discussion of eras and epochs in section 3.1), and an Indian astronomical text will give instructions for how to compute it. The computation of planetary positions, etc., is based on this count of days: knowing how far each luminary and planet travels on average during a day, one can find the average motion during the span of the *ahargaṇa*, and the actual position of the heavenly body at the given time can then be found geometrically from the mean position. Now, in order to convert a date in an Indian calendar to another one, say an Islamic one, one approach, which is essentially what al-Bīrūnī does, would be to find the *ahargaṇa* for the particular date. If the equivalent epoch of the Indian calendar is known in the Islamic calendar, one can basically just use the *ahargaṇa* to find the corresponding date in the Islamic calendar. Such an approach can also be used to, say, convert an Indian date into our modern calendar.

Similarly, to convert a, say, Islamic date to a corresponding date in an Indian calendar, one can start by finding what the epoch of the Indian calendar is in the Islamic calendar. Then one can proceed to count the number of days from that date to the present date, which yields the *ahargaṇa*. The *ahargaṇa*, in turn, can be used to find the current day in the Indian calendar.[31]

While the above sounds relatively simple, in practice it can be more complicated, involving many computations. The fact that the Indian calendar is luni-solar, whereas the western calendar is solar also contributes numerous non-trivial computations. The complexity of the Indian calendar, involving as it does both the motions of the sun and the moon, as well its various eras and epochs, makes converting between calendars a challenging process.

Notes

1. See Yano (2003), p. 378.
2. See Pingree (1981), p. 10.
3. See Yano (2003).
4. For these hypotheses, see Pingree (1973), p. 4, Falk (2000), p. 117, and Ōhashi (2000), p. 344.
5. See Yano (2003), p. 378.
6. See Plofker (2009), p. 33.
7. See Plofker (2009), pp. 34–35.
8. Pingree (1982), p. 355.
9. The time units used for record-keeping are mentioned in *Artha-śāstra* 2.6.12 and 2.7.30, while the end of the fiscal year is specified in 2.7.6, and the prescribed times for intercalation in 2.20.66.
10. See Pingree (1976) and Yano (2003), pp. 383–385.
11. Salomon (1998), pp. 171–173.
12. Salomon (1998), pp. 182–184.
13. Falk (2001), pp. 131–133.
14. Salomon (1998), p. 182. For epochs and descriptions of other historical eras commonly used in Indian dates, see Salomon (1998), pp. 181–195.
15. Salomon (1998), pp. 180–181, Pingree (1963), pp. 238–239.
16. Salomon (1998), pp. 197–198, Pillai (1985), p. 39.
17. Salomon (1998), p. 196.
18. Pingree (1963), pp. 238–240.
19. See Yano (2003), pp. 384–385, and Pingree and Morrissey (1989), p. 104.
20. For a comparison of the parameters of different Classical astronomical schools, see Pingree (1978), pp. 555–618.
21. For more detailed discussion of all the time units described below, see Yano (2003), pp. 384–388, Pillai (1985), pp. 1–8, and Sewell and Dīkshit (1896), pp. 1–7. A translated excerpt from a late 19th-century *pañcāṅga* is shown in Sewell and Dīkshit (1896), pp. 14–15.
22. Yano (2003), pp. 384–386.
23. Pillai (1985), p. 36; Sewell and Dīkshit (1896), p. cxiii.
24. Salomon (1998), p. 174.
25. MS. Oxford (Chandra Shum Shere) d.799(6), f. 21. The conversion program used for most of the following dates is Michio Yano's online 'Pancanga' program available at http://www.cc.kyoto-su.ac.jp/~yanom/pancanga.
26. MS. LD Institute (Ahmedabad) 8261, f. 42.
27. Salomon (1998), p. 179. Yano's 'Pancanga' program finds Saturday 4 June for the date that Salomon, reporting F. Kielhorn's results, gives as Friday 3 June.
28. *Siddhāntaśiromaṇi* I.1.6.1–3, Śastrī (1989), pp. 31–33, my translation.
29. See Pingree (1996) for a comprehensive discussion of *bījas*.
30. See Kennedy et al. (1965).
31. The first known attempt to formulate such a conversion algorithm in an Indian text appears in an early 14th-century arithmetic treatise by a Jain official at the Delhi Sultans' court; see SaKHYa (2009), pp. 166–167.

References

Falk, H., 2000, "Measuring Time in Mesopotamia and Ancient India", *Zeitschrift der Deutschen Morgenländischen Gesellschaft* 150, 107–132.

——, 2001, "The *yuga* of Sphujiddhvaja and the Era of the Kuṣāṇas", *Silk Road Art and Archaeology* 7, 121–136.

Kennedy, E. S., Engle, S., and Wamstad, J., 1965, "The Hindu Calendar as Described in Al-Bīrūnī's

Masudic Canon", *Journal of Near Eastern Studies* 24, 274–284.

Ōhashi, Y., 2000, "Remarks on the Origin of Indo-Tibetan Astronomy", in H. Selin (ed.), *Astronomy Across Cultures: The History of Non-Western Astronomy* (Dordrecht: Kluwer), 341–369.

Pillai, L. D. S., repr. 1985, *Panchang and Horoscope* (New Delhi: Asian Educational Services).

Pingree, D., 1963, "Astronomy and Astrology in India and Iran", *Isis* 54, 229–246.

——, 1973, "The Mesopotamian Origin of Early Indian Mathematical Astronomy", *Journal for the History of Astronomy* 4, 1–12.

——, 1976, "The Recovery of Early Greek Astronomy from India", *Journal for the History of Astronomy* 7, 109–123.

——, 1978, "History of Mathematical Astronomy in India", in C. Gillespie (ed.), *Dictionary of Scientific Biography* (New York: Scribners), vol. 15, 533–633.

——, 1981, *Jyotiḥśāstra: Astral and Mathematical Literature*, History of Indian Literature 6 (Wiesbaden: Otto Harrassowitz).

——, 1982, "A Note on the Calendars Used in Early Indian Inscriptions", *Journal of the American Oriental Society* 102, 355–359.

——, 1996, "Bīja-Corrections in Indian Astronomy", *Journal for the History of Astronomy* 27, 161–172.

——, and Morrissey, P., 1989, "On the Identification of the Yogatārās of the Indian Nakṣatras", *Journal for the History of Astronomy* 20, 99–119.

Plofker, K., 2009, *Mathematics in India* (Princeton and Oxford: Princeton University Press).

SaKHYa, 2009, *Gaṇitasārakaumudī* (Delhi: Manohar).

Salomon, R., 1998, *Indian Epigraphy* (Oxford: Oxford University Press).

Śāstrī, B. D., rev. ed. 1989, *Siddhāntaśiromaṇi*, Kashi Sanskrit Series 72 (Varanasi: Chaukhambha Sanskrit Sansthan).

Sewell, R., and Dīkshit, S. B., 1896, *The Indian Calendar* (London: Swan Sonnenschein).

Shamasastry, R., 1915, *Artha-śāstra of Kauṭilya* (Mysore: University of Mysore Oriental Library).

Yano, M., 2003, "Calendar, Astronomy and Astrology", in G. Flood (ed.), *The Blackwell Companion to Hinduism* (Oxford: Blackwell), 376–392.

The 364-Day Year in the Dead Sea Scrolls and Jewish Pseudepigrapha*

Jonathan Ben-Dov

The Dead Sea Scrolls are a corpus of ancient Jewish writings discovered on the shores of the Dead Sea in caves near the site of Qumran.[1] The scrolls were written between approximately 200 BC and 68 AD. They belong to the period marked in Jewish history as the 'Second Temple Period' (ca. 515 BC – 70 AD). Many of the scrolls are copies of earlier material, most notably books of the Hebrew Bible, while other compositions preserved in the scrolls were written closer in time to the copies found at Qumran, and thus reflect the interests and ideology of a Jewish society in the early Roman period. Some scrolls constitute copies of the Pseudepigrapha, i.e., Jewish writings with an apocalyptic background that were not preserved as part of Scripture but circulated as 'extraneous books'. Some of these writings were preserved through later periods of time, while being transmitted in various translations such as Greek, Latin, Syriac and ancient Ethiopic (Geʿez). A final and significant part of the scrolls corpus represents the writings of a unique Jewish sect who settled at Qumran, and whose scribes produced a great amount of written documents reflecting the ideology and practice of the sect. According to the prevalent theory, it was this group, called the *yaḥad*, who ultimately hid the scrolls in the caves near Qumran.

Like the sectarian writings from Qumran, many Psuedepigrapha attest to a belief in a select group of inspired people and its separation from the rest of the nation. Many other themes, including the calendar, are common to the two textual corpora. However, the sectarian ideology and practice did not reach full implementation in the Psuedepigrapha, while in the sectarian scrolls they are fully fledged. The two main Psuedepigrapha to be discussed here are the Book of 1 Enoch, especially the astronomical section in chapters 72–82, and the book of Jubliees.[2] The Book of 1 Enoch (also called the 'Ethiopic Enoch' on account of its preservation in Ethiopic culture) is a collection of Jewish apocalyptic writings, mostly written around the second century BC. Enoch, a biblical figure from ante-diluvian times, is depicted in the post-biblical apocalyptic literature as the founder of human civilization and transmitter of science and writing to humanity. While fragments of the Aramaic Enochic writings were found at Qumran, and fragments of a Greek translation surfaced elsewhere, a full version of the Book of 1 Enoch only exists in Ethiopic translation. The *Astronomical Book* is considered the earliest part of the work, possibly as early as third century BC, although its final literary form is probably later.[3] The Book

* This article is a revised version of a Hebrew article which appeared in Menahem Kister (ed.), *The Qumran Scrolls and Their World* (Jerusalem: Yad Ben-Zvi Press, 2009), pp. 435–476. I am grateful to the publisher for the kind permission to translate the paper and publish it in English. I would like to express my thanks to my assistant, Niva Dikman, who offered substantial help in preparing this article for print.

of Jubilees takes the form of a retelling of biblical history in apocalyptic spirit, from the creation until the encounter of God and Moses on Mount Sinai. The book was written in Hebrew around the middle of the second century BC. As in the case of 1 Enoch, fragments of the original were found at Qumran and in various translations but the entire book was preserved and transmitted only in Ethiopic.[4]

Among the many fields of interest represented in the sectarian scrolls, such as Bible interpretation, prayer, sectarian law, visionary literature, etc., a group of calendrical documents takes pride of place. The apocalyptic calendar tradition began already in the Pseudepigraphal *Astronomical Book* and continued in various trajectories in the scrolls written by the *yaḥad* and preserved in the caves. This calendrical tradition, as well as the astronomical premises underlying it, is the topic of the present article.

Scholarly discussion on the calendar of the *yaḥad* community interfaces with a wider discussion of other calendars: the luni-solar calendar that later became what is now called 'The Jewish Calendar', as well as calendars in use by surrounding peoples: calendars from Mesopotamia and Greece, the luni-solar calendars used throughout the Ancient Near East in Persian and Hellenistic times, as well as Ptolemaic-Egyptian calendars.[5]

Against the background of all these, the central distinguishing feature of the Qumranic tradition is the number of 364 days in the year. In the hands of different Jewish authors throughout a period of no less than two hundred years, the number 364 served as a basic theme and a ground for variations, culminating in the creation of a rich calendrical tradition. This number, acquiring various elaborations over the generations, was transformed into the focal point of a wide-ranging and sophisticated creativity. Although not based on a particularly advanced astronomical knowledge, this calendar tradition stands out among other ancient calendars in its ability to absorb a wide variety of temporal and religious parameters in an extraordinarily elaborate matrix. Most of these parameters will be discussed below, excluding the Jewish cultic festivals, which will not be surveyed here in detail.

1. Textual Sources Attesting to the 364-Day Year

- "The moon brings about the years precisely, all according to their eternal positions. They come neither early nor late by one day by which they would change: Each is exactly 364 days." (1 Enoch 74:12; cf. 75:2, 82:6, 11–20; ca. 2nd–3rd centuries BC).[6]

- "And you, command the people of Israel that they observe the years according to the number of 364 days." (Jubilees 6:32; cf. verses 23–38; 2nd century BC).

- "and he (King David) wrote: psalms, 3,600; songs to sing before the altar accompanying the daily perpetual burnt-offering, for all the days of the year, 364" (Psalms Scroll 11Q5 XXVII 4–7; copy dated to 1st century AD but probably authored earlier).[7]

- "The year is complete: three hundred s[ixty-four] days." (4QMMT Halakhic Letter[a], 4Q394 fragments 3–7 i 2-3; ca. 2–1 centuries BC).[8] Cf. the similar wording "(Thus) a year of 364 days is completed" in 1 Enoch 82:6.

- "On that day Noah went out from the ark, at the end of an exact year, three hundred and sixty four days" (Commentary on Genesis A, 4Q252 ii 2–3; ca. 1st century BC).[9]

In addition to these explicit mentions of the 364-day year, it is attested less directly in a variety of other sources. After its first appearance in the astronomical section of 1 Enoch (chapters 72–82), the 364-day year is also known from, or at least implied in, another composition of roughly the same period, the Aramaic Levi Document (probably also 3rd century BC); as well as from the somewhat later book of Jubilees, and from a wide range of other compositions from Qumran whose dating varies between the end of the second century BC to the mid-first century AD.[10] The sources related to the 364-day calendar tradition can be divided into a number of categories:

a. Astronomical documents which track the movement of the luminaries using scientific models but do not apply their data to a practical calendar: the Astronomical Book of Enoch and the scroll 4Q317 Phases of the Moon (for which see below, section 7).

b. Calendrical documents.[11] Writings of a technical nature and limited vocabulary which relate to various aspects of the religious calendar.

c. Compositions giving indirect evidence of the calendar. These compositions were not intended to transmit a detailed calendar and most do not even mention the number 364. However, their content is based on the characteristic calendar of the *yaḥad* and each one of them contains elements characteristic of the 364-day calendar tradition. The present article will not cover all oblique reference to the calendar. The more prominent texts discussed below are:
   1. Rewritten Scripture with a chronological emphasis, such as sections from the Aramaic Levi Document, the Book of Jubilees, 4Q252 Commentary on Genesis A.
   2. A legal composition which deals with the cycle of festival days: the Temple Scroll.
   3. Liturgical compositions for various days of the year: 11QPs[a] Psalms Scroll column XXVII, 4Q503 Daily Prayers, the Song of the Seasons in 1QS X, Songs of the Sabbath Sacrifice, various prayers for the festivals.[12]
   4. Polemic statements about the calendar as a key religious and sectarian practice in such foundation documents as the Damascus Document, the *Pesher* literature etc.

The 364-day calendar tradition has undergone considerable development, combining mathematical-astronomical concepts with a calendar perfectly integrated with the religious life of the *yaḥad* community. While this development calls for a heavy diachronic analysis, the entire 364 day calendar tradition retains persistent characteristic features when viewed from a synchronic perspective.

2. The 364-Day Year: General Characteristics

More than any astronomical aspect, the 364-day year is characterized by its numerical harmony. In fact the best definition for the year is neither a 'solar' nor 'luni-solar' year but rather a seven-based (septenary) schematic year. This definition gives the best account for most manifestations of this sectarian reckoning.

The year ideally begins in the spring equinox.[13] It is divided symmetrically into a hierarchical order of time periods, the hierarchical dimension emphasized quite strongly in the textual sources (1 En 82:9–20; Jub 6:29–31; 4Q328, 4Q329). The sources underline the division of the year into 52 weeks and hence into 4 quarters of 13 weeks or 91 days each. The quarters are sometimes designated by the term *tequfah*, 'season, period' or maybe more accurately 'solstice, equinox'.[14] The division into weeks proves especially useful for liturgical means (11QPs[a] XXVII; Songs of the Sabbath Sacrifice);[15] the order of prayers for the service of the Sabbath sacrifice was composed on this basis, containing 13 prayers according to the count of the Sabbaths in the quarter.[16]

Other sources give priority to the division of the year into months. Each quarter comprises three months whose days number 30, 30 and 31. The scroll 6Q17 neatly transmits this order of months: "[the first month, in it 30 days. The] second month, in it 30 [days. The third month, in it 31 days,] and completed are the days of [the quarter]" (see also 1 Enoch chapter 72 passim).[17] Since the 364-day year originated from the ideal 360-day year, which consists solely of schematic 30-day months (see below), some ancient Jewish writers were reluctant to create a 31-day month, and instead counted the last (91th) day of the quarter as an 'additional day'.

The fourfold division of the year, most probably borrowed from the Mesopotamian pattern, was well absorbed in Jewish tradition, as it is attested not only in the sectarian 364-day calendar tradition but also in later rabbinic texts and mosaics from the late Roman period. The *tequfot* are marked by the sun's cardinal points, with each solstice and equinox date standing at the conclusion, or sometimes at the beginning of every quarter. These four added days (sometimes called 'epagomenal' days after the practice of the Egyptian civil year), one in each quarter, constitute the difference between the ideal year of 360 days and the distinctive 364-day year. The emphasis on solar movements and the seasons of the year, at least in the ideal level, is an important characteristic of the 364-day calendar tradition.

The 364-day year contains twelve schematic months. The months are named neither by Canaanite names known from the Bible (Ziv, Bul, Ethanim), nor by the Babylonian-Aramaic names absorbed into later biblical books and into Jewish practice (Tišri, Marḥešwan, etc.).[18] Instead they are numbered according to their order in the year: the first month, the second month etc., similar to the mode of designation in priestly layers of the Pentateuch, such as the laws concerning the festivals in Lev 23 and Num 28–29.[19]

The neat division of the year into 52 weeks had great value in the Jewish culture, where, since biblical times, the number seven has been considered sacred. Some priestly circles in the Second Temple Period cherished the seven-based (septenary) count as a generative principle in producing new temporal frameworks, laying special emphasis on full weeks (Sunday to Sabbath) rather than on nominal weeks of seven days.[20] The septenary character of the 364-day year was a central reason for its acceptance in Jewish circles after its first introduction by way of the *Astronomical Book*. In this respect the 364-day year is greatly advantaged with regard to the standard Jewish luni-solar calendar, in which the number of days in the year is ever changing with observation and the needs of intercalation. In the 364-day year it is impossible for a day of feast to fall on the Sabbath day, an occurrence which would cause great confusion with regard to the correct procedures in the Temple, and which in fact bothered the rabbinic legal experts quite considerably.[21]

Qumran compositions make excessive use of septenary counts. Thus for example the space of seven weeks between the various festivals of first fruits in the Temple Scroll (columns XVIII–XXIII) fits perfectly within the heptadic structure of the year. Above all this structure is recognizable in the corpus of *mishmarot* documents, i.e., rosters of the terms of service of the priestly families in the temple (see below, Section 8). These rosters divide the year into terms of service of one week, constructing a six-year cycle for the assignment of an equal share of service for all twenty-four priestly families:

24 (priestly courses) × 13 (weeks of service) = 2184 (days) = 6 (years) × 364

Owing to the fact that the number 364 divides neatly into seven, and since the day of the week in which the beginning of the year falls is fixed, all the dates, festivals etc. in the year will wittingly occur on the very same day of the week. Various lists of priestly courses (henceforth: *mishmarot*) fix the beginning of the year on the fourth day of the week, the day of the creation of the luminaries, for example: "[...] its light on the fourth day of the wee[k ...] [... the] creation on the fourth day" (4Q319 IV 10–11; cp. 4Q320 1 i 2–3, and below Appendix 1). The days of the week on which the festivals occur are counted in great detail in 4Q320 4 iii–vi, as well as in other similar lists. Several other compositions, not directly connected with the priestly courses, are also based on the perpetual order of the days of the week (4Q317, 4Q252 and perhaps also 4Q503).[22] It thus seems that the 364-day calendar tradition put significant emphasis on the days of the week, long before this element became central in other Jewish calendrical systems. It is doubtful, however, whether this was also the case in the earlier phases of the 364-day calendar tradition such as 1 Enoch and the book of Jubilees, which do not emphasize the days of the week in the calendrical framework.

The data presented above can be summarized in the following table.

Days of the week	Months 1, 4, 7, 10						Months 2, 5, 8, 11						Months 3, 6, 9, 12				
Sunday		5	12	19	26			3	10	17	24		1	8	15	22	29
Monday		6	13	20	27			4	11	18	25		2	9	16	23	30
Tuesday		7	14	21	28			5	12	19	26		3	10	17	24	31
Wednesday	1	8	15	22	29			6	13	20	27		4	11	18	25	
Thursday	2	9	16	23	30			7	14	21	28		5	12	19	26	
Friday	3	10	17	24			1	8	15	22	29		6	13	20	27	
Saturday	4	11	18	25			2	9	16	23	30		7	14	21	28	

An inspection of the table reveals the great numerical possibilities innate within the 364-day year. The structure of days, weeks and months in each of the quarters retains an essential symmetry according to the position in the quarter. Thus, each month is identical to the other similarly-situated months in the other quarters of the year. The first month in each quarter (thus also the first month of the year) begins on a Wednesday and ends on a Thursday. The second month begins on a Friday and ends on Sabbath, and the last month of each quarter, which has 31 days, begins on a Sunday and ends on a Tuesday. The length of each quarter is 12 full weeks and another two half-weeks, in total 13 weeks.

The festival of Unleavened Bread (*Mazzot*, 15th of the first month) constantly falls on the fourth day of the week, and so does the festival of Tabernacles (*Sukkot*), on the 15th of the seventh month. The first day of the first month (i.e., ideally the spring New Year) also occurs on a Wednesday, and thus also the Day of Remembrance on the first of the seventh month (i.e., ideally the autumn New Year). The table enables one to reconstruct the layout of a complete month on the basis of the brief data for one day alone, by dint of its perfect symmetry. This elegant structure can be carried out even further when one goes beyond the bounds of one year to a cycle of three or six years and when the *mishmarot* are integrated into the yearly calendar.[23] The introduction of additional numerical modulæ—24 (courses), 6 (years), 7 (week), 13 (weeks in a quarter)—into the matrix allows for an enormous amount of arithmetical possibilities to be represented in the overall calendrical scheme. One calendrical document (4Q319 Otot) goes even further when calculating *mishmarot* and lunar phenomena along a cycle of six jubilees (6 × 49 = 294 years), a system which exemplifies how much calendar experts of this tradition cherished the numerical harmony innate in it.[24]

3. Calendrical Disputes in the Second Temple Period

From the very outset the evidence for the 364-day year was involved in disputes with other calendrical traditions.[25] The polemics involve in most cases the rival luni-solar calendar tradition, which was current then in Judah as in many other kingdoms of the Hellenistic Levant (see also below, section 4). As pointed out above, the 364-day year was distinct from the luni-solar calendar inasmuch as it allowed for all time periods to be pre-calculated based on an eternal Divine scheme. The luni-solar calendar, in contrast, was ever based on *ad hoc* observations of the moon and intercalations, depending on the astronomical circumstances and the whims of the responsible authority.[26] In accordance with their apocalyptic orientation, the adherents of the 364-day calendar tradition condemned the human involvement in calendrical matters practiced by their rivals. The Rabbinic tradition, in contrast, underscored the conspicuous human involvement in calendar reckoning and its *ad hoc* determination, as can be seen in the Mishnah tractate Roš Haššanah and in later rabbinic sources. This disagreement seems to have begun in the early stages of the second century BC.[27]

Prior to the rise of that polemic, at a stage in which the 364-day calendar tradition was only preliminarily distinct from its ancestor, the 360-day ideal year, some of its practitioners made sure to turn their zeal against those who did not count the four ('additional') days within the year:

> People err regarding them (the four additional days) and do not calculate them in the numbering of the entire world because they err regarding them and people do not understand them precisely (1 En 82:5; cf. 75:2)

It seems, however, that this polemic did not last long, or that a 360-day year was never actually practiced in Judah.[28]

Returning now to the more well-attested polemics with the luni-solar tradition, one recognizes it most clearly in Jubilees and in Qumran literature, even in writings which are not patently calendrical:

> Command the sons of Israel to observe the years according to this reckoning – three hundred and sixty-four days; and these shall make up a complete year. ... But if they neglect the proper order and fail to observe them ... the all the seasons will get out of order and the sequence of the year will be disturbed. .... Yet all the sons of Israel will forget and be ignorant of the progression of the years; they will forget the new moon and festival and sabbath [...] (Jub 6:32–38, cp. 23:19).

Similar words are used by the writer of 4Qpesher Hosea[a] :

> "I will put an end to all of her joy: her pil[grimages, new] moons, Sabbaths, and all her sacred days". This means that [all the sacred] days they will take away in exchange for Gentile sacred days, so that [all] [her joy] will be turned into mourning. (4Q166 ii 14–17)[29]

In the Habakkuk Pesher the controversy appears in the description of an historical incident:

> This (a scriptural verse quoted earlier) refers to the Wicked Priest, who pursued the Teacher of Righteousness to destroy him in the heat of his anger at his place of exile. At the time set aside for the repose of the Day of Atonement he appeared to them to destroy them and to bring them to ruin on the fast-day, the Sabbath intended for their repose. (1QpHab XI 4–8).

The *yaḥad* community members preserved in their historical memory a Day of Atonement (according to their reckoning) on which the Evil Priest came out from Jerusalem to pursue the Teacher of Righteousness in the desert. The background to this enmity must have been the calendrical controversy concerning the actual date of the Day of Atonement, for otherwise how could the high priest in Jerusalem be free from his many duties in the Temple to go out to the desert on this holy day?[30]

Additional documents of the yahad enumerate calendrical disagreements as a decisive cause of their dispute with the rest of Israel. Accordingly, in the Damascus Document:

> And with those remaining of the ones who held the commandments of God He established his covenant [...] to reveal to them the hidden things [...] holy Sabbaths and honourable festivals. (CD III, 12–15)

> And all who were brought into the covenant without coming to the Temple to lighten my altar without cause [...] if they do not keep the law exactly [...] to differentiate between the sacred and the profane and to keep the Sabbath day as interpreted and the festivals and the Day of Atonement (CD VI, 11-19; cf. 4Q266 2 2–6)

The special interest of Jewish authors with the chronology of biblical times intercepted with the above noted calendar polemics. The most pronounced point of disagreement involved the chronology of the biblical Flood (Genesis 6–9), no doubt because the Flood chronology appears to be based on a 364-day year, at least according to some of the ancient versions. Thus in 1 Enoch 106:15 we read:

> And there will be great wrath upon the earth and a flood, and there will be great destruction for a year

In the Massoretic version of Genesis, the flood lasted for a complete year + ten days (Genesis 7:11, 8:14), a number that readily suggests the 354-day lunar year plus an epact of ten days, totally equaling 364 days. However, other versions allow for more ambiguous conclusions. According to the Greek version (Septuagint) the Flood lasted exactly one year, leaving open the question what kind of year it is that Scripture relates to in this case. The scroll 4Q252, a Qumranic commentary on Genesis, states that the Flood lasted for one complete year of exactly "three hundred and sixty-four days", although this figure requires some modifications of the biblical text. Finally, in Jubilees chapter 5 the biblical dates are even further manipulated to account for more than one of the contrasting versions at the same time.[31]

It would appear that the inclusion of a calendrical list at the beginning of the scroll 4Q394, which contains the polemical composition 4QMMT (Halakhic Letter[a]), is connected with the author's contention that the calendar is a central cause for the dispute which is vividly depicted in that treatise on religious law.[32] Indeed, calendrical disagreement would be highly significant in Judea, a land in which worship was conducted by definition at one central Temple only. Any sort of tolerance towards conflicting calendrical traditions would necessarily entail an unbearable chaos in the Temple schedule and is therefore impossible. For this reason, statements of calendrical polemic most often involve the danger of profaning the religious festivals (see quotations from the *Damascus Covenant* [CD] above).[33]

4. The Early History of the Jewish 364-day Calendar in Judea

In a series of scholarly articles (1953–1957) Annie Jaubert analyzed the dates appearing in Jubilees, comparing them with the dates arising from the priestly sources in the Hebrew Bible, which predate Jubilees by three centuries or so.[34] Putting great emphasis on the days of the week as a factor in the priestly calendar, and based on the structure of the 364-day year (above), her surprising conclusion was that the calendar of Jubilees was identical to that which stood behind priestly sources in the Pentateuch, such as the list of the journeys of the Israelites in the Book of Numbers, as well as behind other texts from late books of the Hebrew Bible (ca. 6th century BC). Jaubert discovered that the biblical narratives could be interpreted to show, for example, that the Israelites abstained from travel on the Sabbath day. During the 1950s, preliminary publications of the first scrolls unearthed at Qumran revealed a surprising similarity between the Qumran calendars and those calendars previously studied by Jaubert. Accordingly, Jaubert maintained that the Qumranic 364-day calendar tradition had very early origins in Jewish antiquity, and that the 364-day year was put to practice in the Jerusalem Temple for the first few centuries after its restoration in the late 6th century. She claimed that the luni-solar calendar (later also adopted by the rabbis) gained hold in Jerusalem only gradually in the Hellenistic period. VanderKam (2000), pp. 81–104 (originally published in 1979), corroborated parts of Jaubert's theory, while going even further by connecting the introduction of the luni-solar calendar in the Jerusalem temple with the (admittedly ambiguous) statement on calendar reforms performed by Antiochus IV Epiphanes in Jerusalem (Daniel 7:25).[35] According to this reasoning, the *yaḥad* community members retained the antique Jewish calendar of 364 days, while opposing the Pharisaic circles who had adopted Antiochus' pagan calendar.

Inasmuch as the Jaubert's argument with regard to the dates in the Pentateuch rests on a rather equivocal statistic analysis of her database, it is impossible to determine whether her conclusions are valid.[36] It would be fair to say that they are possible but not necessary. In any case, there is no *positive* proof for the existence of a 364-day calendar tradition in Judah prior to the *Astronomical Book*. The Persian and early Hellenistic periods in this region are so shrouded in obscurity that it is difficult to determine the development of liturgical institutions in practice during this time. If something could be learned from the general history of the early Hellenistic period, it is that small kingdoms in the Levant usually practiced the luni-solar calendar of Babylonia, the Persian Empire and the Seleucids, with minor local modifications.[37] It is hard to conceive that the luni-solar calendar was only introduced in Jerusalem in the second century BC.

It seems that the 364-day year is thus a product of the Hellenistic period. Indeed, some distinct elements of what later became the 364-day calendar tradition may be traced in earlier sources. This is the case mainly with regard to septenary time reckoning, which had been an important temporal marker already at the Persian period, if not before. But the septenary counts in the Hebrew Bible (mainly in Leviticus 23–26) are only minimally reminiscent of the full-fledged septenary reckoning in later apocalyptic literature and should not thus be considered as belonging to the same stage of tradition. In the absence of concrete evidence for an early existence of the 364-day calendar tradition in Jewish sources, one must abstain from unnecessary assumptions about its antiquity.

Furthermore, one has to take in account the nature of the earliest source available to us, i.e., the *Astronomical Book*. In this source religious-priestly concepts like cult, festivals and priests are conspicuously absent, while the heart of the argument concentrates on a 'scientific' attempt to explain the true mechanisms of heaven. By the time of the composition of the *Astronomical Book*, therefore, the 364-day year was not conceived as a cultic-religious year. Thus, although septenary principles were present already at an early stage, they were not developed into a concrete calendrical system before the Hellenistic period, when the apocalyptic *Zeitgeist* called for systematization of these preliminary principles. This systematization of the 364-day calendar tradition was also, at least in part, due to the fruitful encounter with the scientific models of the *Astronomical Book*.

To conclude then, it would appear the 364-day year was *not* practiced in Judah prior to the Hellenistic period. Moreover, it seems not to have fully crystallized as a religious concept before the second century BC. It is thus not a conservative element, preserving the antique national tradition, but rather a revisionist undertaking, aimed to respond to the prevalent reality with a novel development of some antique principles.[38]

5. Extra-Jewish Sources for the 364-Day Calendar Tradition

The *Astronomical Book*, even in its earlier versions which lack the literary apocalyptic framework, is no doubt a Jewish document. A Jewish origin would be the best possible explanation for the fact that in the *Astronomical Book* lunar visibility is measured by units of 1/14, instead of 1/15 as in all other cognate lunar tables from Antiquity (see also below). A Jewish author preferred the number 14 because it divides into seven and would fit well into septenary time frameworks.[39] At the same time, the astronomical book clearly depends on non-Jewish, earlier astronomical sources. What is more, the text lacks any references to specifically Jewish concepts like festivals and priests, and serves more as an ideal calculation of heavenly motions than as a calendar in practical usage.

After some early attempts, Matthias Albani fully proved that many of the calculations of the *Astronomical Book* depend on the traditional, pre-Hellenistic Mesopotamian astronomy, as collected and consolidated in the astronomical compendium Mul.Apin.[40] Recently Drawnel (2007) has demonstrated an even stronger correspondence between the *Astronomical Book* and the lunar visibility tables contained in tablet 14 of the Mesopotamian compendium *Enūma Anu Enlil* (henceforth EAE). These two compositions, assuming textual form around the turn of the first millennium BC but probably edited somewhat later, summarize the traditional astronomy that accumulated in Mesopotamia until that time.[41] Since the present article is about the calendar specifically, I shall delve here only shortly into the details of astronomy. The *Astronomical Book* shares with Mesopotamian science the principal schemes for solar and lunar phenomena.[42] The so-called 'intercalation schemes' of Mul.Apin are echoed in the *Astronomical Book*, focusing on the following components: the fourfold division of the year; the ratio of 2:1 in measuring the length of daylight and nighttime; the three paths of Heaven (presented in the *Astronomical Book* as twelve gates, six each in east and west = six bands that cross the horizon from east to west). In addition, the basic geographical-meteorological scheme of the four winds of heaven (1 Enoch chapter 76) is adopted from Mesopotamian thought, although not directly from Mul.Apin. Finally, the authors of the *Astronomical Book* created an intriguing new variation on the lunar visibility schemes of EAE 14, presented in the Qumran scrolls 4Q208 and 4Q209.[43] A later, Qumranic, stage of the Jewish discipline (4Q320, 4Q321 and 4Q321a), attests additionally to the use of the 'Lunar Three', a standard set of lunar data for each month, used in Mesopotamia since more or less the sixth century BC.[44] This list of parallel themes makes it clear that the Jewish 364-day calendar tradition depended on Mesopotamian influence rather than on Egyptian, Greek, Persian etc., as had been argued in the past.

All of the above astronomical elements taken together yield a rather comprehensive view of the sky, which combines period calculations with a spatial model for the place of the main luminaries in heaven throughout the year. At the height of the Hellenistic period there already existed far more advanced astronomical knowledge, both in Babylonia and in the Hellenistic world. The attachment to an archaic stage of Mesopotamian knowledge may be due to the fact that the cultural contact with Babylonia took place at an early date, or rather that this contact did not go further than the simple astronomy of EAE and Mul.Apin, leaving out newer disciplines of that culture: the observational evidence of the astronomical diaries and the ACT-type mathematical astronomy. Great importance was attached in Judah to an ancient, canonical, body of knowledge in preference to the desire for observable, scientific precision. This line of thought in general characterizes the calendrical and astronomical tenets of the *yaḥad*, which rejected observation and precision and instead preferred arithmetical and schematic dimensions. In these later stages greater emphasis was given to various symmetries within the structure of the 364-day year, as well as to its concordance with new Jewish elements injected into it and their own numerical dimension.

The traditional Mesopotamian astronomy was based on the ideal year of 360 days, which is most suitable for astronomical and administrative calculations. This number was followed in ancient Mesopotamia for calculation purposes and remained the standard in the first millennium BC. There is also some evidence—admittedly debatable—for the use of an average year of 364 days in Mul.Apin, supported also by several other contemporary documents.[45] The introduction of the 364-day year into Jewish sources thus rests on two platforms: 1) an adoption of the Babylonian figure 364 as the length of the year (if indeed that number existed in Babylonian calendar-science), and 2) an inner-Jewish development which adapted the 360-day year, adding to it the four cardinal days, to reach the number of 364.[46] The appeal of the Jewish 364-day year rested on its septenary character, an attractive concept for Jewish apocalyptic writers. The 364-day calendar tradition in Judah is thus a Jewish-apocalyptic adaptation of traditional Mesopotamian knowledge. It is difficult to know how the Mesopotamian knowledge reached Judah, possibly through an intermediary geographical and cultural medium, which should perhaps be sought in the Aramaic speaking region of Syria.

The origin of the 364-day year in the ideal 360-day year is still apparent in some sources within the former tradition.[47] The astrological document 4Q318 functions according to a 360-day year; but this document appears not to be part of the sectarian calendar tradition, as can also be seen from other characteristics. In contrast, the *Astronomical Book* supplies more solid evidence for the 360-day year. The models for solar and lunar movements employed in the *Astronomical Book* (most notably chapter 72, as well as some literary statements in the framework of the book) had been originally devised according the ideal 360-day year and only subsequently implemented with the additional days. Throughout the entire range of the sectarian calendrical literature there is a distinction between 360 days, which are the 'days of the year' in the full sense of the word, and the four additional days. Thus for example the memory of a 360-day year excluding the four additional days occurs in the reference to the 3,600 songs in the Psalms Scroll (11Q5 XXVII 5), a number that is nothing more than a multiple of 360.[48] In this scroll, the additional days were especially marked as times "to play musical songs over the stricken", with special songs authored for this purpose. The lack of stability of the 'additional days' added to the 360-day year can also be recognized from the doubt arising as to whether they should be placed at the beginning or end of each quarter according to 1 Enoch, Jubilees and the calendrical scrolls from Qumran.

6. Sun and Moon

Within the Mesopotamian tradition, the number of 360 days was conceived as an ideal figure for controlling all of the heavenly luminaries: sun, moon, stars, planets. The number 364, if indeed present in that tradition, was conceived as a mean number resulting from a calculation of the epact over three years. Accordingly, these numbers were intended to correlate neither the length of the lunar year only, nor the solar or sidereal years. Although it was soon realized that the application of schematic numbers in reality deviates from the actual periods of the luminaries, the numerical scheme was retained because it kept yielding interesting arithmetical models, which, in turn, were used by astronomers to achieve yet more accurate results.[49]

The use of the number 364 in the *Astronomical Book* is not far from this concept. It is applied throughout the book to both the sun and the moon, and in a more moderate way also to the stars. Although some scholars claimed that the 364-day year in the *Astronomical Book* is primarily a solar year,[50] possibly because they overstated the primacy of the solar model in chapter 72, this is certainly not the case. The 364-day year is not designated a solar year anywhere in the *Astronomical Book*, nor is there a preference for the sun over the moon in the determination of times. On the contrary, it is the purported aim of the astronomical book to achieve a harmony between all heavenly luminaries by means of the Divine mechanism of the 364-day year. The author of the *Astronomical Book* was so satisfied having attained a lunar application of the 364-day year that he stated: "The moon brings about the year precisely, [...]They come neither early nor late by one day by which they would change the year; each is exactly 364 days" (1 Enoch 74:12).[51] Moreover, the 364-day year was accepted in Jewish literature not on account of a preference for any particular luminary over another, but rather on account of the perfect septenary traits of this number and of the arithmetical possibilities innate in it. Nor is the number 364 identical with the length of ca. 365.24 days in the tropical year, because the margin of ca. 1.24 days between the two measurements accumulates to a significant difference within a short period of time. The 364-day year thus came into being not as a solar year, but as a schematic year which is suitable for the entire heavenly sphere.

The view that the Qumran calendar is a solar calendar which opposed any use of the moon in calendar reckoning cannot be maintained anymore. The role of the moon in time-reckoning is supported by many documents in Qumran which record lunar phases—calendars, astronomical documents, and collections of prayers. A triennial cycle was devised in the Qumran *mishmarot* texts in order to synchronize the 364-day year with the schematic lunar calendar (see below, Section 7). Other documents from Qumran prefer neither the sun nor the moon but rather concentrate on numerical aspects of the year, detached from the actual luminaries. Thus for example in the Temple Scroll, the Commentary on Genesis A (4Q252), the Damascus Document and the *pesharim*. Thus, the characterization of the 364-day year as a solar year alone does not cater for all of its various aspects.

The only source in the 364-day calendar tradition which clearly favours the sun against the moon in the determination of times is the Book of Jubilees (2:9, 6:32–38). In fact it is on the basis of the quotations from Jubilees that the 364-day year was for many years considered a solar calendar in scholarship. However, the tendency in Jubilees does not characterize the entire 364-day calendar tradition and must be accounted for separately.

Further clarifications are due here with regard to the role of the moon in time-reckoning. The many documents enumerating lunar phases do this for the sake of astronomical precision or in order to add a stronger dimension to the regular structure of the cycles of years. However, there is no function for the lunar phases in the ritual calendar. The religious life of the community was dictated by the 364-day calendar alone; the *yahad* had no festival or sacrifice which depended on lunar movements, such as the first of the month, the full moon, etc. (see further below on 4Q503). Also, when the phases of the moon are indicated in the calendrical documents, they are always indicated schematically and never by actual observation.[52] In sectarian circles, the schematic year remained the exclusive mechanism to calibrate sacred time, although some other calculations were maintained alongside it for various other purposes.

7. The Three-year Cycle

Employing the model of the *Astronomical Book*, some later writings devised their calendrical calculations on the basis of a single schematic year. In these documents, even when reference was made to the lunar phases, which would require a concordance of these phases with the 364-day year, the framework of a single schematic year was not interrupted. A good example is the scroll 4Q503, a collection of daily prayers which consists of praises for the Lord about the creation of Time and the luminaries. In this collection, the prayer for each day of the month counts the lunar phases pertinent to that day. This scroll did not know the three-year cycle known from the *mishmarot* scrolls.[53] Had the author of that scroll—which is unfortunately very badly preserved—continued his record of lunar phases throughout the course of an entire year, he would have found difficulty accounting for the difference between the numbers 364 and 354. However so, there are no signs that any longer year cycle was ever maintained in 4Q503.

In contrast, other scrolls do employ such a longer cycle of years. In order to reach a reasonable concordance between the 364-day year and the lunar year of 354 days, a simple cycle was devised, which is clearly used in some Qumran texts but appeared most probably already in the Astronomical Book. The lunar year and the 364-day year are synchronized at the end of every three years by means of the addition of a 30-day month:

$$3 \times 364 = 1092 = 3 \times 354 + 30$$

The triennial cycle, which was a marginal component (if any) in Mul.Apin (II ii 10–12), and a subsidiary interest (if any) in 1 Enoch 74:10–16,[54] consequently became a central component in the Jewish 364-day calendar tradition. Scrolls from Qumran perfected the application of this triennial cycle within the yearly calendar. A significant advance in this direction is to be found in the scroll 4Q317, a single copy of an otherwise unknown document, penned in Hebrew in a particular cryptic script. The fact that an effort was taken to encrypt the document apparently reveals its sectarian nature. The main subject of this document is a description of the daily lunar phases—whether the periods of lunar visibility as in the *Astronomical Book* or simply the waxing and waning of the moon.[55] Below is an excerpt from the beginning of this document:

3. On the sixth of the month,]
4. Thir[teen] parts are obscured. [And thus the moon enters the day.]
5. On the seventh of the month, [fourteen parts] are obscure[ed. And thus]
6. The moon enters the day. *Vacat*
7. On the eighth of the month, the moon [rules all the day in the midst]
8. of the sky [fourteen-and –one-half (?) being obscured. And when the sun sets] its light [ceases]
9. to be obscured, [and thus the moon begins to be revealed]
10. on the first day of the week (the eighth of the month). *vacat* [On the ninth of the month,]
11. on[e] part [is revealed. And thus the moon enters the night.]
12. On the tenth of the month, [two parts are revealed. And thus the moon enters]
13. the night. *vacat*

(4Q317 1 ii 3–13)

This fragment is part of a continuous description of the daily phases of the moon. One part of light is diminished every day until the completion of all fourteen parts (or, according to a recurrent correction in 4Q317, fourteen and a half parts). In accordance with the models of the *Astronomical Book*, the moon sets during daytime ("and so it enters the day") on the second part of the lunation. On the eighth day of the month (lines 7–9), which is also the first day of the week, in a month whose name and number are not mentioned, the moon is entirely invisible; only at the end of the same day with the setting of the sun is it beginning to be revealed. From here onwards the moon (or: the moon's period of visibility) grows by one 'part' for each day, setting during nighttime throughout the length of its waxing phase ("and so it enters the night").

The document 4Q317 is very fragmentary and replete with errors and corrections which make its precise interpretation difficult. In spite of this, it is possible to grasp its structure and importance. Firstly, the author of the 4Q317 omitted the description of the passing of the sun through the heavenly gates, an element which occupies an important place in the *Astronomical Book*—both in the Ethiopic (chapter 72) and the Aramaic (4Q209 7 iii 1–2) versions. In fact this text omits all references to the movement of the luminaries in heaven, relating to period schemes only. It would appear that this aspect of Enochic astronomy was discarded as a consequence of the author's failure to give a full explanation for the movement of the luminaries throughout the 364-day year. Secondly, the dates in 4Q317 are numbered according to the schematic months of the 364-day year, in contrast to the *Astronomical Book* where they are numbered in the 29/30 alternating order of lunar months.[56] The document 4Q317 made, therefore, a decisive contribution to the consolidation of the three-year cycle and prepared the way for the full integration of the moon within the calendrical system at Qumran.

In other lunar texts from Qumran—4Q320, 4Q321, 4Q321a—the three-year cycle is embedded within the six-year cycle of priestly courses, constituting exactly one half of the latter cycle. In these texts the daily phases of the moon are no longer recorded, and instead only two lunar events for every month are noted. One of these events is called in the scrolls *dwq*, and the second remains unnamed in the scrolls but designated conveniently here as X.[57] So for example in a line from 4Q321:

> (X occurs) on the fifth (day) in (the week of) Immer (which falls) on the twe[n]ty-third in the te[nth month]; and its *dwq* [is] on the sixth (day) in (the week of) Je]šebab (which falls) [on the tenth in i[t (=the tenth month) (4Q321 I 3–4)

This line mentions two lunar events occurring within one schematic month: the tenth month of the first year in the triennial cycle. The first event, X, is not given a name, but only dated as the fifth day in the week of the priestly duty of Immer, which is the twenty-third day of the month. The second event, *dwq*, falls on the sixth day of the week of the priestly duty of Ješebab, on the tenth of the same month. From the date of X until the following *dwq* 16/17 days pass—in accordance with the length of the lunar month at 29/30 days. Note that X is recorded first in the line even though it occurs 13 days after *dwq*. This order pertains to approximately a half of the three-year cycle, whereas in the other half of the cycle, the order of recording the two lunar phenomena within the month concurs with their actual order of occurrence.

The identification of X and *dwq* may be elucidated by comparing them with the Mesopotamian data of the Lunar Three.[58] Two figures, transmitted in 4Q320 (X only) and 4Q321–321a (X and *dwq*) relate to the moon's visibility in key points of the month:

1. The date after full moon in which the moon first sets in the morning after sunrise (Babylonian NA = Qumran *dwq*). This phase marks the onset of the moon's waning.
2. The date at the end of the lunation in which the moon last rises in the morning before sunrise (Babylonian KUR = Qumran X)

The third piece of data, noted only in 4Q320, is the number of days in the preceding lunar month, a standard component in the notation of every month in the Babylonian astronomical diaries and other related texts.[59]

The majority scholarly opinion with regard to the identification of X and *dwq* remains different, however, than the one suggested here. Most scholars would identify X with the full moon and *dwq* with the New Moon (see below Appendix 1).[60]

The three documents discussed here show that the calendar experts of the *yahad*, although diligently conducting their religious life according to the 364-day year, did not altogether discard the synchronization of this year with the lunar phases. Their interest in lunar movements was retained not in order to sanctify lunar occasions such as the first of the month or the full moon, because, as said, cultic occurrences were determined by the 364-day year exclusively. The days of X and *dwq* were not religious festivals but rather scientific pieces of data without cultic implication.

The three-year cycle, as embedded in the *mishmarot* six-year cycle, became an inseparable part of the 364-day calendar tradition at Qumran. The beginning of the first six-year cycle in world history, which occurred at the very day of the creation of the luminaries, is depicted in the prologue to 4Q320 (see below, Appendix 1). Like the prologues attached at the beginning and end of the lunar sections of *Enūma Anu Enlil*, this short literary passage commemorates the creation of the luminaries at the perfect time of creation, before nature was corrupted by human sinfulness.

A further elaboration of this tradition appears in a list called "Otot" (Signs) in 4Q319, columns IV-VI. This list includes all the year-cycles of various lengths known from Qumran—calendrical and non-calendrical texts alike—within an all-encompassing cycle of six jubilees or 294 years (6 × 49 = 294).[61] The beginning of every triennial cycle within this time span (i.e., the beginning of every year 1 and 4 in the *mishmarot* cycle), is specified as a 'sign'. These signs are understood as events of cosmic significance worthy of being indicated in the sacred year, since they revive (in a schematic way) the conjunction of sun and moon at the very beginning of creation. On account of the particular structure of the cycle of *mishmarot* the signs always occur in the period of the families Gamul and Šekaniah in an alternate order. The years are not counted according to their order in the six-year cycle (as was usual in the *mishmarot* documents), but rather according to their order in the sabbatical cycle (*šemitah*, the year of Release, a fallow year declared every seventh year according to Pentateuchal legislation). At the end of every jubilee there is a summary of the number of signs that occurred within that jubilee (16 or 17) as well as a special record for the signs, among those noted above, which occurred in years of the *šemitah* (3 or 4). The distinctive numerical structure of the 364-day year dictated the complex form of the mishmarot throughout the length of the list of signs.[62]

One cannot but wonder what the purpose is of the various counts of multiple years in this list. It seems that the author of the list of signs intended to integrate all of the possible year cycles within one super-structure, as a means to express the great essential unity of all time frameworks under one general principle. He was mainly concerned with integrating the six-year mishmarot cycle with the seven-based *šemitah* and jubilee cycles, whose sanctity was acknowledged from biblical times and which was far more widespread than the newly-introduced six-year cycle. The integration of the various cycles was brought about by means of a precise count of the points of congruence between them: signs, *mishmarot*, sabbatical years, and jubilees.

8. The Priestly Families (*mishmarot*)

A passage in the Hebrew Bible (1 Chronicles 24:7–18) lists twenty-four priestly families which participated in the Temple service.[63] These families are called in rabbinic sources *mishmarot*, 'watches, guards'; this term is mentioned neither in 1 Chron 24 nor in the calendrical scrolls from Qumran, but appears in the War Scroll (1QM II 1–4 and parallels).[64] In a similar way to the Athenian *prytaneia* or the Assyrian *līmu*, this administrative cycle was used as a constituent factor of the Jewish sectarian calendar. From rabbinic sources (the late Roman period) and the writings of Josephus (first century AD), it is known that the division of *mishmarot* was used to control the temple service during the Second Temple period. This division, in turn, formed the basis for the later Jewish non-priestly divisions of *maʿamadot*, a central element of the liturgical calendar for many centuries after the destruction of the temple.[65] The *mishmarot* cycle perfectly fits the needs of the 364-day calendar tradition because it works with units of weeks. It is less easily applied to the standard Jewish luni-solar calendar, where the number of weeks in a year is not fixed. However, some sources attest to its use in the latter system too, in a way which is not entirely clear today.[66]

The calendrical documents assign consecutive Temple service for the *mishmarot*, each for a period of one week. Accordingly, the perfect symmetry of the 364-day year was utilized in order to unify the sacred time with the sacred body of the priesthood. The cycle of the *mishmarot* was not only a technical means for the organization of religious administration, but was also understood to reflect the natural order. Even more so because the cycle of the *mishmarot* coincided with the lunar and solar cycles. Thus every new beginning of the priestly cycle was considered to be a reenactment of the situation which prevailed in heaven at the time of the creation of the luminaries. Therefore it was declared, in the introduction to the scroll 4Q319, that "[the] Creation in the fourth (day) in Ga[mul]" (IV 11; compare the parallel opening of 4Q320). The authors of calendrical texts saw a need to anchor the cycle of *mishmarot* already in the creation of the world, before the erection of the Temple on earth! The cycle of the *mishmarot*, just like the movements of the sun, moon and other markers of the march of Time, was a natural force to be hallowed and commemorated. This conceptual element is one of the sources for the formation of the later genre known as *ʿavodah* in the *piyyut* literature, a series of liturgical poems which associate the theme of creation with the theme of priestly service in the temple.[67]

The time for shifting the *mishmarot*, in the Qumran texts as in the Bible and the rabbinic traditions (2 Kings 12:5–7; Mishnah *Sukkah* 5:5; Tosephta, *Sukkah* 4:24–25; Josephus, *Antiquities*, 7.367) was on the Sabbath afternoon, which fell at the beginning of the family's service and was called by its name (such as the "Sabbath of Jedaʿjah" in 4Q320 2 13). The following days of that week were also called by the name of the priestly family in service. The calendrical documents meticulously record which course was serving in each of the religious festivals of the year, in order, among other reasons, to ascertain that the division of the *mishmarot* is evenly distributed.

9. Intercalation

As stated above, the use of the triennial cycle arose from the need to synchronize the 364-day year with the lunar year of 354 days. However, the difference of 1.24 days from the true solar year does not allow the 364-day year a complete correlation with the actual course of the seasons. Accordingly, if no means were taken for adjusting the length of the year, community members would have lost, within a very short time, all connection with the seasons of the year. They would find themselves, for example, celebrating Passover, the spring festival, in the middle of the winter after 100 years of practicing the 364-day year. This problem was even more serious with respect to the 364-day calendar tradition, whose protagonists repeatedly claimed for its outstanding accuracy, based on its Divine origin. In addition, the special festivals celebrated by the members of the community such as the festivals of the first fruits mentioned in the Temple Scroll, were dependent on the agricultural year. Thirdly, from a conceptual point of view, the fourfold division of the year into seasons was a constituent factor in the consolidation of the 364-day year, forming the subject for such hymns as the Song of the Seasons in 1QS X. It is difficult to imagine that there was no attempt to solve this problem by the community members.

Nevertheless, in the entire Qumran corpus and beyond it there is no explicit statement of any change whatsoever in the perfect scheme of the 364-day year. Furthermore, the 364-day calendar tradition rests on the perfect harmony between the various arithmetical components contained in it. It would have been impossible for any adaptation of the year—by means of an additional day, week or month—not to have affected the perfect harmony of the these components. For example, the addition of a week to the year would undermine the cycle which allocated exactly equal periods of service to each of the *mishmarot*, for it would be necessary to assign that particular additional week to one of the priestly courses, thus ruining the preconceived cycle.

Three modes of solving this problem have been presented in scholarly research, as summarized by Albani:[68]

a. The 364-day calendar tradition remained purely theoretical and was never intended for actual use. There was no need to adapt the year because it had no practical implications.[69]

b. The 364-day year, although practiced in reality, was never corrected because it was based from the outset on calculation rather than observation. Related to this is the statement in 1 Enoch 80:2–8: "In the days of the sinners the years will grow shorter [...] the moon will change its order and will not appear at its (normal) time . [...]Many heads of the stars will stray from the command."

Every deviation of the ideal year from reality was considered to be an unpreventable result of human sinfulness. At the end of days, so the sectaries hoped, the matter would be corrected with "the new Creation" (Jub 1:29; Temple Scroll 11QTa XXIX). Until then the 364-day year served as a wandering year, floating among the seasons.[70]

c. Members of the community adjusted the year by means of the addition of a week or weeks at various points.[71] Uwe Glessmer suggested a detailed model for such an adjustment which, in his opinion, was based on the list of signs in 4Q319.[72] Such suggestions of adjustment, in addition to the fact that they disrupt the cycle of the priestly service and the perfect symmetry of the year, are beset by one major disadvantage: they do not have any basis in the written sources, not even in 4Q319.

In the light of all this, one cannot accept that the *yaḥad* employed a fixed mechanism for intercalation. It appears that the power of the scheme was so great that it overcame the obvious discrepancy with the seasons. What is more, the importance of the observational element in the 364-day calendar tradition was minor from the very outset. However, the possibility that *ad hoc* adjustments were made at times when the gap increased to an unreasonable extent cannot be rejected. A similar practice is found, for example, in Roman history. When Julius Caesar came to introduce a calendar reform in Rome in 46 BC, he found that the calendar that was being used had the equinox occurring almost three months earlier than it should have been. He was thus forced to intercalate these days in an *ad hoc* manner before he could enact an orderly correction.[73] From this we learn firstly, that members of any society are reluctant to introduce corrections to the traditional calendars; and secondly, that the solution to the accumulated gap was sometimes found in local adjustments rather than in an ordered system, which would necessarily imply a declaration of the defective nature of the traditional calendar.

Appendix 1: The prologue of 4Q320

4Q320 is a collection of various types of calendrical documents: phases of the moon (frgs. 1–2), signs (frgs. 3, 5, 7), length of each month and the name of the priestly course that begins it (frgs. 3–4), festival calendar (frg. 4), as well as some other, less clear calculations (frg. 6). These lists are interconnected with sections written in a literary style, deviating from the technical wording of the calendrical documents. As indicated above, some literary passages appear as introductions in the Mesopotamian collection *Enūma Anu Enlil*, which may shed light on the similar practice in the Qumran scrolls.[74] The introduction to the entire scroll (4Q320 1 i 1–5) should be considered in detail:

1. [...] to its being seen (or: appearance) from the east
2. [] to shine [in] the middle of the heavens at the foundation of
3. [Creatio]n from evening to morning on the 4th (day) of the week (of service)
4. [of Ga]mul, in the first month in the [fir]st (solar)
5. year. (vacat)

It is difficult to tell whether this introduction was preceded by other words or whether the preserved text begins the literary passage. This passage contains a description of the rising of one of the heavenly bodies "from the east" and the continuation of its march to the "middle of the heavens", i.e., the meridian. All this took place at the "foundation of [Creatio]n", i.e., at the time of the creation of the luminaries.

The phrase "from evening to morning" in line 3 can be naturally interpreted to refer to the moon because obviously the sun does not stay in heaven during this time. More precisely, the expression can be interpreted to refer to the full moon, for this is the one day in the month in which the moon is seen in heaven throughout the whole night, whereas on other days its period of night time visibility diminishes. Immediately after the introduction, the scroll continues with a list of X and *dwq* dates, commencing directly with the first X date. It thus seemed reasonable to assume that, since the prologue recounts the creation of the full moon, that date is also the date of the first X occurrence. According to this interpretation, X = full moon. Furthermore, this interpretation gave rise to the theory that the *yahad* celebrated the beginning of the month at the day of full moon.[75] This view is sometimes supported with evidence for such an odd practice, from the biblical period up to the medieval sect of the Magharia, reported in Muslim sources.[76]

Above (section 7) I expressed my opinion that X and *dwq* should be identified otherwise, in accordance with the Mesopotamian Lunar Three. Since these lunar data are mere astronomical figures without cultic significance, it would be useless to connect them with that way or another of celebrating the beginning of the month. The very idea of celebrating any lunar event as the beginning of the month does not conform to the spirit of the sectarian calendar, where the sacred festivals were marked by the schematic 364-day year exclusively. It does remain, however, for me to account for the expression "from evening until morning" in line 3, which inadvertently relates to the night of full moon. One needs to weigh the possibility that what is at issue here is a general literary introduction to the scroll, which does not necessarily relate to the specific list which follows it, but rather lays down the basic setting for the content of the entire collection.[77] Accordingly, one cannot draw conclusions concerning the *yahad*'s practice of the new moon celebration from the prologue to the scroll 4Q320.

Appendix 2: The Six-Year *Mishmarot* Service Cycle

- The sign > indicates the entrance of a priestly course into the Temple on the afternoon of the Saturday preceding its first day of service.
- X refers to the lunar phenomenon defined only by date in 4Q320-4Q321a.
- D refers to the lunar phenomenon designated *dwq* in 4Q321 and 4Q321a.
- The Festival of Wood Offering is recorded on the twenty-ninth of the sixth month, precisely a week after the Festival of Oil. While this dating is not entirely detemined, it was selected here for convenience (cp. 4Q394 1-2 v).
- In this table the term 'Passah' indicates also the seven subsequent days of the Feast of Unleavened Bread. In some scrolls, however, the two festivals are separately enumerated.

Year 1

Month 1

	Sun	Mon	Tue	Wed	Thu	Fri	Sat	
גמול				1^{x}	2	3	4	
<דליה	5	6	7	8	9	10	11	
<מעוזיה	12	13	14*	15	16	17^{D}	18	*Passah
<יהויריב	19	20	21	22	23	24	25	
<ידעיה	26*	27	28	29	30^{x}			*Waving of the Omer

Month 2

	Sun	Mon	Tue	Wed	Thu	Fri	Sat	
						1	2	
<חרים	3	4	5	6	7	8	9	
<שעורים	10	11	12	13	14*	15	16	* Second Passah
<מלכיה	17^{D}	18	19	20	21	22	23	
<מימין	24	25	26	27	28	29	30^{x}	

Month 3

	Sun	Mon	Tue	Wed	Thu	Fri	Sat	
<הקוץ	1	2	3	4	5	6	7	
<אביה	8	9	10	11	12	13	14	
<ישוע	15*	16^{D}	17	18	19	20	21	*Festival of Weeks
<שכניה	22	23	24	25	26	27	28	
<אלישיב	29^{x}	30	31					

Month 4

	Sun	Mon	Tue	Wed	Thu	Fri	Sat
				1	2	3	4
<יקים	5	6	7	8	9	10	11
<חופה	12	13	14	15^{D}	16	17	18
<ישבאב	19	20	21	22	23	24	25
<בלגה	26	27	28^{x}	29	30		

Month 5

	Sun	Mon	Tue	Wed	Thu	Fri	Sat	
						1	2	
<אמר	3*	4	5	6	7	8	9	*Festival of Wine
<חזיר	10	11	12	13	14^{D}	15	16	
<הפצץ	17	18	19	20	21	22	23	
<פתחיה	24	25	26	27^{x}	28	29	30	

Month 6

	Sun	Mon	Tue	Wed	Thu	Fri	Sat	
<יחזקאל	1	2	3	4	5	6	7	
<יכין	8	9	10	11	12	13	14^{D}	
<גמול	15	16	17	18	19	20	21	
<דליה	22*	23	24	25	26	27^{x}	28	*Festival of Oil
<מעוזיה	29*	30	31					*Festival of Wood Offering

Month 7

	Sun	Mon	Tue	Wed	Thu	Fri	Sat
				1*	2	3	4
<יהויריב	5	6	7	8	9	10*	11
<ידעיה	12^{D}	13	14	15*	16	17	18
<חרים	19	20	21	22	23	24	25^{X}
<שעורים	26	27	28	29	30		

*Day of Remembrance
*Day of Atonement
*Festival of Booths

Month 8

	Sun	Mon	Tue	Wed	Thu	Fri	Sat
						1	2
<מלכיה	3	4	5	6	7	8	9
<מימין	10	11	12^{D}	13	14	15	16
<הקוץ	17	18	19	20	21	22	23
<אביה	24	25^{X}	26	27	28	29	30

Month 9

	Sun	Mon	Tue	Wed	Thu	Fri	Sat
<ישוע	1	2	3	4	5	6	7
<שכניה	8	9	10	11^{D}	12	13	14
<אלישיב	15	16	17	18	19	20	21
<יקים	22	23	24^{X}	25	26	27	28
<חופה	29	30	31				

Month 10

	Sun	Mon	Tue	Wed	Thu	Fri	Sat
				1	2	3	4
<ישבאב	5	6	7	8	9	10^{D}	11
<בלגה	12	13	14	15	16	17	18
<אמר	19	20	21	22	23^{X}	24	25
<חזיר	26	27	28	29	30		

Month 11

	Sun	Mon	Tue	Wed	Thu	Fri	Sat
						1	2
<הפצץ	3	4	5	6	7	8	9^{D}
<פתחיה	10	11	12	13	14	15	16
<יחזקאל	17	18	19	20	21	22^{X}	23
<יכין	24	25	26	27	28	29	30

Month 12

	Sun	Mon	Tue	Wed	Thu	Fri	Sat
<גמול	1	2	3	4	5	6	7
<דליה	8	9^{D}	10	11	12	13	14
<מעוזיה	15	16	17	18	19	20	21
<יהויריב	22^{X}	23	24	25	26	27	28
<ידעיה	29	30	31				

Year 2

Month 1

	Sun	Mon	Tue	Wed	Thu	Fri	Sat	
				1	2	3	4	
<חרים	5	6	7^{D}	8	9	10	11	
<שעורים	12	13	14*	15	16	17	18	*Passah
<מלכיה	19	20^{X}	21	22	23	24	25	
<מימין	26*	27	28	29	30			*Waving of the Omer

Month 2

	Sun	Mon	Tue	Wed	Thu	Fri	Sat	
						1	2	
<הקוץ	3	4	5	6	7^{D}	8	9	
<אביה	10	11	12	13	14*	15	16	* Second Passah
<ישוע	17	18	19	20^{X}	21	22	23	
<שכניה	24	25	26	27	28	29	30	

Month 3

	Sun	Mon	Tue	Wed	Thu	Fri	Sat	
<אלישיב	1	2	3	4	5	6^{D}	7	
<יקים	8	9	10	11	12	13	14	
<חופה	15*	16	17	18	19^{X}	20	21	*Festival of Weeks
<ישבאב	22	23	24	25	26	27	28	
<בלגה	29	30	31					

Month 4

	Sun	Mon	Tue	Wed	Thu	Fri	Sat
				1	2	3	4
<אמר	5^{D}	6	7	8	9	10	11
<חזיר	12	13	14	15	16	17	18^{X}
<הפצץ	19	20	21	22	23	24	25
<פתחיה	26	27	28	29	30		

Month 5

	Sun	Mon	Tue	Wed	Thu	Fri	Sat	
						1	2	
<יחזקאל	3*	4^{D}	5	6	7	8	9	*Festival of Wine
<יכין	10	11	12	13	14	15	16	
<גמול	17^{X}	18	19	20	21	22	23	
<בלגה	24	25	26	27	28	29	30	

Month 6

	Sun	Mon	Tue	Wed	Thu	Fri	Sat	
<מעוזיה	1	2	3	4^{D}	5	6	7	
<יהויריב	8	9	10	11	12	13	14	
<ידעיה	15	16	17^{X}	18	19	20	21	
<חרים	22*	23	24	25	26	27	28	*Festival of Oil
<פתחיה	29*	30	31					*Festival of Wood Offering

Month 7

	Sun	Mon	Tue	Wed	Thu	Fri	Sat
				1*	2^{D}	3	4
<מלכיה	5	6	7	8	9	10*	11
<מימין	12	13	14	15^{X*}	16	17^{D}	18
<הקוץ	19	20	21	22	23	24	25
<אביה	26	27	28	29	30^{X}		

*Day of Remembrance
*Day of Atonement
*Festival of Booths

Month 8

	Sun	Mon	Tue	Wed	Thu	Fri	Sat
						1	2
<ישוע	3	4	5	6	7	8	9
<שכניה	10	11	12	13	14	15^{X}	16^{D}
<אלישיב	17	18	19	20	21	22	23
<יקים	24	25	26	27	28	29	30

Month 9

	Sun	Mon	Tue	Wed	Thu	Fri	Sat
<חופה	1^{D}	2	3	4	5	6	7
<ישבאב	8	9	10	11	12	13	14^{X}
<בלגה	15	16	17	18	19	20	21
<אמר	22	23	24	25	26	27	28
<חזיר	29	30	31^{D}				

Month 10

	Sun	Mon	Tue	Wed	Thu	Fri	Sat
				1	2	3	4
<הפצץ	5	6	7	8	9	10	11
<פתחיה	12	13^{X}	14	15	16	17	18
<יחזקאל	19	20	21	22	23	24	25
<יכין	26	27	28	29^{D}	30		

Month 11

	Sun	Mon	Tue	Wed	Thu	Fri	Sat
						1	2
<גמול	3	4	5	6	7	8	9
<דליה	10	11	12^{X}	13	14	15	16
<מעוזיה	17	18	19	20	21	22	23
<יהויריב	24	25	26	27	28	29^{D}	30

Month 12

	Sun	Mon	Tue	Wed	Thu	Fri	Sat
<ידעיה	1	2	3	4	5	6	7
<חרים	8	9	10	11	12^{X}	13	14
<שעורים	15	16	17	18	19	20	21
<מלכיה	22	23	24	25	26	27	28^{D}
<מימין	29	30	31				

Year 3

Month 1

	Sun	Mon	Tue	Wed	Thu	Fri	Sat	
				1	2	3	4	
<הקוץ	5	6	7	8	9	10^{X}	11	
<אביה	12	13	14*	15	16	17	18	*Passah
<ישוע	19	20	21	22	23	24	25	
<שכניה	26*	27^{D}	28	29	30			*Waving of the Omer

Month 2

	Sun	Mon	Tue	Wed	Thu	Fri	Sat	
						1	2	
<אלישיב	3	4	5	6	7	8	9	
<יקים	10^{X}	11	12	13	14*	15	16	* Second Passah
<חופה	17	18	19	20	21	22	23	
<ישבאב	24	25	26^{D}	27	28	29	30	

Month 3

	Sun	Mon	Tue	Wed	Thu	Fri	Sat	
<בלגה	1	2	3	4	5	6	7	
<אמר	8	9^{X}	10	11	12	13	14	
<חזיר	15*	16	17	18	19	20	21	*Festival of Weeks
<הפצץ	22	23	24	25	26^{D}	27	28	
<פתחיה	29	30	31					

Month 4

	Sun	Mon	Tue	Wed	Thu	Fri	Sat
				1	2	3	4
<יחזקאל	5	6	7	8^{X}	9	10	11
<יכין	12	13	14	15	16	17	18
<גמול	19	20	21	22	23	24^{D}	25
<דליה	26	27	28	29	30		

Month 5

	Sun	Mon	Tue	Wed	Thu	Fri	Sat	
						1	2	
<מעוזיה	3*	4	5	6	7^{X}	8	9	*Festival of Wine
<יהויריב	10	11	12	13	14	15	16	
<ידעיה	17	18	19	20	21	22	23	
<חרים	24^{D}	25	26	27	28	29	30	

Month 6

	Sun	Mon	Tue	Wed	Thu	Fri	Sat	
<שעורים	1	2	3	4	5	6	7^{X}	
<מלכיה	8	9	10	11	12	13	14	
<מימין	15	16	17	18	19	20	21	
<הקוץ	22*	23^{D}	24	25	26	27	28	*Festival of Oil
<אביה	29*	30	31					*Festival of Wood Offering

Month 7

	Sun	Mon	Tue	Wed	Thu	Fri	Sat
				1*	2	3	4
ישוע>	5^{X}	6	7	8	9	10*	11
שכניה>	12	13	14	15*	16	17	18
אלישיב>	19	20	21	22^{D}	23	24	25
יקים>	26	27	28	29	30^{X}		

*Day of Remembrance
*Day of Atonement
*Festival of Booths

Month 8

	Sun	Mon	Tue	Wed	Thu	Fri	Sat
						1	2
חופה>	3	4	5^{X}	6	7	8	9
ישבאב>	10	11	12	13	14	15	16
בלגה>	17	18	19	20	21^{D}	22	23
אמר>	24	25	26	27	28	29	30

Month 9

	Sun	Mon	Tue	Wed	Thu	Fri	Sat
חזיר>	1	2	3	4^{X}	5	6	7
הפצץ>	8	9	10	11	12	13	14
פתחיה>	15	16	17	18	19	20	21^{D}
יחזקאל>	22	23	24	25	26	27	28
יכין>	29	30	31				

Month 10

	Sun	Mon	Tue	Wed	Thu	Fri	Sat
				1	2	3^{X}	4
גמול>	5	6	7	8	9	10	11
דליה>	12	13	14	15	16	17	18
מעוזיה>	19^{D}	20	21	22	23	24	25
יהויריב>	26	27	28	29	30		

Month 11

	Sun	Mon	Tue	Wed	Thu	Fri	Sat
						1	2^{X}
ידעיה>	3	4	5	6	7	8	9
חרים>	10	11	12	13	14	15	16
שעורים>	17	18	19^{D}	20	21	22	23
מלכיה>	24	25	26	27	28	29	30

Month 12

	Sun	Mon	Tue	Wed	Thu	Fri	Sat
מימין>	1	2^{X}	3	4	5	6	7
הקוץ>	8	9	10	11	12	13	14
אביה>	15	16	17	18^{D}	19	20	21
ישוע>	22	23	24	25	26	27	28
שכניה>	29	30	31				

Year 4

Month 1

	Sun	Mon	Tue	Wed	Thu	Fri	Sat	
				1^{x}	2	3	4	
<אלישיב>	5	6	7	8	9	10	11	
<יקים>	12	13	14*	15	16	17^{D}	18	*Passah
<חופה>	19	20	21	22	23	24	25	
<ישבאב>	26*	27	28	29	30^{x}			*Waving of the Omer

Month 2

	Sun	Mon	Tue	Wed	Thu	Fri	Sat	
						1	2	
<בלגה>	3	4	5	6	7	8	9	
<אמר>	10	11	12	13	14*	15	16	* Second Passah
<חזיר>	17^{D}	18	19	20	21	22	23	
<הפצץ>	24	25	26	27	28	29	30^{x}	

Month 3

	Sun	Mon	Tue	Wed	Thu	Fri	Sat	
<פתחיה>	1	2	3	4	5	6	7	
<יחזקאל>	8	9	10	11	12	13	14	
<יכין>	15*	16^{D}	17	18	19	20	21	*Festival of Weeks
<גמול>	22	23	24	25	26	27	28	
<דליה>	29^{x}	30	31					

Month 4

	Sun	Mon	Tue	Wed	Thu	Fri	Sat
				1	2	3	4
<מעוזיה>	5	6	7	8	9	10	11
<יהויריב>	12	13	14	15^{D}	16	17	18
<ידעיה>	19	20	21	22	23	24	25
<חרים>	26	27	28^{x}	29	30		

Month 5

	Sun	Mon	Tue	Wed	Thu	Fri	Sat	
						1	2	
<שעורים>	3*	4	5	6	7	8	9	*Festival of Wine
<מלכיה>	10	11	12	13	14^{D}	15	16	
<מימין>	17	18	19	20	21	22	23	
<הקוץ>	24	25	26	27^{x}	28	29	30	

Month 6

	Sun	Mon	Tue	Wed	Thu	Fri	Sat	
<אביה>	1	2	3	4	5	6	7	
<ישוע>	8	9	10	11	12	13	14^{D}	
<שכניה>	15	16	17	18	19	20	21	
<אלישיב>	22*	23	24	25	26	27^{x}	28	*Festival of Oil
<יקים>	29*	30	31					*Festival of Wood Offering

Month 7

	Sun	Mon	Tue	Wed	Thu	Fri	Sat
				1*	2	3	4
<חופה	5	6	7	8	9	10*	11
<ישבאב	12[D]	13	14	15*	16	17[D]	18
<בלגה	19	20	21	22	23	24	25[X]
<אמר	26	27	28	29	30		

*Day of Remembrance
*Day of Atonement
*Festival of Booths

Month 8

	Sun	Mon	Tue	Wed	Thu	Fri	Sat
						1	2
<חזיר	3	4	5	6	7	8	9
<הפצץ	10	11	12[D]	13	14	15	16
<פתחיה	17	18	19	20	21	22	23
<יחזקאל	24	25[X]	26	27	28	29	30

Month 9

	Sun	Mon	Tue	Wed	Thu	Fri	Sat
<יכין	1	2	3	4	5	6	7
<גמול	8	9	10	11[D]	12	13	14
<דליה	15	16	17	18	19	20	21
<מעוזיה	22	23	24[X]	25	26	27	28
<יהויריב	29	30	31				

Month 10

	Sun	Mon	Tue	Wed	Thu	Fri	Sat
				1	2	3	4
<ידעיה	5	6	7	8	9	10[D]	11
<חרים	12	13	14	15	16	17	18
<שעורים	19	20	21	22	23[X]	24	25
<מלכיה	26	27	28	29	30		

Month 11

	Sun	Mon	Tue	Wed	Thu	Fri	Sat
						1	2
<מימין	3	4	5	6	7	8	9[D]
<הקוץ	10	11	12	13	14	15	16
<אביה	17	18	19	20	21	22[X]	23
<ישוע	24	25	26	27	28	29	30

Month 12

	Sun	Mon	Tue	Wed	Thu	Fri	Sat
<שכניה	1	2	3	4	5	6	7
<אלישיב	8	9[D]	10	11	12	13	14
<יקים	15	16	17	18	19	20	21
<חופה	22[X]	23	24	25	26	27	28
<ישבאב	29	30	31				

Year 5

Month 1

	Sun	Mon	Tue	Wed	Thu	Fri	Sat	
				1	2	3	4	
בלגה>	5	6	7^{D}	8	9	10	11	
אמר>	12	13	14*	15	16	17	18	*Passah
חזיר>	19	20^{X}	21	22	23	24	25	
הפצץ>	26*	27	28	29	30^{X}			*Waving of the Omer

Month 2

	Sun	Mon	Tue	Wed	Thu	Fri	Sat	
						1	2	
פתחיה>	3	4	5	6	7^{D}	8	9	
יחזקאל>	10	11	12	13	14*	15	16	* Second Passah
יכין>	17	18	19	20^{X}	21	22	23	
גמול>	24	25	26	27	28	29	30	

Month 3

	Sun	Mon	Tue	Wed	Thu	Fri	Sat	
דליה>	1	2	3	4	5	6	7	
מעוזיה>	8	9	10	11	12	13	14	
יהויריב>	15*	16	17	18	19^{X}	20	21	*Festival of Weeks
ידעיה>	22	23	24	25	26	27	28	
חרים>	29	30	31					

Month 4

	Sun	Mon	Tue	Wed	Thu	Fri	Sat
				1	2	3	4
שעורים>	5^{D}	6	7	8	9	10	11
מלכיה>	12	13	14	15	16	17	18^{X}
מימין>	19	20	21	22	23	24	25
הקוץ>	26	27	28	29	30		

Month 5

	Sun	Mon	Tue	Wed	Thu	Fri	Sat	
						1	2	
אביה>	3*	4^{D}	5	6	7	8	9	*Festival of Wine
ישוע>	10	11	12	13	14	15	16	
שכניה>	17^{X}	18	19	20	21	22	23	
אלישיב>	24	25	26	27	28	29	30	

Month 6

	Sun	Mon	Tue	Wed	Thu	Fri	Sat	
יקים>	1	2	3	4^{D}	5	6	7	
חופה>	8	9	10	11	12	13	14	
ישבאב>	15	16	17^{X}	18	19	20	21	
בלגה>	22*	23	24	25	26	27	28	*Festival of Oil
אמר>	29*	30	31					*Festival of Wood Offering

Month 7

	Sun	Mon	Tue	Wed	Thu	Fri	Sat
				1*	2^{D}	3	4
חזיר>	5	6	7	8	9	10*	11
הפצץ>	12	13	14	15^{X}*	16	17^{D}	18
פתחיה>	19	20	21	22	23	24	25
יחזקאל>	26	27	28	29	30^{X}		

*Day of Remembrance
*Day of Atonement
*Festival of Booths

Month 8

	Sun	Mon	Tue	Wed	Thu	Fri	Sat
						1	2^{D}
יכין>	3	4	5	6	7	8	9
גמול>	10	11	12	13	14	15^{X}	16
דליה>	17	18	19	20	21	22	23
מעוזיה>	24	25	26	27	28	29	30

Month 9

	Sun	Mon	Tue	Wed	Thu	Fri	Sat
יהויריב>	1^{D}	2	3	4	5	6	7
ידעיה>	8	9	10	11	12	13	14^{X}
חרים>	15	16	17	18	19	20	21
שעורים>	22	23	24	25	26	27	28
מלכיה>	29	30	31^{D}				

Month 10

	Sun	Mon	Tue	Wed	Thu	Fri	Sat
				1	2	3	4
מימין>	5	6	7	8	9	10	11
הקוץ>	12	13^{X}	14	15	16	17	18
אביה>	19	20	21	22	23	24	25
ישוע>	26	27	28	29^{D}	30		

Month 11

	Sun	Mon	Tue	Wed	Thu	Fri	Sat
						1	2
שכניה>	3	4	5	6	7	8	9
אלישיב>	10	11	12^{X}	13	14	15	16
יקים>	17	18	19	20	21	22	23
חופה>	24	25	26	27	28	29^{D}	30

Month 12

	Sun	Mon	Tue	Wed	Thu	Fri	Sat
ישבאב>	1	2	3	4	5	6	7
בלגה>	8	9	10	11	12^{X}	13	14
אמר>	15	16	17	18	19	20	21
חזיר>	22	23	24	25	26	27	28^{D}
הפצץ>	29	30	31				

Year 6

Month 1

	Sun	Mon	Tue	Wed	Thu	Fri	Sat	
				1	2	3	4	
פתחיה<	5	6	7	8	9	10^{X}	11	
יחזקאל<	12	13	14*	15	16	17	18	*Passah
יכין<	19	20	21	22	23	24	25	
גמול<	26*	27^{D}	28	29	30			*Waving of the Omer

Month 2

	Sun	Mon	Tue	Wed	Thu	Fri	Sat	
						1	2	
דליה<	3	4	5	6	7	8	9	
מעוזיה<	10^{X}	11	12	13	14*	15	16	* Second Passah
יהויריב<	17	18	19	20	21	22	23	
ידעיה<	24	25	26^{D}	27	28	29	30	

Month 3

	Sun	Mon	Tue	Wed	Thu	Fri	Sat	
הרים<	1	2	3	4	5	6	7	
שעורים<	8	9^{X}	10	11	12	13	14	
מלכיה<	15*	16	17	18	19	20	21	*Festival of Weeks
מימין<	22	23	24	25	26^{D}	27	28	
הקוץ<	29	30	31					

Month 4

	Sun	Mon	Tue	Wed	Thu	Fri	Sat
				1	2	3	4
אביה<	5	6	7	8^{X}	9	10	11
ישוע<	12	13	14	15	16	17	18
שכניה<	19	20	21	22	23	24^{D}	25
אלישיב<	26	27	28	29	30		

Month 5

	Sun	Mon	Tue	Wed	Thu	Fri	Sat	
						1	2	
יקים<	3*	4	5	6	7^{X}	8	9	*Festival of Wine
חופה<	10	11	12	13	14	15	16	
ישבאב<	17	18	19	20	21	22	23	
בלגה<	24^{D}	25	26	27	28	29	30	

Month 6

	Sun	Mon	Tue	Wed	Thu	Fri	Sat	
אמר<	1	2	3	4	5	6	7^{X}	
חזיר<	8	9	10	11	12	13	14	
הפצץ<	15	16	17	18	19	20	21	
פתחיה<	22*	23^{D}	24	25	26	27	28	*Festival of Oil
יחזקאל<	29*	30	31					*Festival of Wood Offering

Month 7

	Sun	Mon	Tue	Wed	Thu	Fri	Sat
				1*	2	3	4
יכין>	5^{X}	6	7	8	9	10*	11
גמול>	12	13	14	15*	16	17	18
דליה>	19	20	21	22^{D}	23	24	25
מעוזיה>	26	27	28	29	30		

*Day of Remembrance
*Day of Atonement
*Festival of Booths

Month 8

	Sun	Mon	Tue	Wed	Thu	Fri	Sat
						1	2
יהויריב>	3	4	5^{X}	6	7	8	9
ידעיה>	10	11	12	13	14	15	16
חרים>	17	18	19	20	21^{D}	22	23
שעורים>	24	25	26	27	28	29	30

Month 9

	Sun	Mon	Tue	Wed	Thu	Fri	Sat
מלכיה>	1	2	3	4^{X}	5	6	7
מימין>	8	9	10	11	12	13	14
הקוץ>	15	16	17	18	19	20	21^{D}
אביה>	22	23	24	25	26	27	28
<ישוע'	29	30	31				

Month 10

	Sun	Mon	Tue	Wed	Thu	Fri	Sat
				1	2	3^{X}	4
שכניה>	5	6	7	8	9	10	11
אלישיב>	12	13	14	15	16	17	18
יקים>	19^{D}	20	21	22	23	24	25
חופה>	26	27	28	29	30		

Month 11

	Sun	Mon	Tue	Wed	Thu	Fri	Sat
						1	2^{X}
ישבאב>	3	4	5	6	7	8	9
בלגה>	10	11	12	13	14	15	16
אמר>	17	18	19^{D}	20	21	22	23
חזיר>	24	25	26	27	28	29	30

Month 12

	Sun	Mon	Tue	Wed	Thu	Fri	Sat
הפצץ>	1	2^{X}	3	4	5	6	7
פתחיה>	8	9	10	11	12	13	14
יחזקאל>	15	16	17	18^{D}	19	20	21
יכין>	22	23	24	25	26	27	28
גמול>	29	30	31				

Notes

1. For a general introduction to the Dead Sea Scrolls see VanderKam and Flint (2005), García-Martínez (1996). The scrolls are published with commentary in the series Discoveries in the Judaean Desert (Oxford, 1955–2009). Quotations from the Scrolls (transcriptions and translations) are conveniently taken from Parry and Tov (2004–2005).
2. Yet another pseudepigraphon which suggests calendrical statements is 2 (Slavonic) Enoch. However, the calendar in that book underwent numerous corrections and redactions. See Stökl Ben-Ezra (forthcoming).
3. Citations from 1 Enoch follow Nickelsburg and VanderKam (2004) unless otherwise stated.
4. Quotations from Jubilees are taken from VanderKam (1989).
5. For a survey of various calendars, see Bickerman (1980), pp. 13–61, Hannah (2005), Stern (2001), pp. 25–46.
6. For the variant readings of the words "the moon" at 74:12 in the Ethiopic version, see Ben-Dov (2008), p. 124.
7. Parry and Tov (2004), vol. 5, pp. 196–197.
8. Parry and Tov (2004), vol. 4, pp. 56–57. The number of days in a year was not fully preserved in the Scroll. However, the reconstruction is certain enough in the light of other documents mentioned here as well as of calendrical lists similar to the one appended to the beginning of the 4QHalakhic Letter[a].
9. Parry and Tov (2004), vol. 2, pp. 108–109.
10. The paleographic dating is too limited because it is based on the script of particular copies and cannot disclose the date of authorship. Special difficulties arise on an attempt to give a paleographical date for the documents written in cryptic script. However, a concentration of manuscripts in a limited period could imply as to their distribution and function. The earliest calendrical scroll is 4Q320, dated to the last quarter of the second century BC, whereas the latest of those discussed here is the Psalms Scroll from Cave 11 (11Q5), dated to the first half of the first century AD. A large group of calendrical scrolls is dated on the basis of script to the middle of the first century BC. See the tables in Tov (2002), pp. 385, 403–404, 426.
11. For a critical edition of the calendrical texts from Qumran, see Talmon, Ben-Dov and Glessmer (2001).
12. Most of these texts are concentrated in Parry and Tov (2004), vol. 4.
13. Thus, the festival of Passover always falls in the first month, following the biblical decree in Exodus chapter 12.
14. In Jewish sources of the Roman period, both textual and artistic like the zodiac mosaic floors from various synagogues, the term *tequfah* indicates the day of transition (Greek *tropē*) rather than a whole season of the year. It is hard to tell the exact meaning of the word *tequfah* in Qumran Hebrew because of the fragmentary state of formulas which end the seasons of the year in such calendars as 4Q394 1–2 and the cryptic scroll 4Q324d.
15. In addition, for the special importance of the 52-week construction in the Book of Jubilees, see Ben-Dov (2009).
16. For the text of the prayers, see Parry and Tov (2004), vol. 4. Maier thought that the thirteen songs were composed not only for the first term of the year but were intended to be repeated at each term. See Maier (1992); for further discussion and bibliography see Ben-Dov and Saulnier (2008), p. 132.
17. Parry and Tov (2005), vol. 5, pp. 190–191); Quoted also in Talmon, Ben-Dov and Glessmer (2001), p. 7. For the reconstruction compare 4Q320 frags. 3–4. A month of 31 days at the end of the quarter is mentioned explicitly in 1 Enoch 72: 13, 19, 25, 31, but no mention of it is preserved intact in the calendrical scrolls. Such a reference needs to be reconstructed with great probability in 4Q321 II 5–6; see also 4Q252 I 20. For the reluctance of the Book of Jubilees to count a 31st day in the month, see Ben-Dov (2009).
18. The names of Babylonian months are preserved in Qumran literature in one or two places only. In 4Q332 line 2, the name of the month 'Shevat' is preserved. It is possible that the date 'X of M[arḥešw]an

is preserved in 4Q322a 2 5. See, however, the reservations of the editor, Tigchelaar (2001), p. 127.

19. On month-names in biblical literature see generally VanderKam (1998), pp. 8–11.
20. Naeh (1992).
21. For example, b. Pesaḥim 66:1; see Baumgarten (1977), pp. 127-128; Beckwith (1996), p. 103.
22. See Ben-Dov (2008), pp. 62–67.
23. For details on this structure, see Elior (2004), pp. 44–58.
24. The resulting symmetries in 4Q319 are presented graphically in Talmon, Ben-Dov and Glessmer (2001), pp. 203, 207.
25. Talmon (1989), pp. 147–185, esp. 186–199. Talmon's article (originally published in 1958!) is still valuable, although recent research calls for more careful distinctions between older materials like Jubilees and 1 Enoch and the later Qumran texts. In addition, the extent of the dispute between followers of the solar and the lunar calendars must be reevaluated (see below).
26. For this aspect of the debate, see Elior (2005), pp. 201–206.
27. Cf. VanderKam (2000), pp. 121–127.
28. For some reflections on the difference between a 360 and a 364-day year see Boccaccini (2002).
29. Cf. Bernstein (1991). The language of the book of Jubilees is also echoed in 4Q390 1 8, "and they will forget the law and the festival, the Shabbat and the covenant" (cf. 4Q390 2 i 10; Parry and Tov (2004), vol. 6, pp. 114–115; also Tigchelaar (2005)).
30. This interpretation of the passage in Pesher Habakkuk was suggested by Talmon in 1951 (see Talmon (1989), pp. 186–199). Although recently challenged by Stern (2000), pp. 184–185, it remains accepted in the study of the Dead Sea Scrolls.
31. See further details and bibliography on the Flood chronology in Kister (1999), pp. 360–363; Ben-Dov (2008), pp. 41–43; Ben-Dov and Saulnier (2008), p. 129.
32. Kister (1999), p. 360; von Weissenberg (2009), pp. 33–38, 129–133.
33. In fact, this kind of religious argumentation is quite common in calendrical disputes throughout the Hellenistic Near East, as for example in the Ptolemaic decree of Canopus 239 BC.
34. The studies by Jaubert were conveniently collected in English in Jaubert (1965).
35. For a summary of the methods of Jaubert and VanderKam, see VanderKam (1998), pp. 54–58; for subsequent research see Ben-Dov and Saulnier (2008), pp. 135–142.
36. Baumgarten (1977), pp. 101–114; Wacholder and Wacholder (1995), pp. 4–25; Abegg (2001), p. 147.
37. Stern (2001), pp. 27–31.
38. See, for example, Kister (1999), p. 361.
39. In fact, in the *Astronomical Book* the fractions are not indicated as 1/14, 2/14 etc., but rather as sevenths: 0.5/7, 1/7, 1.5/7, etc.
40. Albani (1994).
41. For a summary of the astronomy of Mul.Apin and *Enūma Anu Enlil*, see Hunger and Pingree (1999), pp. 32–83.
42. The stars, which take a significant part in Mul.Apin and *Enūma Anu Enlil* are far less central in the worldview of Jewish astronomical writing. Jewish monotheism tends to avoid the stars because of the danger of them being hallowed as deities.
43. For a summary of the relations between the *Astronomical Book* and Mesopotamian astronomy, see Ben-Dov (2008), pp. 181–196.
44. For this element see below section 7, as well as Ben-Dov and Horowitz (2005); Ben-Dov (2008), p. 232.
45. Horowitz (1996); Ben-Dov (2008), pp. 164–167.
46. In this formulation I have slightly modified my opinion with respect to earlier publications.
47. Some Jewish documents use schematic 30-day months on account of their convenience for long-term calculation. So, for example, the period of 150 days mentioned in the Flood story (Gen 8:3–4) is equal to five consecutive months of 30 days each. This may be the background for the similar figure in Jubilees 5:27 (but see Ben-Dov (2009), pp. 288–289).

48. VanderKam (1999), pp. 214*–216*.
49. See Brown (2000), p. 113; Brack-Bernsen (2007), pp. 93–98. Brown, however, puts more stress on divinatory uses of ideal period schemes.
50. For example Albani (1994), p. 97.
51. For the different readings of this verse see above, note 6.
52. Contra Stern (2000), pp. 179–186.
53. See in detail with earlier bibliography Ben-Dov (2008), pp. 132–139.
54. The passage as it is now depicts an 8-year cycle (*octaeteris*), but there are good grounds to believe that this reflects a later Hellenistic redaction, while the original form of the passage in fact related to a 3-year cycle. See Ben-Dov (2008), pp. 125–129.
55. The translation of the Hebrew formulas in the text depends on this exegetical choice. The translation by Abegg, quoted here from Parry and Tov (2004), vol. 4, pp. 58–59, reflects the latter possibility, that 4Q317 simply measures the amount of light in the moon. However, if 4Q317 is to be understood as measuring the periods of lunar visibility, then the translation should be modified to read: "on day X of the month, it (= the moon) is obscured / revealed (during) Y parts". In this case the number of parts (Y) must be understood as modifying the verb "obscure" or "reveal", serving as an adverbial clause. Although this is not a very straightforward Hebrew syntax, it might be possible here because of the mathematical context, which is extremely rare in ancient Hebrew texts.
56. Ben-Dov (2008), pp. 141–144.
57. The nominal form *dwq* is always written with a pronominal suffix. The etymology of the term remains debated. Despite the opinion of most scholars, who derive the term from the root DWQ, 'observe, view' (mainly in Aramaic; see Wise (1994), pp. 222–228), it now seems preferable to derive it from the root DQQ, 'diminish, thin'. This possibility was first raised by Talmon and Knohl (1991), pp. 505–521. It seems to be cognate to the Akkadian term *maššartu* (*Enūma Anu Enlil* 14, table B), relating to the waning of the moon or to the shortening of its period of visibility; see Ben-Dov (2008), p. 219.
58. See Ben-Dov (2008), pp. 236–239. This identification of X and *dwq* was first suggested by Talmon and Knohl (1991), before the analogy with the Lunar Three arose.
59. Note that although the same data is used in the Babylonian and Qumranic texts, it is indicated differently. See Ben-Dov (2008), p. 236.
60. See, for example, VanderKam (1998), pp. 79–80; Gillet-Didier (2001–2002); Glessmer (1999), pp. 250–252.
61. An inexplicable fact is the designation of the jubilees in the list by the ordinal numbers 2–7 rather than 1–6 as one would expect. See Talmon, Ben-Dov and Glessmer (2001), pp. 208.
62. See the complex structure of the list, as expressed graphically in Talmon, Ben-Dov and Glessmer (2001), p. 203.
63. The list in 1 Chronicles opens with the family of Joiarib, placing the family of Gamul in the 22nd position. In contrast, all sources from Qumran place Gamul in the first position, as the family which served at the creation of the world. So far no satisfactory explanation has been found for this anomaly. A common opinion in scholarship suggests that Joiarib was dethroned from the first position because of the sectaries' opposition to the Hasmonean clan, the rulers of Judah at that time, whose members were descendants of Joiarib. Beckwith (1996), p. 89 suggested further that the biblical list commencing with Joiarib was indeed followed at Qumran, but that Joiarib served at the autumn New Year, with the result that Gamul served at the first spring New Year, the time of the Creation. This suggestion is worth further consideration.
64. 1QM 2:1–4 reads as follows: "the congregation's clans are fifty-two. They shall rank the chiefs of the priests after the Chief Priest and his deputy; twelve chief priests to serve in the regular offering before God. The chiefs of the courses, twenty-six, shall serve in their courses. After them the chiefs of the Levites serve continually, twelve in all, one to a tribe. The chiefs of their courses shall serve each man in his office." From this section it can be understood that the scroll recognized twenty-six priestly courses, exactly congruent with the length of a 52-week year in which each course could serve exactly twice per year. This number is different from that described in the book of Chronicles and the Qumran calendri-

cal documents, which recognize only twenty-four priestly courses. It is impossible to determine whether the visionary statement in the War Scroll was meant to convey a valid calendrical principle, or whether its significance was confined to this place alone.

65. Sperber (1971); Tabori (2003).
66. See for example the statement by Rabbi Abahu about the mishmar that served at the beginning of each Jubilee (*y. Sukkah*, 5:8, [folio 55.4]), and that by Rabbi Hiyya about a full number of weeks service counted in the 49 days between Passover and the Feast of First Fruits (*Midrash Leviticus Rabbah* 28:2 [ed. Margalioth, p. 653]).
67. Yahalom (1999), pp. 107–130; Kister (2001).
68. See Albani (1997), pp. 103–110; Ben-Dov and Saulnier (2008), pp. 146–152.
69. Thus recently Wacholder and Wacholder (1995), p. 36–37.
70. See Beckwith (1996), pp. 133–140. On 1 Enoch 80: 2–8 see also Albani (1994), pp. 108–112; VanderKam (2006).
71. See a survey of suggested modes of intercalation in Beckwith (1996), pp. 126–127.
72. Glessmer (1999), pp. 263–268; see my response in Talmon, Ben-Dov and Glessmer (2001), pp. 210–211.
73. Bickerman (1980), p. 46.
74. For the introductions in *Enūma Anu Enlil*, see Brown (2000), pp. 234–235.
75. For example VanderKam (1994), pp. 380–383.
76. See for example Koch and Glessmer (1999).
77. The prologue to *Enūma Anu Enlil* seems to fulfill a similar function; see in greater detail Ben-Dov (2008), pp. 240–241.

References

Abegg, M.G., 2001, "The Calendar at Qumran", in A.J. Avery-Peck et al. (eds.), *Judaism in Late Antiquity* (Leiden: Brill), Part 5, Vol. 1, 145–171.

Albani, M., 1994, *Astronomie und Schöpfungsglaube: Untersuchungen zum astronomischen Henochbuch* (Neukirchen-Vluyn: Neukirchener Verlag).

——, 1997, "Zur Rekonstruktion eines Verdrängten Konzepts: Der 364-Tage-Kalender in der gegenwärtigen Forschung" in M. Albani et al (eds.), *Studies in the Book of Jubilees* (Tübingen: Mohr Siebeck), 103–110.

Baumgarten, J. M., 1977, *Studies in Qumran Law* (Leiden: Brill).

Beckwith, R., 1996, *Calendar and Chronology, Jewish and Christian: Biblical, Intertestamental and Patristic Studies* (Leiden: Brill).

Ben-Dov, J., 2008, *Head of All Years: Astronomy and Calendars at Qumran in their Ancient Context* (Leiden: Brill)

——, 2009, "Tradition and Innovation in the Calendar of Jubilees", in G. Boccaccini and G. Ibba (eds.), *Enoch and the Mosaic Torah. The Evidence of Jubilees* (Grand Rapids, Michigan: Eerdmans), 276–293.

——, and Horowitz, W., 2005, "The Babylonian Lunar Three in Calendrical Scrolls from Qumran", *Zeitschrift für Assyriologie* 95, 104–120.

——, and Saulnier, S., 2008, "Qumran Calendars: A Survey of Research 1980-2007", *Currents in Biblical Research* 7, 124–168.

Bernstein, M.J., 1991, "'Walking in the Festivals of the Gentiles': 4QpHosea[a] 2.15-17 and Jubilees 6:34-38", *Journal for the Study of the Pseudepigrapha* 9, 21–34.

Bickerman, E. J., 1980, *Chronology of the Ancient World* (London: Thames and Hudson). (revised edition)

Boccaccini, G., 2002, "The Solar Calendars of Daniel and Enoch", in J. J. Collins and P. W. Flint (eds.), *The Book of Daniel: Composition and Reception* (Leiden: Brill), Vol. 2, 311–328.

Brack-Bernsen, L., 2007, "The 360-Day Year in Mesopotamia", in J. M. Steele (ed.), *Calendars and Years. Astronomy and Time in the Ancient Near East* (Oxford: Oxbow Books), 83–100.

Brown, D., 2000, *Mesopotamian Planetary Astronomy-Astrology* (Groningen: Styx).
Elior, R., 2005, *The Three Temples: On the Emergence of Jewish Mysticism*, trans. D. Louvish (Oxford: Littman Library of Jewish Civilization).
García Martínez, F., 1996, *The Dead Sea Scrolls Translated: The Qumran Texts in English*, trans. G. W. E. Watson (Leiden: Brill).
Gillet-Didier, V., 2001–2002, "Calendrier lunaire, calendrier solaire et gardes sacerdotales: Recherches sur 4Q321", *Revue de Qumran* 20,2, 171–205.
Glessmer, U., 1997, "Explizite aussagen über kalendarische Konflikte in Jubiläenbuch: Jub 6, 22-32.33-38", in M. Albani et al. (eds.), *Studies in the Book of Jubilees* (Tübingen: Mohr Siebeck), 127–164.
——, 1999, "Calendars in the Qumran Scrolls", in P. W. Flint and J. C. VanderKam (eds.), *The Dead Sea Scrolls after Fifty Years: A Comprehensive Assessment* (Leiden: Brill), II, 213–278.
Hannah, R., 2005, *Greek and Roman Calendars. Constructions of Time in the Classical World* (London: Duckworth).
Hunger, H. and Pingree, D., 1999, *Astral Sciences in Mesopotamia* (Leiden: Brill).
Jaubert, A., 1965, *The Date of the Last Supper*, trans. I. Rafferty (New York: Society of St. Paul).
Kister, M. 1999, "Studies in 4QMiqṣat Maʿasei HaTorah and Related Texts", *Tarbiz* 68, 317–371 (in Hebrew).
——, 2001, "5Q13 and the Avodah: A Historical Survey and its Significance", *Dead Sea Discoveries* 8, 136–148.
Koch, K. and Glessmer, U., 1999, "Neumonds-Neujahr oder Vollmonds-Neujahr? Zu spätisraelitischen Kalender-Theologien", in B. Kollmann, W. Reinbold and A. Steudel (eds.), *Antikes Judentum und frühes Christentum: Festschrift für Hartmut Stegemann zum 65. Geburtstag* (Berlin: de Gruyer), 114–136.
Maier, J. 1992, "Shîrê ʿOlat hash-Shabbat: Some Observations on the Calendric Implications and on their Style", in J. Trebolle Barrera and L. Vegas Montaner (eds.), *The Madrid Qumran Congress: Proceedings of the International Congress on the Dead Sea Scrolls II* (Leiden: Brill), 543–560.
Naeh, S., 1992, "Did the Tannaim Interpret the Script of the Torah Differently from the Aurhorized Reading?" *Tarbiz* 61, 401–448 (in Hebrew).
Nickelsburg, G. W. E. and VanderKam, J. C., 2004, *1 Enoch. A New Translation*, (Minneapolis: Fortress Press).
Parry, D.W. and Tov, E., 2004–2005, *The Dead Sea Scrolls Reader*, 6 vols. (Leiden: Brill).
Sperber, D., 1971, "Mishmarot and Maʿmadot: Talmudic Data", in *Encyclopaedia Judaica*, (Jerusalem: Keter Pub. House), XII, cols. 90–92.
Stern, S., 2000, "Qumran Calendars: Theory and Practice", in T. H. Lim (ed.), *The Dead Sea Scrolls in their Historical Context* (Edinburgh: T&T Clark), 179–186.
——, 2001, *Calendar and Community: A History of the Jewish Calendar 2nd Century BCE – 10th Century CE* (Oxford: Oxford University Press).
D. Stökl Ben-Ezra, forthcoming, "Halakha, Calendars and the Provenances of 2 Enoch", in A. Orlov (ed.), *Proceedings of the Enoch Seminar 2009* (forthcoming).
Tabori, J., 2003, "Maʿamadot: A Second Temple Non-Temple Liturgy", in E.G. Chazon (ed.), *Liturgical Perspectives: Prayer and Poetry in Light of the Dead Sea Scrolls: Proceedings of the Fifth International Symposium of the Orion Center for the Study of the Dead sea Scrolls and Associated Literature* (Leiden: Brill), 235–261.
Talmon, S., 1989, *The World of Qumran from Within* (Jerusalem and Leiden: Magnes and Brill).
——, 1999, "Anti-Lunar-Calender Polemic in the Covenanters' Writings", in M. Becker and W. Fenske (eds.), *Das Ende der Tage und die Gegenwart des Heils. Festschrift für Heinz-Wolfgang Kuhn zum 65* (Leiden: Brill), 29–40.
——, Ben-Dov, J. and Glessmer, U., 2001, *Qumran Cave 4 XVI: Calendrical Texts*, Discoveries in the Judaen Desert 21 (Oxford: Clarendon).
——, and Knohl, I., 1991, "A Calendrical Scroll from Qumran Cave IV — Miš Ba (4Q321)", *Tarbiz* 60, 505–521. (in Hebrew)
Tigchelaar, E. J. C., 2001, "322a. 4QHistorical Text H?", in D. M. Gropp, M. Bernstein et al. (eds.),

Wadi Daliyeh II: The Samaria Papyri from Wadi Daliyeh; Qumran Cave 4, XXVIII, Miscellanea Part 2, Discoveries in the Judaen Desert 28 (Oxford: Clarendon), 125–128.

——, and Garcia Martinez, F., 2000, "4QAstronomical Enoch[a] ar" in P. S. Alexander et al. (eds.), *Qumran Miscellanea, Part I*, Discoveries in the Judaean Desert 36 (Oxford: Clarendon), 104–171.

——, 2005, "A Cave 4 Fragment of Divre Moshe (4QDM) and the Text of 1Q22 1:7-19 and Jubilees 1:9, 14", *Dead Sea Discoveries* 12, 303–312.

Tov, E., 2002, *The Texts from the Judaen Desert: Indices and An Introduction to the Discoveries in the Judaean Desert Series*, Discoveries in the Judaean Desert 39 (Oxford : Clarendon).

VanderKam, J. C., 1989, *The Book of Jubilees: A Critical Text and Translation*, (2 vols. Leuven: Peeters).

——, 1994, "Calendrical Texts and the Origins of the Dead Sea Scroll Community", in M. O. Wise et al. (eds.), *Methods of Investigation of the Dead Sea Scrolls and the Khirbet Qumran Site* (New York: NYAS), 371–386.

——, 1998, *Calendars in the Dead Sea Scrolls: Measuring Time* (London: Routledge).

——, 1999, "Studies on 'David's Compositions' (11QPs[a] 27:2-11)", *Eretz Israel* 26 (Festschrift F. M. Cross) *212–*220.

——, 2000, *From Revelation to Canon: Studies in the Hebrew Bible and Second Temple Literature* (Leiden: Brill).

——, 2006, "1 Enoch 80 within the Book of the Luminaries", in F. García Martínez et al., (eds.), *From 4QMMT to Resurrection, Mélanges qumraniens en hommage à Émile Puech* (Leiden: Brill), 333–355.

——, and Flint, P.W., 2005, *The Meaning of the Dead Sea Scrolls: Their Significance for Understanding the Bible, Judaism, Jesus, and Christianity* (London: T&T Clark).

Wacholder, B. Z. and Wacholder, S., 1995, "Patterns of Biblical Dates and Qumran's Calendar: The Fallacy of Jaubert's Hypothesis", *Hebrew Union College Annual* 66, 4–25.

von Weissenberg, H., 2009, *4QMMT: Reevaluating the Text, the Function and the Meaning of the Epilogue* (Leiden: Brill).

Werman, C., 1995, "The Story of the Flood in the Book of Jubilees", *Tarbiz* 64, 183–202. (in Hebrew).

Yahalom, Y., 1999, *Poetry and Society in Jewish Galilee of Late Antiquity* (Tel Aviv: Hakibbutz Hameuchad). (in Hebrew).

The 'Well-Known Calendars': al-Khāzinī's Description of Significant Chronological Systems for Medieval Mathematical Astronomy in Arabic

Clemency Montelle

In memory of Professor David Pingree

1. Introduction

Sometime around AD 1115, the scholar Abū Manṣūr ʿAbd al-Raḥmān al-Khāzinī, originally a slave-boy of Byzantine origin, composed in Arabic what was to be one of the major works in mathematical astronomy of the medieval period, the *Zīj al-Sanjarī*. As its title implies, al-Khāzinī wrote this work for the Sulṭān Sanjar ibn Malikshāh, who ruled from AD 1118 until he died almost forty years later in 1157. In his childhood, al-Khāzinī was owned by Abu'l-Ḥusayn ʿAlī ibn Muḥammad al-Khāzin al-Marwazī, the treasurer of Merv, who made provisions so that his young charge received a first-class education in mathematics and philosophy. Al-Khāzinī obviously excelled in his studies as in his adulthood he served as an astronomical practitioner in the Seljuk court. It is supposed that he was based in Merv, which was, at this time, a flourishing centre of scientific and literary activity.[1]

In addition to his abilities as a mathematician, al-Khāzinī was one of about twenty Islamic astronomers who performed original observations.[2] He was amongst the succession of significant scholars in the Eastern Islamic astronomical tradition. His work was inspired by his predecessors, including ʿUmar al-Khayyām, al-Bīrūnī, and al-Asfizārī, and his successors were Naṣīr al-Dīn al-Ṭūsī and others who worked at the Marāgha Observatory, as well as those from the Samarkand observatory, including al-Kāshī and Ulugh Beg. His *zīj* was well used in the Islamic world, and was transmitted to Byzantium, where it was used in particular by astronomer and geographer George Chrysococces (fl. ca. 1335) and through him as an intermediary, reached Theodore Meliteniotes, an astronomer working in Constantinople (fl. ca. 1360).[3] In addition, al-Khāzinī refers to astronomical and mathematical techniques that originated in other cultures. Thus, this work is a rich and vital source for increasing our understanding of the transmission and reception of scientific ideas through the Islamic Near East.

Zīj is a term derived from middle-Persian that refers to compositions containing mathematical tables and accompanying explanatory discussion intended for practical astronomical use. Works of this character provide a significant portion of knowledge we have concerning medieval Islamic mathematical astronomy. Such 'handbooks' are substantial works, usually up to 200 folia, and contain much astronomical and mathematical information such as mean motion calculations, chronological systems and calendar conversion, tabulations of trigonometric functions, stellar coordinates, planetary longitudes and latitudes, and so on; material which directly reflects the abilities, preoccupations, and talents of working scientists of the day. Indeed, the *Zīj al-Sanjarī* is a particularly good example of this format;[4] it contains extensive mathematical and astronomical tables and detailed accompanying explanation not only on how to use the tables but also, on occasion, about their construction and notable features.

Chronology was a key topic in a *zīj*, and it was often covered first in works of this format. Notably, al-Khāzinī shows a great interest in relaying the details of other societies' calendrical systems and chronological conventions. His discussion on the various manipulations of calendars and their arrangement is thorough and unusually comprehensive. Through al-Khāzinī's eyes then, we will explore the various details of calendars that were important to Islamic practitioners of the time, and gain a unique insight into their features and circumstances through such primary source exposition.

1.1 The Wajīz of al-Khāzinī

The full title of al-Khāzinī's *zīj* is *al-Zīj al-muʿtabar al-Sanjarī al-Sulṭānī* (lit. 'The Tested Astronomical Tables Related to the Sultan Sanjar'),[5] which, due to the fact that it contains a significant amount of calendrical information with tables for holidays, fasts, rulers, and prophets, was also known as the *Jāmiʿ al-tawārīḵ li'l-Sinjarī* (lit. 'The Collection of the Chronologies for Sanjar').[6] Later though, in 1130/1131, al-Khāzinī wrote an abridgement of this work and its tables, called *Wajīz al-Zīj al-muʿtabar al-Sulṭānī* (lit. 'Summary of the Tested Astronomical Tables Related to the Sultan').[7]

The *wajīz* covers the following subjects over twelve books: calendars, mathematical foundations, the two declinations and the rising times in *sphaera recta*, the equations of day and oblique ascensions, the fixed stars, local time, the mean motions of the planets, their true longitudes, retrogressions and latitudes, parallax, syzygies and eclipses, the sighting of the lunar crescent, the revolutions of the years, the casting of the rays, and prorogations.

The chronological material opens al-Khāzinī's *wajīz* and is notably extensive and diverse. He describes both contemporary and ancient calendars, as well as referring to pertinent historical details to support his exposition. He covers the Hijra, Yazdijird, Seleucid, Persian, Jalali, Hindu, Alexandrian, Nabonassar, and Byzantine calendars and provides a detailed account of how to convert from one calendar to any other. Furthermore, he draws from a variety of cultures and groups in societies to support and enrich his account. Al-Khāzinī refers to Arab, Persian, Byzantine, Hebrew, Christian, Indian, Sassanian, Egyptian, and Coptic sources, among others.

His audience is also multi-layered. He provides details relevant to 'the common people' (*al-ʿāmma*) as well as the so-called 'masters of science' (*āṣḥāb al-tanjīm*). He also includes tables of Muslim, Zoroastrian, Christian, Persian, and Jewish holidays, feast-days, and fasts, and a table of lunar mansions. In addition, he devotes a large portion of his exposition to various calendrical manipulations, such as how to establish the week-day for the beginning of particular months and years, calendar conversions, intercalation schemes, and how to use the tables provided to compute these chronological details efficiently.

As was common, al-Khāzinī organizes his work into the following divisions: *maqāla* (books), which are divided into *bāb* (chapters) that are further subdivided into *faṣl* (sections). These are usually numbered, but occasionally not. The contents of al-Khāzinī's chapter on chronology is shown in table 1.

There are some notable features of his exposition on chronology. As well as the main tables which cover the chronological material included with the other tables at the end of

Chapter	BOOK ONE: On the Well-Known Calendars Title (with section number where given)
1	On the nature of the night and the day and the month and the year
	On the nature of the year
2	On the description of the ancient calendars
	On the description of the well-known calendars in our days.
	i) The calendar of the Hijra
	ii) The calendar of al-Muʿtaḍid
	iii) The calendar of the Seleucids
	iv) The calendar of the Persians
	v) The calendar of Mālik Shāh
	vi) The calendar of 'Buḵtinaṣir'
	vii) The calendar of 'Bilibbus'
3	On the yearly entrances of the calendar and its months in week-days
	1. [Table]
	2. On the extension of the calendar
	3. On the knowledge of the days occurring in an unknown calendar to a known one
	4. On the elimination of the days producing years and months
4	On the knowledge of the entrances of the months in the week-days and the knowledge of the calendars—one from the other—according to the table
	1. On the knowledge of the entrances of the months in the week-days
	2. On the derivation of three calendars from the Hijra calendar by means of tables
5	On the festivals of the nations and their established days
	1. On the rising of the mansions of the moon
	2. On the big fast (Lent) of the Christians
	3. [On the beginning of Lent]
	4. On the Muslim festivals and their well-known days
	5. On the Persian festivals and their well-known days
	6. On the names of the days of the Persians for each month
	7. On the Christian festivals and their well-known days

TABLE 1. The Contents of the first book of the *wajīz*.

1	ا	10	ي	100	ق
2	ب	20	ك	200	ر
3	ج	30	ل	300	ش
4	د	40	م		
5	ه	50	ن		
6	و	60	س		
7	ز	70	ع		
8	ح	80	ف		
9	ط	90	ص		

TABLE 2. Arabic alphabetic (*abjad*) notation.

0	٠
1	١
2	٢
3	٣
4	٤
5	٥
6	٦
7	٧
8	٨
9	٩

TABLE 3. Arabic place-value notation.

the work, al-Khāzinī positions several calendrical tables in amongst his prose exposition. This is presumably for ease of comprehension, as the prose is closely linked to the content of the tables which need to be frequently consulted when reading. To represent numbers, al-Khāzinī commonly uses the Arabic alphabetic (*abjad*) numerals (see table 2), particulary for those numbers expressed sexagesimally. For large integers, such as large quantities of days, he uses the Hindu-Arabic base ten place-value notation (see table 3). In addition, al-Khāzinī will frequently express a number in words, particulary if it is the length of a year or a month.

2. Al-Khāzinī's Discussion of Calendars and Chronology

2.1 Book One: Introductory Material

At the outset of the first book, al-Khāzinī explains that he will cover:

> ...the well-known calendars and...the nature of the night and the day and the month and the year and the calendar and the entrance of the years and the months in days of the week and the knowledge of one from the other, the holidays and the dates of the well-known days for each nation... (T: f. 2)

First, he defines the preliminaries and basic units of time. He begins with a *nychthemeron* (*al-yaum bi-lailahi*; lit. 'the day and its night') with its beginning at sunset.[8] He states the months are based on the motion of the moon and they begin with the sighting of the lunar crescent. He contrasts the nychthemeron with the so-called canonical day (*al-yaum al-šarʿī*) which starts at dawn and ends at sunset. Such a definition of the canonical day he ascribes to the Persians, the Byzantines, and the 'common people'. He notes, though, that for the 'masters of the science of the stars', a *nychthemeron* is when the sun crosses the meridian to the next crossing.

He then discusses the nature of the years, beginning by defining the solar year as the return of the sun on the zodiacal circle to that same point, stating that this is 365 days and a quarter 'approximately' (*taqrīb*). He notes this is commonly divided into four seasons. Next, he gives the length of the synodic month which he states can be derived from the mean velocities of the sun ($\bar{v}_s$) and the moon ($\bar{v}_m$) as follows:

$$360 \div (\bar{v}_m - \bar{v}_s) = 29;31,50$$

He then describes the lunar year which he states is 354;22,1 days in length, which contains 12 rotations of the moon and is 'approximately' 11 days shorter than the solar year. He also notes there is a year composed of the two (i.e., a luni-solar year), which he says is preferred by 'a few of the nations'. He is more explicit later on when he describes those systems of the Indians and the Hebrews.

At this point too, al-Khāzinī summarises the various conventions for intercalation. The Hebrews, Byzantines, and Christians have years of 12 months which are 354 days long, and occasionally one of 13 months which is 384 days long. He cites the term *ʿibūr* which is the Arabic transliteration of the term 'intercalation' in Hebrew, to refer to this 13-month year. Al-Khāzinī also describes the Indian practice, stating their year begins at conjunction around the point of the vernal equinox, which is indeed their convention. He provides the reader with the Arabic transliteration for the Indian intercalary month as *ādamāsa* which he says is equivalent to the Arabic intercalary month (*al-šahr al-kabīsa*). Here al-Khāzinī has reported correctly as the Sanskrit term for intercalary month is *adhimāsa* (lit. 'additional month'). Al-Khāzinī gives the beginning of the year according to the Hebrews as the conjunction around the autumnal equinox, which should fall, he states, between 24 Ābu and 27 Ulūlu. Al-Khāzinī notes that feast days (*al-ʿīd*) and fasts (*al-ṣiyām*) are in accordance with the lunar calendar.

2.2 Book Two: On Ancient and Contemporary Calendars

Having established this basic information, al-Khāzinī describes various types of 'calendars'. First, he covers the ancient calendars (*al-tawārīḵ al-qudamāʾ*), followed by various prominent contemporary calendars. Al-Khāzinī selects seven in this latter category and gives a description of varying length for each of them. He names these seven calendars as the Hijra, the calendar of al-Muʿtaḍid, the Seleucid calendar, the Persian calendar, the calendar of Mālik Shāh, the calendar of 'Buḵtinaṣir' (Nabonassar), and the calendar of 'Bilibbus' (Philip), and discusses them in that order. Al-Khāzinī is earnest in his exposition. He endeavors to present his reader with much background information and coverage of the topic. His accounts may include details on their structure, their epoch, their origin, who used them, intercalation details, among other pertinent features. What is notable about al-Khāzinī's descriptions is the accuracy of his accounts as well as the level of precision he gives. He thus provides insight into the state of chronological knowledge at the time he was active. Furthermore, he offers a distinctly 'Arabic' perspective on the state of the craft, giving a real sense of what calendars were deemed important, how well they were known, and the ways in which they might have been used.

2.2.1 The 'Ancient' Calendar

Al-Khāzinī argues that the ancient knowledge of the months arose from repeated observation of the lunar crescent, and of the years, from the seasonal variations due to the motion of the sun, rotation by rotation. He notes the difficulty for those early peoples:

> ...[to achieve] an exactness with respect to the intervals of heat and cold, feasts, transactions, and all that is necessary for naming the time intervals and the formation of appointed dates and so on.
> (T: f. 1, I: f. 3)

This ancient calendar, al-Khāzinī notes, was determined from the motion of the luminaries. In addition, he observes that the earliest calendars were measured from a beginning (epoch) year and were shaped by major historical or natural events, which obviously due to their infrequency were useful chronological landmarks. He even gives examples; the emergence of a saint, the uprising of a king, the destruction of a nation, or the transitional period of a dynasty have all served as such chronological boundaries.

2.2.2 Hijra Calendar

Al-Khāzinī makes a clear distinction between these ancient time-keeping systems and the ones in his day. This difference was the use of computation and of astronomical observations and tracking to organize the calendar in the latter case, rather than unpredictable events in the former, such as natural disasters or political turbulence, to define the passing of time. Al-Khāzinī opens his description of the contemporary calendars with the Hijra calendar, but his account here is relatively concise in comparison to his treatment of the other calendars. He notes the Hijra began with the flight of the prophet Muḥammad from Mecca to Medina. The years are lunar 'employed by observation (*al-ru'ya*) and not by calculation (*al-ḥusbān*)' by which he means that the first day of the month is determined by the actual sighting of the lunar crescent.

Al-Khāzinī notes the centrality of this calendar to the Islamic faith. He states that the calendar's beginning is Friday but gives no further details. Its epoch indeed is Friday 16 July 622 AD. Al-Khāzinī notes that the number of days in each month is variable and the middle of the month is determined by calculation. He notes there is a 30-day month and a 29-day month and raises the potential problem with a calendar based on observation—one can't guarantee that conditions will be right for the sighting of the new crescent. Indeed, the average length from one new moon to the next (the synodic month) is a little over 29½ days. True lunar months have a variable number of days due to the complexities of the moon's orbit which entails that the arrangement of 29- and 30-day months is difficult to predict. Al-Khāzinī states that he has listed the month names and the days in the table, both summarily and in detail (see table 4). These are found at the end of the *zīj* with all of the tables. In order to appreciate the original format of this table, its rendition in each manuscript (T: f. 23v and I: f. 39) is reproduced in figures 1 and 2.[9]

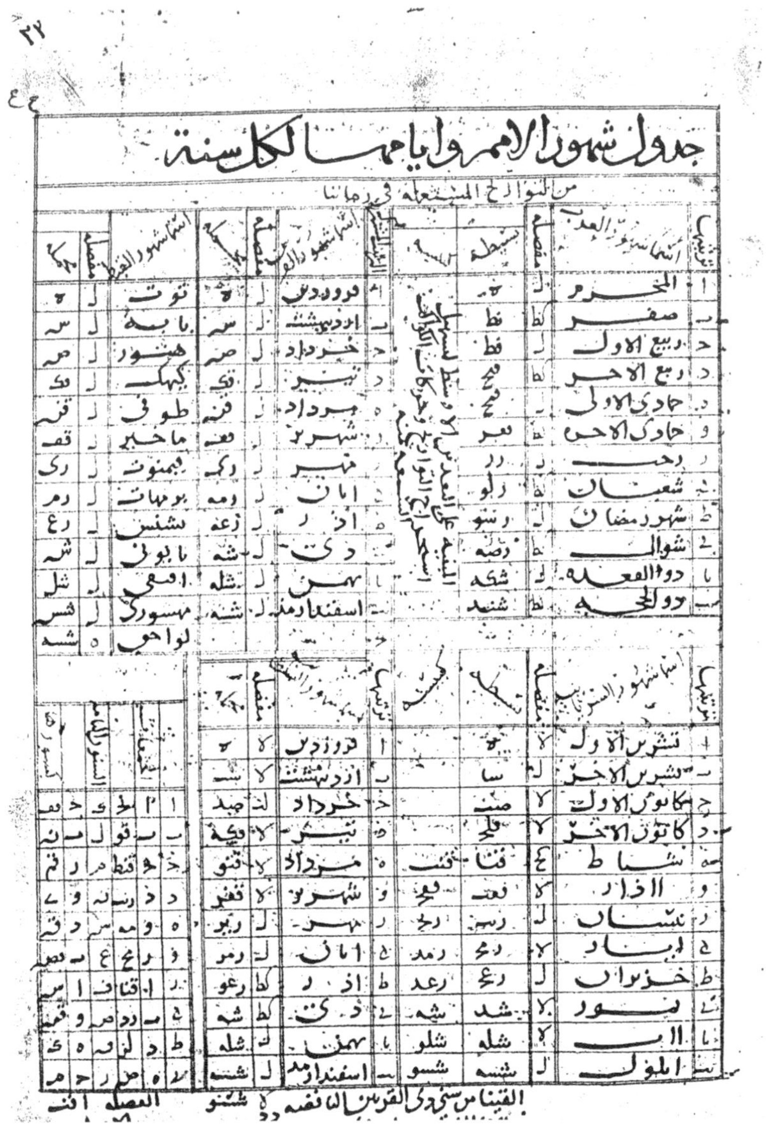

FIGURE 1. The Table of the Months of the Nations and their days for each year in MS T. (Image reproduced by kind permission of the Sipahsālār Mosque, Teheran)

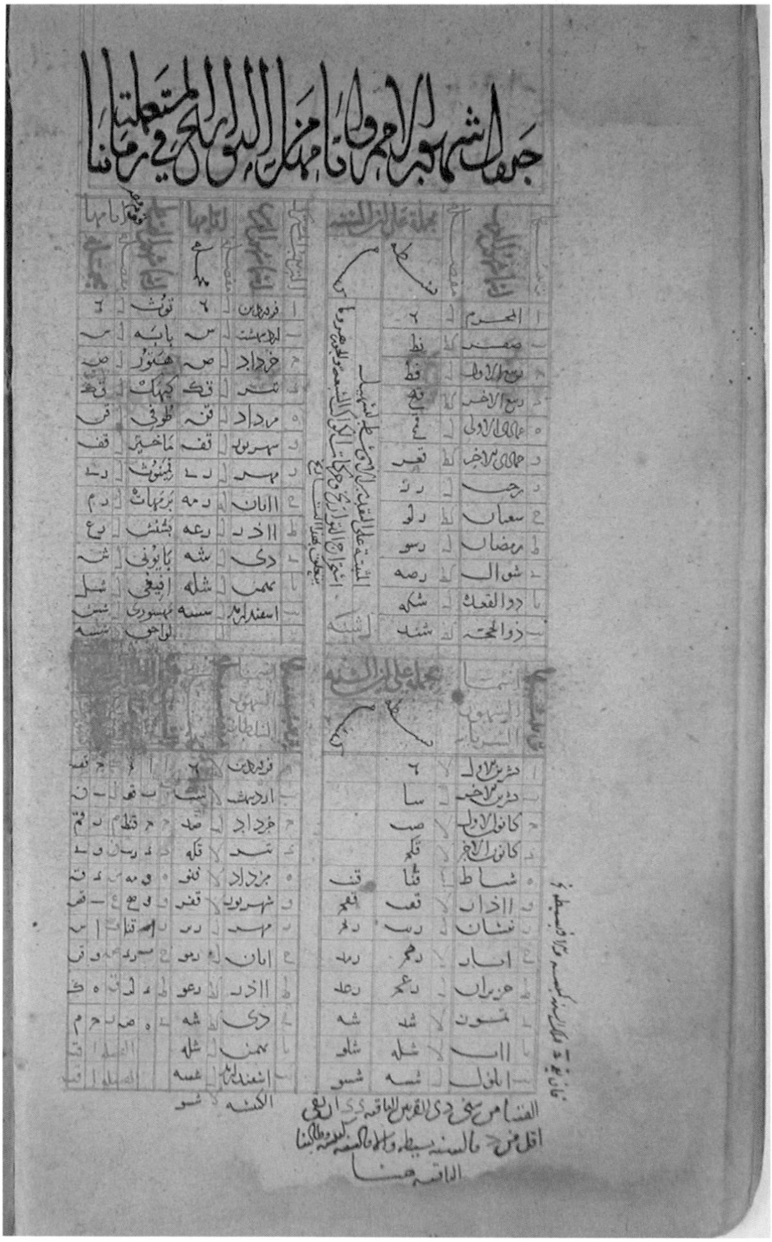

FIGURE 2. The Table of the Months of the Nations and their days for each year in MS I. (Image reproduced by kind permission of the Hamidiye Library, Istanbul)

	Month Name	Length	Total Day Count
1.	muharram	30	0
2.	ṣafar	29	59
3.	rabiᶜ al-awwal	30	89
4.	rabiᶜ al-akar	29	118
5.	jumādā al-awwal	30	148
6.	jumādā al-akar	29	177
7.	rajan	30	207
8.	ša'abān	29	236
9.	ramaḍān	30	266
10.	shawwal	29	295
11.	dhu al-qiᶜdah	30	325
12.	dhu al-ḥijjah	29	354

TABLE 4. Arabic Months.[10]

2.2.3 al-Muᶜtaḍid

The second system is the calendar of al-Muᶜtaḍid, an ᶜAbbāsid Caliph who ruled from 892–902. Al-Khāzinī characterizes this calendar as follows: the years are Byzantine and the months are Persian (for the Persian months see below, table 6). It begins on the 11th of Hazīrān 'always' and there are five epagomenal (lit. 'stolen' *al-mustaraqa*) days in Ābān. Indeed, this calendar is a solar calendar, and the reason as to why al-Muᶜtaḍid, an Islamic Caliph, might value a purely solar calendar is perhaps because he was particularly interested in the Greek sciences.[11]

2.2.4 Seleucid

The third system is the Seleucid (Byzantine) calendar (*ta'rīk al-rūm*). Al-Khāzinī characterizes this as based on solar years and 'Syrian' (*al-sarīniya*) months (see table 5). This refers to the Syrian calendar which bases its month names on the Aramaic versions of the Babylonian months.

Al-Khāzinī states that the calendar begins on a Monday and each year is 365¼ days. The epoch is indeed Monday 1st October 312 BC. Al-Khāzinī also notes that originally this began at the autumnal equinox, but since they adopted Syrian month names, they started with the appropriate Syrian month which corresponded with October. Al-Khāzinī briefly describes the procedure for intercalating an extra day which is to be added in February (*šubāṭ*) when appropriate. He also notes that every 110 years the solar year advances one day; thus an additional day must be added, so that the year length is:

$$365 + 1/4 + 1/110 = 6,5;15,32,44...$$

	Month Name	Length	Total Day Count
1.	tišrīn al-awwal	31	0
2.	tišrīn al-aḵar	30	61
3.	kānūn al-awwal	31	92
4.	kānūn al-aḵar	31	123
5.	šubāṭ	28	151
6.	ʾāḏār	31	182
7.	nīsān	30	212
8.	ʾayyār	31	243
9.	ḥazīrān	30	273
10.	tammūz	31	304
11.	ʾāb	31	335
12.	aylūl	30	365

TABLE 5. Syrian Months.

2.2.5 The Persian Calendar: Yazdijird

The fourth system is the Persian calendar (*taʾrīḵ al-furs*), or, as al-Khāzinī reports, that of Yazdijird ibn Šaharyār, the 'last king of the barbarians' by which al-Khāzinī means non-Arabs. Indeed, Yazdijird III was the twenty-ninth and last king of the Sassanid dynasty. Al-Khāzinī reports that the beginning of this calendar is Tuesday which correctly refers to Tuesday 16 June 632 AD, the ascension of Yazdijird III. Al-Khāzinī relates that there are two systems according to which the year is organized: the simple (*basīṭa*) and the so-called *makbūsa*.[12] The simple consists of 365 days; each month has thirty days and five extra (epagomenal) days (here referred to simply as *al-ḵamsa* 'the five') are added at the end of Ābān. He gives the names and details of these months (see table 6) in the table (T: f. 23v and I: f. 39).

The other, the *makbūsa*, al-Khāzinī notes, takes into account agricultural estates, the time of plowing, and other related conventions.[13] This system has several characteristics. Firstly, al-Khāzinī relates that each month has thirty days, each day of the month has a particular name, and the five epagomenal days are added at the end of the year. Secondly, the first day of the first month of the year occurs when the sun arrives at the vernal equinoctial point, which is the beginning of Farwardīn. Thirdly, an intercalary month is to be added every 124 years. The year length then is:

$$365\ 30/124 \text{ days} = 365;14,30,58,\ldots$$

Of this second calendar though, there are two versions: 'Solar' and 'Persian'. The first of the two is based on a fixed month, that is months aligned with the four seasons of the year. It begins in Farwardīn and ends in Isfandārmah and the five epagomenal days always are placed at this end. In this version, the 'famous days', that is holidays, feasts, and the

	Month Name	Length	Total Day Count
1.	farwardīn	30	0
2.	ardībihišt	30	60
3.	ḵurdāḏ	30	90
4.	tīr	30	120
5.	murdāḏ	30	150
6.	šahrīwar	30	180
7.	mihr	30	210
8.	ābān	30	245
9.	āḏar	30	275
10.	dai	30	305
11.	bahman	30	335
12.	isfandārmah	30	365

TABLE 6. Persian Months.

like, are arranged in the same way in the months throughout the year.

The second version has so-called 'wandering months', that is, the months are not fixed with respect to the seasons. Al-Khāzinī describes the resulting seasonal drift in this version, carefully explaining how in this arrangement each month shifts slowly until those days which were once in spring now occur in winter. He notes the entire length of the cycle, observing that by the 1494th year wandering Farwardīn returns to the beginning of fixed Farwardīn and the sun occupies the first minute of Aries.

Al-Khāzinī then describes some of the circumstances of this calendar. He references another very early epoch, that of 'the beginning of the creation of human beings' (*nušū' al-isān al-awwal*), and relates this to the epoch of Yazdijird, giving the difference between the two as 4336 years. This would place this so-called ancient epoch at 3705 BC. The only other well-known epoch close to this date is that on which the Hebrew calendar is based at 3761 BC.

Next, he refers to the period of the 'Kisra' which is an Arabic transliteration for 'Caesars'. This term was used by Persians and Arabs as an honorific to refer to the Roman and Byzantine emperors. At this point, al-Khāzinī reports, when the sun was at the spring equinoctial point, wandering Āḏar was corresponded to fixed Farwardīn, and the five epagomenal days were placed in (wandering) Ābān, which corresponded to fixed Isfandārmah.

Following this, al-Khāzinī relates the circumstances at the beginning of the calendar of Yazdijird. At this point, wandering Dai corresponded to the beginning of fixed Farwardīn. Al-Khāzinī explains how to compute this 'shift' between fixed and wandering:

> To determine the month-shift, we take completed Yazdijird years and we add to them 123[14] and a half. We double the result and we divide this double by 249. There results in integers the *makbūsa* months. We subtract them from Āḏar. Then we add the five epagomenal days to the end of its successor and it will be in agreement with fixed Farwardīn.
> (I: f. 4r; T: f. 3)

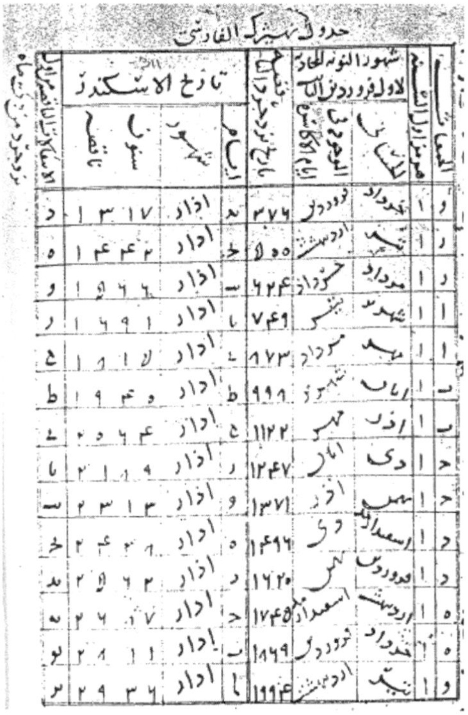

FIGURE 3. The Table of the *Nachizak* for the Persians in MS T. (Image reproduced by kind permission of the Sipahsālār Mosque, Teheran)

The process al-Khāzinī is referring to is

$$\text{Month-Shift} = 2(\text{Y} + 123.5) \div 249$$

where Y is the number of completed Yazdijird years. The reason for the factor of two may be to avoid dividing by a fraction. This relation seems to be based on the fact that one month is added every 124 years in the fixed-month system which shifts it with respect to the wandering-month system.

Al-Khāzinī reports that due to particular religious opinion, such as that of the Zoroastrians (lit. 'the religion of the Magi' *dīn al-majūsya*), who did not permit any such alterations to the calendar, a few regions kept the placement of the epagomenal days at the end of Ābān.

Al-Khāzinī gives a historical note, invoking the last days of the Persian people and the destruction of their dynasty by the Arabs. This refers to the Sassanian Dynasty which was overthrown in 651. At this point al-Khāzinī states that the five epagomenal days remained at the end of Ābān up to the year 375 for Yazdijird, which is 1006 AD. Indeed, initiatives had been proposed to shift the placement of these epagomenal days at this earlier time, but these were interrupted by invasion.

Al-Khāzinī relates that at sunrise at the vernal equinox, Persian year 500 (i.e., 1131 AD), for the longitude of the *qubba*, that is the Cupola (i.e., Ujjain),[15] which was the beginning of wandering Ardībihišt, scholars transferred the five days to the end of wander-

Table of the Nachizak for the Persians								
Months of the Shift					Seleucid Calendar			
Weekday	Beginning of the Year	Months	Base point in the days of the Kisras	Calendar of Yazdijird incomplete (years)	Days	Months	Incomplete Years	Incomplete wandering (months) from the beginning of Yazdijird from dai
6	1	kurdāḏ	farwardīn	376	14	*aḏār*	1317	4
7	1	tīr	ardībihišt	500	13	*aḏār*	1445	5
7	1	murdāḏ	kurdāḏ	624	12	*aḏār*	1466	6
1	1	šahrīwar	tīr	749	11	*aḏār*	1691	7
1	1	mihr	murdāḏ	873	10	*aḏār*	1815	8
2	1	ābān	šahrīwar	998	9	*aḏār*	1940	9
2	1	āḏar	mihr	1122	8	*aḏār*	2064	10
3	1	dai	ābān	1247	7	*aḏār*	2189	11
3	1	bahman	āḏar	1371	6	*aḏār*	2313	12
4	1	isfandārmah	dai	1496	5	*aḏār*	2438	13
4	1	farwardīn	bahman	1620	4	*aḏār*	2562	14
5	1	ardībihišt	isfandārmah	1745	3	*aḏār*	2687	15
5	1	kurdāḏ	farwardīn	1869	2	*aḏār*	2811	16
6	1	tīr	ardībihišt	1994	1	*aḏār*	2936	17

TABLE 7. The Table of the Nachizak for the Persians.

ing Farwardīn. The beginning of wandering Ardībihišt corresponded at this point to the beginning of fixed Farwardīn.

All these details and further years and their circumstances were summarized in a table that al-Khāzinī included in his prose text (see figure 3 and table 7). This table documents the fixed month and its corresponding wandering month equivalent starting from the beginning of Yazdijird 376, the weekday, and the corresponding position in the Seleucid Calendar (where 14 *āḏār* 1317 corresponds to 376 Farwardīn 1st Yazdijird which corresponds to 15 March 1007 AD) in increments of 124 years. Impressively, al-Khāzinī has computed these circumstances right up to the middle of the twenty-seventh century!

2.2.6 Mālik Shāh

The fifth calendar al-Khāzinī describes is the calendar of Sultan Mālik Shāh. Al-Khāzinī is obviously impressed with the Sultan as he considers him as 'possessed of an excellent character'! This praise is understandable, given that this is the father of the very individual to whom this work is addressed, the Seljuk Sulṭān Jalāl al-Dīn Mālik Shāh I (d. 1092) and Sanjar was his third son. Al-Khāzinī describes the features of this calendar as follows: its years are solar and thus it 'contains' the four seasons. The epoch of this calendar is when the greater luminaries are in conjunction at the spring equinoctial point. The months are delimited by the sun's entries into the beginning of each zodiacal sign, a practice al-Khāzinī contrasts with the Byzantines and the Persians. The epoch he gives as the first day of Šaʿabān 468 which corresponds to Thursday 10 March 1076. The intercalation is organized as follows: in 220 solar years there are 53 intercalary days distributed so that 45 are placed as a fourth-year intercalation and 8 as a fifth-year.[16] The year length is thus:

$$365\ 53/220 \text{ days} = 365;14,27,...$$

Indeed, this calendar was commissioned by the Sultan in 1073 and implemented on 15 March 1079, slightly different to the epoch al-Khāzinī gives. The motivation for it arose from the inadequacies of the Islamic calendar being lunar and its asynchrony with respect to the seasons which required constant adjustments. It was developed by a group of astronomers, including ʿUmar al-Khayyām, at the observatory in Iṣfahān.[17] The year begins at the vernal equinox and the months are based on solar transits through the zodiac. Because of this, the seasonal discrepancy is never greater than one day, nor is there a need for a leap year. Given the variation of the sun's motion, months could be 29, 30, 31 or even 32 days long. However the drawback of this system was that detailed and accurate ephemerides as well as regular observations were required to track the sun's motion.

The solar transit model is similar to models used in India, particularly that set out in the *Sūryasiddhānta*.[18]

2.2.7 The Calendar of Buktinasir

The sixth calendar al-Khāzinī describes is that of the named *Buḵtinaṣir* the first. Here, al-Khāzinī refers to the famous work, Ptolemy's *Almagest*, stating that the *Almagest* was computed according to the calendar of *Buḵtinaṣir*. This leads us to infer that the so-called *Buḵtinaṣir* is in fact Nabonassar,[19] an individual who founded his kingdom in Babylon in 747 BC, on whom the main chronological system of the *Almagest* is based. Indeed, Ptolemy used Nabonassar's rise to establish an epoch which corresponded with Thoth 1, the beginning of the Egyptian Year; Nabonassar's was the reign that included the earliest observation Ptolemy invoked.[20] Al-Khāzinī also states the years are Egyptian[21] and the months are Coptic (with respect to their name). Al-Khāzinī gives these in a table (see table 8).

He mentions that the beginning is Thursday. He is correct; the epoch of this calendar is Thursday 26 February 747 BC. He gives the number of days between this calendar and the epoch of the Hijra as 499,800,[22] and with the beginning of Yazdijird 503,425. These

	Month Name	Length	Total Day Count
1.	tūt	30	0
2.	bāba	30	60
3.	hatūr	30	90
4.	kākab	30	120
5.	ṭūbī	30	150
6.	mīẖīr	30	180
7.	babmanūt	30	210
8.	barmahāt	30	240
9.	bašnas	30	270
10.	ififī	30	300
11.	ififī	30	330
12.	mīsūrī	30	360
12.	lawāẖu	35	365

TABLE 8. Egyptian Months.

are given in days presumably to facilitate conversions between dates in one calendar to another. Al-Khāzinī discusses this further, later in this chapter.

2.2.8 The Calendar of Bilibbus

The seventh and final calendar al-Khāzinī describes is the calendar of an individual called 'bīlibbus'. Al-Khāzinī further qualifies this individual by explaining that he is the brother of *al-askandar*, 'the builder'. This, then, must refer to Alexander the Great (d. 11 June 323 BC), the 'empire-builder', and his brother, Philip (ca. 359 BC – Dec 25th 317 BC). Indeed, this is confirmed by a set of tables which were well-known by early astronomers, Ptolemy's *Handy Tables*.[23] Included in the *Handy Tables* is Ptolemy's 'king-list' which gives epochs of various kings, beginning with Nabonassar. In this list Ptolemy includes an epoch entitled 'Philip who succeeded Alexander the founder' (the 'founder' or 'builder': ὁ κτίστης). This is the Greek equivalent of the description al-Khāzinī gives, nearly word for word. In addition, Ptolemy gives a special emphasis to this epoch. When he reaches this entry in his table, he begins a new, third column in the 'king-list' which begins a new cumulative year-count total, calculated from the beginning of Philip and all those beyond. This is presumably why it has been treated as an epoch in its own right by later scholars such as al-Khāzinī.

Al-Khāzinī relates that this calendar also uses Egyptian years and Coptic months and its beginning is Sunday. From other sources, we know that the epoch of this calendar is Sunday 12th November 324 BC. As for the previous calendar, al-Khāzinī gives us the difference in days between this and other known calendars:

Hijra	345,041 days
Yazdijird	348,665 days

3 Concluding Remarks

In his account of chronology, al-Khāzinī is ambitious in his attempt to provide an expansive description. In addition to the details of ancient calendars, he describes seven different types of calendars that he deems had contemporary significance, each in their own section, and in the process of this exposition refers to the calendrical practices of many more cultures. In chronological order, the epochs al-Khāzinī presents, with their pertinent details are as follows:

Beginning Year	First Day	Julian Date	Week-day	Year Type	Months
Beginning of humans		3705 BC			
Nabonassar	Thoth 1	BC 747 Feb 26	Thursday	Egyptian	Coptic
Philip	Thoth 1	BC 324 Nov 12	Sunday	Egyptian	Coptic
Seleucid	Tishri 1	BC 312 Oct 1	Monday	Luni-Solar	Syrian
Hijra	Muharram 1	AD 622 Jul 16	Friday	Lunar	Arabic
Yazdijird	Farwardīn	AD 632 June 16	Tuesday	Egyptian	Persian
al-Muʿtaḍid	Hazīrān 11	AD 892?		Luni-Solar	Persian
Mālik Shāh	Muharram	AD 1076 Mar 10	Thursday	Solar	Arabic

However, these are notably not in the order that al-Khāzinī presents them. He seems to have ordered them according to importance, and in turn grouped together those calendars which have similarities. For example, the Hijra features first, but is given a relatively concise treatment; al-Muʿtaḍid and the Seleucid are both luni-solar calendars; the calendar reform of Mālik Shāh and the Persian are closely connected; the calendars of Nabonassar and Philip are different epochs of the same system. Al-Khāzinī's most detailed description is of the Persian calendar. He not only sets out the multiple versions of this calendar, but also describes its circumstances at various key instances in time and provides details for well into the future.

What is unique about al-Khāzinī's exposition is that it offers insight into the important chronological systems from the perspective of one who was active at the time that these calendars were begin used. Furthermore, al-Khāzinī is correct for the most part in the details and he includes historical context in his account. He discusses a lesser known calendar (in contemporary times), that of al-Muʿtaḍid, although he is succinct in his description. Another notable feature of al-Khāzinī's accounts is that he simply mentions the week-days of the epochs, and rarely the actual dates referenced to some other system.

In many ways, the discussion of calendars al-Khāzinī sets out captures the broader political history and circumstances of the Middle East. Babylon was to be overtaken by the Persians, who were in turn defeated by the Macedonians. Byzantine and Sassanid (Persian) empires flourished anew but again came under Islamic rule. That these transitions have left their mark on the scientific scene is notable: traces of the earlier prominence of cultures are preserved in the calendrical systems of this time. Al-Khāzinī's motivations to include these various calendrical systems appear multifaceted. His exposition reflects a typical scholarly interest in the history of their discipline, and with it, a desire to preserve the details for future generations. Furthermore, because of his coverage, al-Khāzinī appeals to a wide readership, in keeping with the cultural diversity of the members of the Islamic empire. His *zīj* is directly relevant to representatives of different cultures who can use the tables for the application to their own cultural context and chronology. By extension, the breadth of the chronology of this *zīj* serves as a guide for those designated as part of the Islamic empire to formulate and implement administrative rules to handle bureaucracy for multicultural jurisdictions.

Furthermore, al-Khāzinī epitomises some contemporary reflections on the state of Arabic science during this critical period of flourishing, namely that the science practised during this time was consciously international.[24] Al-Khāzinī's exposition on chronology emblematises the early sentiments such that the exact sciences in the Islamic Near East were 'the sciences shared among all the nations', and, as expressed by Arab historian Ibn Khaldun (1332–1406) in his *Muqaddima* (Introduction [to the science of history])[25] that

> the intellectual sciences are natural to man, inasmuch as he is a thinking being. They are not restricted to any particular religious group. They are studied by the people of all religious groups who are all equally qualified to learn them and do research in them.

al-Khāzinī helps us more broadly to appreciate the significance of this. Indeed, his facility and his expertise in the calendars of diverse early peoples reinforces this evaluation of Islamic scientific culture.

Notes

1. For further biographical details see Hall (1973), pp. 335–351; Pingree (1999) p. 105.
2. Kennedy (1956), p. 169.
3. See Pingree (1985).
4. Kennedy (1956) p.129.
5. See Hall (1973) p. 337.
6. See Kennedy (1956) p. 129.
7. The *wajīz* is preserved in two manuscripts. One is number 859 in the Hamadiye Collection in the Suleymaniye Library in Istanbul (henceforth I): ff. 1v–27 and 29–38 and tables on ff. 39–79. On f. 38 the date this manuscript was copied is given as Rabīʿ al-ākhir in AH 667, which corresponds to 8 December 1268 to 5 Jan 1269. The second copy is number 682 in the Library of the Sipahsālār Mosque in Teheran (henceforth T), which is 125 pages. On p. 123 it is noted by the scribe that this was copied at Mawṣil in Ramaḍān in AH 631 which corresponds to 31 May to 29 June 1234. See Pingree (1999) p. 110–111, who also comments that this *wajīz* is useful for editing the original *zīj*. A Greek version of the *wajīz* was prepared by Gregory Chionidades at Tabrīz in the late 1290s which Pingree estimates is a "faithful if not very intelligent rendering of the Arabic" (p. 112), and tables exist in various states in at least three other Greek manuscripts. For an exposition on eclipse theory in the *wajīz* see Montelle (2010). See Leichter (2009) for its translation by Chionidades into Greek.
8. A nychthemeron is a 24-hour period, called thus to avoid any ambiguity with the term 'day' in the astronomical context. The term derives from the Greek νυχθήμερον, a compound from the Greek word for 'night' (*nukt-*) and 'day' (*hemera*). Accordingly, the Arabic term (a-day-and-its-night) linguistically mirrors the Greek compound.
9. Their contents are largely reproduced in Tables 4–6 and 8.
10. Where the total day count is the total number of days since the beginning of the year of the end of the month. The first entry in this column, 0, appears incorrect. One would expect to read 30. But 0 appears as the first entry in each of the tables consistently, and in both manuscripts. It seems, then, this error was in an earlier manuscript and has not been corrected.

11. Gutas (1999) p. 125.
12. A derivative of this root is used to mean 'intercalary', but it is unclear how to translate this form, which in other contexts means to preserve, to exert pressure on, to attack, to conserve.
13. How this manifests itself more precisely is left unexplained by al-Khāzinī. Perhaps this calendar is like a modern day farmer's almanac and includes agricultural and meteorological phases alongside the calendrical material.
14. This number is illegible in T and I. The complete *zīj* appears to read 123;0,2.
15. Ujjain was the base location for Indian Astronomers for their various computations. It was set to define the zero meridian. This convention was transmitted to the Islamic Near East; among other instances, it formed the basis for the calculations made in the *Zīj al-Sindhind*, a work produced in the eighth century originally based on an intermediary of Brahmagupta's *Brahmasphuṭasiddhānta* (628 AD) which was translated into Arabic by al-Fazārī (fl. second-half of eighth century) under orders from Caliph al-Manṣūr.
16. Al-Khāzinī says nothing more about the precise distribution of these fourth-year and fifth-year intercalations. In fact, this is a slightly different intercalation scheme than was proposed by the originators of Mālik Shāh's calendar. This original cycle, as proposed by al-Khayyām and others, was based on a cycle of 33 years in which every fourth year (and occasionally every fifth), that is, in years 4, 8, 12, 16, 20, 24, 28, and 33, there was a leap year of 366 days (see, for example, Youschkevitch and Rosenfeld (1973), p. 324)—seven 4-year intervals followed by one 5-year interval. Presumably, al-Khāzinī intercalation system would be arranged as 5 fourth-year intervals followed by 1 fifth-year interval, repeated nine times to fill out the 220-year intercalation cycle.
17. See Youschkevitch and Rosenfeld (1973), p.324.
18. See Plofker and Knudsen's article in this work.
19. Another possibility might be Nebuchadnezzar which arguably fits some elements of the transliteration slightly better (but not others). Note that the character 'n' and 'b' in Arabic script differ only by the placement of the diacritic dot.
20. For further details, see Evans (1998), pp. 176–178.
21. That is, 365 days long.
22. T has 499, 802. I appears to be correct.
23. See the 'Canon Basileon' in the Byzantine versions of Theon of Alexandria's revision of the Handy Tables f. 16v and 17r.
24. Dallal (1999), p. 158.
25. As cited by Dallal (1999), p. 157.

References

I: Istanbul Manuscript; Hamidiye MS. 859.

T: Teheran Manuscript: Sipahsālār Mosque of Teheran in the MS number 681.

Vat. Graec. 1291 (ca. 813/820) Handy Tables.

Dallal, A., 1999, "Science, Medicine, and Technology: The Making of a Scientific Culture", in J. L. Esposito (ed), *The Oxford History of Islam* (Oxford: Oxford University Press), 155–213.

Evans, J., 1998, *The History and Practice of Ancient Astronomy* (Oxford: Oxford University Press).

Gutas, D., 1999, *Greek Thought Arabic Culture: The Graeco-Arabic Translation movement in Baghdad and Early 'Abbāsid Society (2nd–4th/8th–10th centuries)* (New York: Routledge).

Hall, R. E., 1973, "Al-Khāzinī", in C. C. Gillipsie (ed.), *Dictionary of Scientific Biography* (New York: Charles Scribner's Sons), vol. 7, 335–351.

Kennedy, E. S., 1956, "A Survey of Islamic Astronomical Tables", *Transactions of the American Philosophical Society*, n.s., 46, pt. 2: 121–177.

Leichter, J., 2009, "The Zij as-Sanjari of Gregory Chioniades" (as accessed February 2010 from http://www.archive.org/details/TheZijAs-sanjariOfGregoryChioniades).

Montelle, C., 2010, *Chasing Shadows: Mathematical Astronomy and the Early History of Eclipse Reckoning* (Baltimore: Johns Hopkins University Press).

Pingree, D., 1985, *The Astronomical Works of Gregory Chioniades* (Amsterdam: Gieben).

——, 1999, "A Preliminary Assessment of the Problems of Editing the Zīj al-Sanjarī of al-Khāzinī", in Y. Ibish (ed.), *Editing Islamic Manuscripts on Science* (London: Al-Furqan Islamic Heritage Foundation), 105–113.

Youschkevitch, A. P. and Rosenfeld, B. A., 1973, "Al-Khayyāmī", in C. C. Gillipsie (ed.), Dictionary of Scientific Biography (New York: Charles Scribner's Sons), vol. 7, 323–334.

The Maya Calendar Correlation Problem

Gerardo Aldana

> I feel sure that no real progress can be made by assuming a [historical Christian to Maya] correlation and then trying to force agreements out of the inscriptions. By that method almost any correlation can be made to look plausible, provided no one examines it too closely. The work must proceed from the other direction, assuming that we do not know equivalent Christian dates unless and until our accumulated knowledge from the inscriptions forces them on us.
> — John Teeple, *Maya Astronomy*, 1930.

> In many cases the validity of a purely astronomical correlation is difficult to judge on its own ground. Quite like the question of building orientation, there is an inherent temptation to play with the numbers. Given enough tolerance, a fit with any astronomical data is possible.
> — Anthony Aveni, *Skywatchers of Ancient Mexico*, 1980, p. 208.

> I think the greatest problem posed by astronomical interpretation is the existence of structural realities that are interlocked and that may fit several correlations. The Maya use of intervals with multiple properties leading to dates of multiple astronomical phenomena means that a correlation based on one sort of valid criterion will include some other phenomena, even if the correlation is incorrect. To the scholar proposing the correlation, this seems to be good evidence that his or her correlation is correct; to others, it suggests that chance can do very strange things; to me, it suggests that the particular supporting evidence probably points to a valid phenomenon.
> — David Kelley, "The Maya Calendar Correlation Problem", 1983, p. 172.

The first two epigraphs to this essay are in a sense incommensurable. From the perspective of the early twentieth century chemical engineer turned Maya calendar enthusiast, John Teeple, the astronomical data was all that might one day be reliable in solving the calendar correlation problem since the historical data was inconclusive and internally inconsistent. Near the end of the same century, the astrophysicist turned archaeoastronomer, Anthony Aveni, claimed that the historical data controlled the debate; it was the astronomical data that was under-constrained.

Now, if the consensus in the field at both times was the same (either that the problem was solved, and this simply presented one renegade opinion, or that the problem was unsolved in both cases), then the history of the calendar correlation in Maya Studies likely would be relatively straightforward to recount. But this is not the case. Rather, at the time of Teeple's assessment, and through the late twentieth century, the problem was considered unsolved with different solutions competing for favourable status. Yet during the "final decades of the twentieth century", the consensus opinion in the field has been that the problem is solved—at least to within three days.[1] As Michael Coe puts it:

> In spite of oceans of ink that have been spilled on the subject, there is now not the slightest chance that these three scholars ([John Goodman, Juan Martínez Hernández, and Eric Thompson] conflated to GMT when talking about the correlation) were not right; and that when we say, for instance, that Yax Pac, King of Copán died on 10 February 822 in the Julian Calendar, he did just that.[2]

This essay starts with the resolution of the Mayan to Christian calendar correlation problem derived by Floyd Lounsbury in the 1980s. It then progressively excavates each individual artefact[3] constituting the conceptual assemblage that represented Lounsbury's solution. Namely, this essay examines the individual histories of Mayanist considerations of the Dresden Codex Venus Table, the Landa equation, the Katun sequence in the Chronicle of Oxkutzcab, and a subset of the calendric data in the Books of Chilam Balam.

The critical distinction to be made here is that this essay takes a history of science approach in order to inhabit the intersection between what Peter Novick describes as internalist versus externalist histories.[4] The challenge, then, becomes one of balancing the healthy skepticism and attention to context of an 'outsider' against a recognition of the subtleties of disciplinary methods and assumptions visible primarily from within. This methodologically interstitial excavation reveals critical aspects of the problem's genealogy that have been buried within the literature, and so rendered invisible to late 20th and early 21st century scholarship. Bringing these aspects to light tips the scales back in favour of the more intellectually conservative view of the calendar correlation problem held before mid-century. That is, a closer examination of the data considered to form the basis of the solution strongly suggests that the problem has not yet been solved.

To find the late twentieth century resolution of the calendar correlation problem beyond its declaration in the popular literature, we must look to its core within the late twentieth century literature on the 'Venus pages' (24 and 46 – 50) in the Precontact hieroglyphic manuscript known as the Dresden Codex. We will find both the formulation of the problem to be solved and its solution respectively in Eric Thompson's *A Commentary on the Dresden Codex*, and in Floyd Lounsbury's "The Base of the Venus Table of the Dresden Codex, and its Significance for the Calendar-Correlation Problem". Because these are relatively specialized publications, and because there are many different calendric components involved in the overall problem, we should defer Lounsbury's solution for a consideration first of Mayan calendrics.

Mayan Calendrics

Mayan civilization is generally broken up into four periods, which in turn find characterization by the calendric records produced in each: the Preclassic (500 BC – AD 100), the Classic (AD 100 – 900), the Postclassic (AD 900 – 1500), and the less-consistently labeled 'Postcontact' (AD 1500 – present; also broken up into sub-periods relating to the Colonial period and national independence). These dates are relatively secure as round figures to within a century or so either way, anchored to C-14 and other dating techniques. A refinement of this periodization to the point of aligning a specific Mayan date with its Julian counterpart is the principal concern of this essay. Both aiding and complicating this

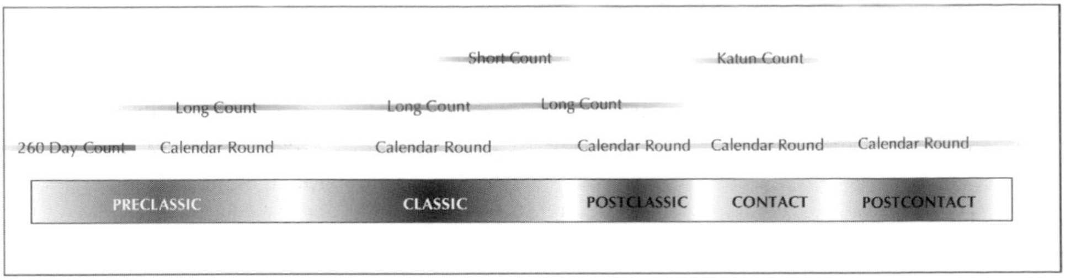

FIGURE 1. Calendric components and the periods from which records survive.

project is that each period is in part discernable based on the types of calendric records produced within it.

Numerous calendric constructs found their way into hieroglyphic texts over the course of Mayan history, but here we focus only on those that have been used in the attempt to solve the Calendar Correlation problem. These are: the 260-Day Count, the 365-Day Count, the Long Count (including the Lunar Series), and the Katun Count. The 260-Day Count, found as early as 600 BC at San José Mogote in Oaxaca, is also evidenced in the Maya area at San Bartolo—here in murals without further calendric complement. The Preclassic, then, is somewhat bracketed by San José Mogote and San Bartolo. The Long Count also finds its origins outside of the Mayan area proper; the first Long Count dates show up on Stela 1 at La Mojarra and Stela C at Tres Zapotes, both from modern day Veracruz, Mexico. These monuments record dates corresponding to events a few hundred years before the first Mayan Long Counts, the latter attested at Early Classic Tikal and Waxaktun (7.16.6.16.18 versus 8.14.10.13.15; see below). The Classic period contains the 'fullest' or at least most elaborated calendric system. The hieroglyphic records from monuments contain Long Count, Calendar Round, Lunar Series along with the aforementioned other calendric components. The record from the Postclassic is much sparser, containing some Long Count records (including those in the Dresden Codex—itself a key manuscript), Calendar Round records, and some Short Count dates. From the Postcontact period, we have only Katun Count dates and Calendar Rounds—in many cases we have only 260-Day Count dates.

One of the key questions governing any attempt to solve the calendar correlation problem is how one addresses the shifts in calendric record keeping. Below, we review each of these calendric components.

The 260-Day Count

Also referred to in the Mayanist literature as the Sacred Round, the tzolkin, or the *chol qiij*, Ernst Förstemann recovered the 260-Day Count from the Dresden Codex during the late nineteenth century. Therein, he found thirteen numerals expressed in 'bar-and-dot' notation cycling along with a set of twenty hieroglyphs now called Day Signs (see figure 2). Isomorphic to the *tonalpohualli* of Central Mexican codices, the *chol qiij* was used both to represent days (without other calendric accompaniment) and for naming historical figures and deities. The latter practice alludes to the symbolic value of the Day Signs, which carried distinct omens as documented by Contact-era chroniclers and twentieth-century ethnographers.[5]

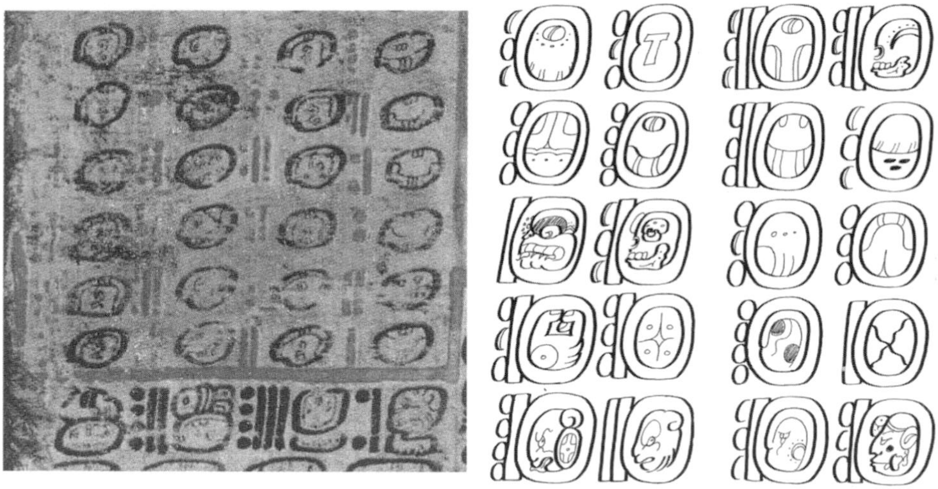

FIGURE 2. a) Table of dates from the Venus Table of the Dresden Codex: Kib, Kimi, Kib, and K'an with various coefficients; below the horizontal line are the haab' months [4] Yaxk'in, 14 Sak, 19 Tzek, 7 Xul (image reproduced from the Forstemann edition by permission of the Foundation for the Advancement of Mesoamerican Studies, Inc.). b) A sequence through the 260 Day Count (read in paired columns, top to bottom): 1 Imix, 2 Ik', 3 Ak'bal, 4 K'an, 5 Chikchan, 6 Kimi, 7 Manik, 8 Lamat, 9 Muluk, 10 Ok, 11 Chuwen, 12 Eb, 13 Ben, 1 Ix, 2 Men, 3 Kib, 4 Kaban, 5 Etz'nab, 6 Kawak, 7 Ajaw (the next day would be 8 Imix).

At some level, we may analogize the Day Signs to 'Western' days of the week, which themselves carry 'omens' of sorts (TGIF; Monday as the first day of the workweek; Sunday as a day of rest). There is also something of a numerical analogue in that Friday the 13th carries a particular cultural meaning distinct from, say Friday the 14th or Monday the 11th. In any case, its symbolic value and its pedestrian utility likely are what has made this count the most robust of calendric records, existing in the earliest of records from Preclassic Oaxaca, and showing up in late twentieth century ethnographic data, often without any other vestiges of the 'full' Mayan calendar.

For all of its robustness, however, the 260-Day Count by itself is limited in its ability to provide a correlation between Christian and Mayan chronologies. Because it repeats every 260 days, we cannot know with certainty what any deviation from a continuous count might mean. That is, if we have a span of time greater than 260 days without any other correlated component of the calendar, then a difference between two counts can have multiple different causes and there is no rigorous means available to determine which was the actual process generating the deviation. What may appear to be a shift of one day can actually have been multiple shifts of larger periods, the net effect of which is to result in a 'one-day' shift within the count. This is a factor that we will encounter below within the consideration of historical and ethnographic records.

The 365-Day Count

Also known as the *haab'*, this count is analogous to the Gregorian tropical year and so

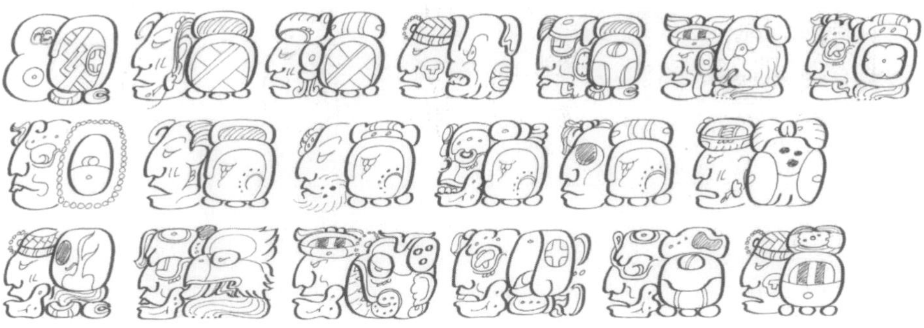

FIGURE 3. A sequence through the 365 Day Count, with 'head variants' in place of bar-and-dot coefficients: 0 Pop, 1 Wo, 2 Sip, 3 Zotz, 4 Tzek, 5 Xul, 6 Yaxk'in, 7 Mol, 8 Ch'en, 9 Yax, 10 Sak, 11 Kej, 12 Mak, 13 K'ank'in, 14 Muwan, 15 Pax, 16 K'ayab, 17 Kumk'u, 3 Wayeb. The sequence is of 21 day intervals except for a final 6 day interval bringing the sequence into the last month (which only has 5 days).

functioned as the 'secular' counterpart to the 260-Day 'Sacred' Round (see figure 3). Eighteen 'months' contain twenty days each to produce a period of 360 days. A final period of five days completes the cycle. It should be noted from the outset that during the Classic Mayan period, no effort was made to compensate for the deviation of this count from the actual tropical year. That is, no 'leap days' were inserted into every fourth year in order to preserve a specific date relative to solar 'stations'—i.e. the solstices or equinoxes. While it is clear that tropical years were recognized and probably held ritual significance—as exemplified architecturally[6]—the *haab'* was allowed to wander through the tropical year during the entire Classic period. Whether or not this drift was allowed after the Classic period is insufficiently determined from the available data, but the question does arise as will be considered below.

The Calendar Round

When combined with the 260-Day Count, the 365-Day Count creates the Calendar Round, a cycle that repeats every 18,980 days (or approximately 52 years). Clearly, this provides researchers with an advantage over 260-Day Count records alone since 'errors' can be more readily detected. Such is the case as we will see in Juan Xiu's manuscript, the "Chronicle of Oxkutzcab", where we confront a list of Julian dates recorded next to Calendar Rounds.

While presenting a more robust check on the attempt to correlate Mayan and Christian chronologies, though, the Calendar Round data is lacking. As noted above, it can only uniquely identify a date within a 52-year period. More significantly, however, we do not have clear continuous records throughout the period of interest. That is, because of calendric redundancies from the Classic period, we can be reasonably confident that the same Calendar Round was maintained by various cities. On the other hand, we have

Chol Qiij Day Sign	Classic Period Haab' Month Coefficient
Imix, Kimi, Chuwen, Kib	4, 9, 14, 19
Ik', Manik, Eb, Kaban	0, 5, 10, 15
Ak'bal, Lamat, Ben Etzn'ab	1, 6, 11, 16
K'an, Muluk, Ix, Kawak	2, 7, 12, 17
Chikchan, Ok, Men, Ajaw	3, 8, 13, 18

TABLE 1: Tropical year groupings of the 260 Day Count Day Signs

no *haab'* data for the earliest times, and we have only partial and/or inconsistent evidence of its maintenance into modern times. Complicating matters is that there are changes in practice documented during the interim period between the early Postclassic and late Colonial periods. Some of this evidence can be found in the Year Bearer mechanism.

Year Bearers

Because there are twenty Day Signs in the 260-Day Count and 365 days in the *haab'*, a unique relationship exists between a subset of the Day Signs and the *haab'* coefficient. That is, twenty divides evenly into 360, but the 'extra' five days create a partitioning within the set of Day Signs. Those extra five days mean that only four of the twenty Day Signs can fall on the first of any given year—and by extension the seating of any given month. One set of four Day Signs will fall on a *haab'* coefficient of 1, 6, 11, or 16, another on 2, 7, 12, and 17, and others on 3, 8, 13, 18, and 4, 9, 14, 19, and 0, 5, 10, and 15 (see table 1). During the Classic period, the Day Signs that could fall on the haab' date 0 Pop were Ik', Manik, Eb, and Kaban. These are therefore known as the Year Bearers of the Classic period. But during the sixteenth century, we will find that Landa recorded the use of the K'an, Muluk, Ix, Kawak set. Still other Year Bearer sets show up in the ethnographic data. It is clear, then, that some slippage between the *chol qiij* and the *haab'* did occur, and it may have been temporally determined, or it may simply have been geographical. Both of these possibilities will concern us in our further deliberations.

The Long Count

The ultimate key to any hopes of a calendar correlation lies in the ability to go beyond cyclic constructs and get to a measure that can identify days uniquely in time. The Long Count does this by simply counting off the number of elapsed days from a 'zero date'. The two complications in the Long Count relative to Indo-European numeration are: i) that the numerical system is vigesimal (or base 20); and ii) the third register is modified from a strict base 20 progression. Specifically, the most commonly recorded periods in the Long Count are given in table 2. Larger periods follow the strict vigesimal pattern, though these occur very infrequently in the Classic period inscriptions and do not directly impact the calendar correlation problem.

The vast majority of historical dates from the Classic period are in the tenth baktun,

Traditional Mayanist Terms	Relative Value	Hieroglyphic Terms	Christian Equivalents
1 k'in		= 1 k'in	= 1 day
1 winal	= 20 k'in	= 1 winik	= 20 days
1 tun	= 18 winal	= 1 haab	= 360 days
1 katun	= 20 tun	= 1 winikhaab	= 7,200 days
1 baktun	= 20 katun	= 1 pih	= 144,000 days

TABLE 2. The Mayan Long Count

with only a few venturing back into the ninth baktun, and a few forward into the eleventh. The implied 'zero date' (some 9 × 400 haab' earlier) is recorded explicitly at Palenque with time intervals ('distance numbers') leading from it into historical times. Rather than mark it as a 'zero date', the Palenque scribes recorded it as the close of thirteen baktuns. While fascinating in its own right (and as it forms the basis of the 2012 hoopla), the subtleties of the 'zero date' do not affect the calendar correlation problem and so will be considered no further here.

Of most import is that Long Count dates are combined with Calendar Round dates in the Classic period inscriptions to provide a robust calendric system that is sufficiently redundant to allow for solid reconstruction even with only partial information surviving erosion. They furthermore allow for the Calendar Correlation problem to be defined as the match of these Long Count/Calendar Round dates with their equivalent dates in the Julian calendar. Scholars have taken to calling this the Ajaw Equation, and expressed it as: LC + X = JD, where X is the Ajaw Constant and JD the Julian Day number. The problem, of course, as shown in figure 1, is that the Long Count fell out of use before Europeans established contact with Mesoamerica. Thus, there is little hope of finding a date recorded both with its Long Count and its Julian equivalents.

The Katun Count

During the Terminal Classic period, a shorthand was developed to record dates that was more elaborate than simply a Calendar Round, but not quite as elaborate as a Long Count. Evidenced at Tikal and Chich'en Itza, these dates specified the katun containing a given Calendar Round date by noting the Ajaw date on which it ended. That is, in the Long Count, the fourth katun of the tenth baktun would be written 9.4.0.0.0 13 Ajaw 18 Yax and called a Katun 13 Ajaw. Stela 22 at Tikal begins with 13 Ajaj 18 Kamk'u. u-17-WINIKHAAB' "13 Ajaw 18 Kamk'u. It is the 17th k'atun". Similarly, a tenth tun-end would be called the close of a lahuntuun, written 9.4.10.0.0 12 Ajaw 8 Mol and called a Tun 12 Ajaw. In each case, the end of the period coincides with an Ajaw date from which to the name is taken. For katuns, the periods repeat in the manner shown in table 3.

When a katun-ending is specified, and the full Calendar Round given, then we essentially have as much information as if we had a full Long Count, since any given katun end repeats only every 6,832,800 days (18,720 haab').

Yet there is a complication that arises between this 'Short Count' of the late Inscriptional Period and the Katun Count of the early Colonial Period. Specifically, the overall

Long Count	Calendar Round	Classic Period Katun Name
9.5.0.0.0	11 Ajaw 18 Tzek	Katun 11 Ajaw
9.6.0.0.0	9 Ajaw 3 Wayeb	Katun 9 Ajaw
9.7.0.0.0	7 Ajaw 3 K'ank'in	Katun 7 Ajaw
9.8.0.0.0	5 Ajaw 3 Ch'en	Katun 5 Ajaw
9.9.0.0.0	3 Ajaw 3 Sots'	Katun 3 Ajaw
9.10.0.0.0	1 Ajaw 8 K'ayab	Katun 1 Ajaw
9.11.0.0.0	12 Ajaw 8 Keh	Katun 12 Ajaw
9.12.0.0.0	10 Ajaw 8 Yaxk'in	Katun 10 Ajaw
9.13.0.0.0	8 Ajaw 8 Wo	Katun 8 Ajaw
9.14.0.0.0	6 Ajaw 13 Muwaan	Katun 6 Ajaw
9.15.0.0.0	4 Ajaw 13 Yax	Katun 4 Ajaw
9.16.0.0.0	2 Ajaw 13 Tzek	Katun 2 Ajaw
9.17.0.0.0	13 Ajaw 18 Kumk'u	Katun 13 Ajaw

TABLE 3: Classic period katun progression

count moves from tallying 20 katuns and tabulating them as baktuns in the Long Count, to a cyclical format in which there are only 13 katuns in each cycle, and they then repeat cyclically without differentiation.

This bears repeating: during the Inscriptional Period, katuns were tallied from zero through nineteen, and kept track of within larger baktun cycles; during the early Colonial Period (and presumably the Late Postclassic), the larger tallies had been dropped, and a Katun Round was introduced, which without additional data could not distinguish one Katun 1 Ahau from any other Katun 1 Ahau. The transition between these two modes of counting time is critical to the consideration of the calendar correlation problem yet we have little data (and that contested) speaking to the transition.

If the Long Count had been dropped and a cyclic tun count had been introduced to accompany the Calendar Round, should we expect that there was strict continuity in any component through the transition? Should we assume that synchrony was maintained across geographical regions without the Long Count? Regarding the dual assumptions behind continuity—that "a single unified calendar was kept", and that "no attempt was made to alter" it—Aveni concedes that "[b]oth assumptions have only the advantage that they are simple".[7]

Lunar Records

Since its earliest records in the Classic period, the Long Count was accompanied by lunar information (see figure 4). Specifically, the hieroglyphic elements of the 'Supplementary Series' known as Glyphs A, B, X, C, D, and E all recorded aspects of the moon age. While Glyphs B, X, and C were primarily numerological, Glyphs D and E provided very straightforward records of the Moon Age, or the number of days elapsed from first visibility of the moon, within a cycle of 29 or 30 days—the latter captured by Glyph A.

There are a few inscriptions that give narrative descriptions of New Moon instead of providing a numerical representation (see e.g. the Copan Str. 10L-11 record in figure 5), but the vast majority provide glyph D as a combination of a bar-and-dot number less than

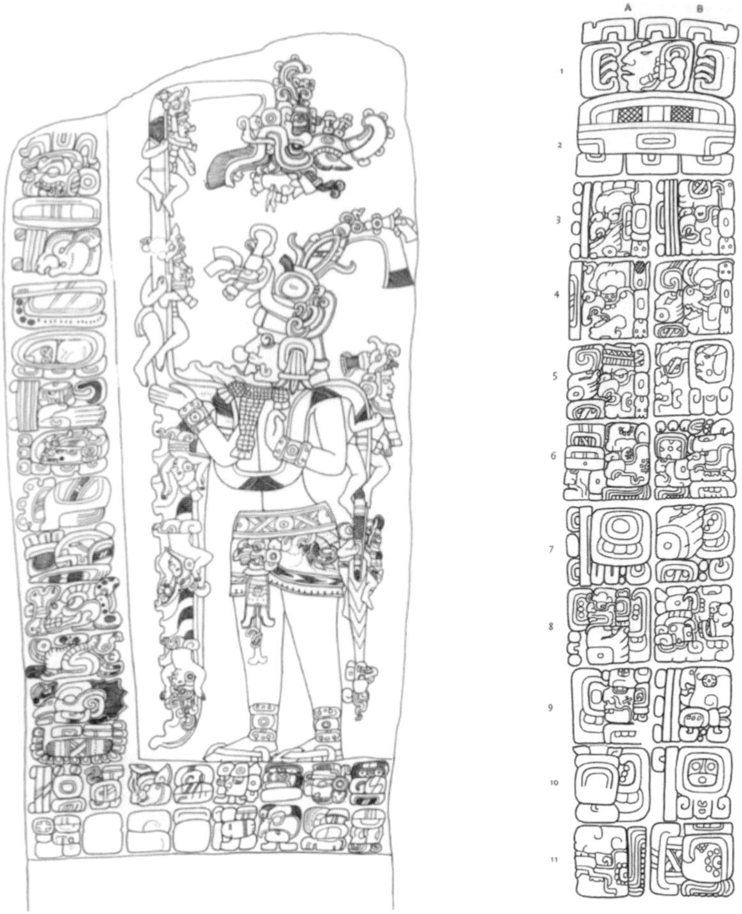

FIGURE 4. a) Hauberg Stela with the earliest known Lunar Series glyphs, fifth glyph block from the top (A5), 17-**K'AL-K'UH-UH** (Drawing by Linda Schele; reproduced by permission of the Foundation for the Advancement of Mesoamerican Studies, Inc.); b) Classic period Lunar Series from Quirigua Stela A, starting with A7, Glyph E = 26 days ago; B7, Glyph D = **HUL-li-ya** (it arrived); A8, Glyph C = u-2-**K'AL-[JGU]-UH** (it is the 2nd period of the Jaguar God of the Underworld Moon); B8, Glyph X = name of the moon; A9, Glyph A = **20** + **10-na** (30 day lunar period) (Drawing by Matthew Looper; reproduced by permission of the author).

twenty and the conjugated verb **HUL-li-ya**, 'to arrive' (here huliiy, or *hul-iiy-ø*, arrive. [COM].3sA). Loosely translated: "[the New Moon] arrived 15 days ago". If the Moon Age was twenty days or greater, 'Glyph E' was included, which provided the scribe an extra glyph block to write the 20+ coefficient of the verbal portion of Glyph D (see figure 4).

For the calendar correlation problem, the utility of the Lunar Series is that overall, it is relatively consistent in recording moon ages both from city to city and over time so that we might readily take the vast majority of them to have been derived from observation.[8] This provides the important restriction that any proposed calendar correlation must pre-

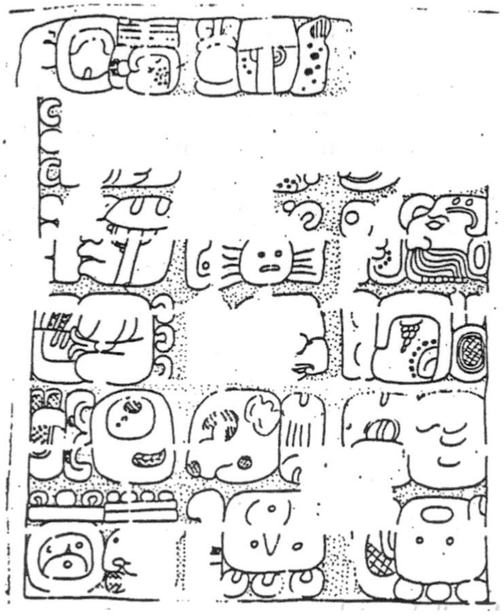

FIGURE 5. New Moon record from Copan Structure 10L-11. From A4, **i-IL-hi** [eroded] **tu-NAH-UH ch'o-ko** 'It was seen [eroded] [PREP] the moon house. It is the New Moon.' (Drawing by Linda Schele; reproduced by permission of the Foundation for the Advancement of Mesoamerican Studies, Inc).

dict (or 'post-dict' as Aveni terms it) the Moon Ages within the Lunar Series to within a day or two. Unfortunately, this is not as tremendous a constraint as it may at first seem given the over 300 lunar records we have from the Classic period. A calendar correlation only has to postdict one for the rest to follow within a reasonable tolerance.

Aside from the regular periodization of synodic lunar months, there have been a few texts from the Classic period that modern scholars have interpreted as eclipse records, but only one of them is directly related to an eclipse representation; the others are inferences based on the fact that the date fell on what has been reconstructed as the date of a visible eclipse after a calendar correlation has been assumed. We will address these records below.

The major source of lunar data utilized as evidence for the correlation problem, then, has come from the Eclipse Table of the Dresden Codex. The Eclipse Table works by starting with a Long Count anchor, and then proceeding through intervals readily recognizable as lunar cycles (177, 178, and 148 days). Again, though, this data does not add much. For one thing, the Long Count dates already match the progress of the Moon Ages recorded in the Classic period inscriptions. There is a strict continuity here suggesting no need for back-calculation in order to connect the two time periods. But more importantly, there are no readily recognizable historical eclipse records within the Dresden Codex Eclipse Table. Rather than recording historical events, the table seems to record possible events or 'warning' dates.[9] Without specific historical records within the Table, its utility has become akin to the Moon Age records from the Classic period inscriptions and essentially redundant to them for purposes of a calendar correlation.

Venus Records

The most important astronomical records with bearing on the calendar correlation problem, at least in its latest considerations, come from the Venus Table in the Dresden Codex. To be sure, there are some important complications with the interpretation of parts of the Venus Table, but the basic constraint that it imposes is relatively straightforward.

The Table breaks up (approximate) synodic periods of Venus into sub-periods of 236, 90, 263, and 8 days. This generates a Venus Round (VR) of 584 days, and counts them off for a period of 37,960 days, or approximately 104 years. For most interpretations of the Venus Table, this provides a sufficient ephemeris for one 104-year period. Yet the average synodic period of Venus is 583.9214 days, not the even 584 days approximated by the Table. As a result, strict adherence to the Table's progression would result in a consistently increasing discrepancy between prediction and observation. It is here that the 'Preface' to the Venus Table (page 24) comes into play. This page provides increasing multiples of the basic VR in a table of intervals, along with narrative anchors of VRs to Long Count dates (with Calendar Rounds), and a series of four intervals that are mathematically recognizable as 'correction intervals'.

The relationships of the Long Count anchors to the Venus Table will be addressed below; here, though, we may cover the recognition of the correction intervals as their interpretation has not changed significantly over the last century. That is, in the 1920s, John Teeple recognized that the correction intervals could be interpreted as modified multiples of Venus Rounds. Three of the four intervals (the fourth has been largely ignored or dismissed as scribal error) fall a few days short of an integral number of Venus Rounds. Teeple suggested that this was intentional in order to make up for the accumulating error between computed prediction and observation. That is, a shift in the Table could be generated by introducing a correction interval, which would maintain the base on a day 1 Ajaw, but would cut out 4, 8, or 12 days from the ephemeris. This would have the effect of compensating for the 5 days of error accumulating every 65 VRs.

Several schemes have been proposed for integrating correction intervals with uncorrected VR in idealized schemes, but for the most part, these proposals rely on the invocation of a specific calendar correlation, so we will explore them below. It should be noted at this point, though, that with correction intervals, scholars have proposed that the Venus Table could remain accurate to within hours over a century's time. Clearly, this degree of accuracy along with the odd sub-periods of the Venus Round yields the ostensible potential of a very tight constraint on any proposal for a calendar correlation.

Thompson's Test

With this review of the critical components of the Mayan calendar, we may now turn to the historical consideration of the calendar correlation problem. In order to see the problem as it was resolved in the late twentieth century, we turn to Thompson's *Commentary on the Dresden Codex*, a volume of the American Philosophical Society's publication series, coming at the end of Thompson's career, and tailored to his reputation as a calendar aficionado.

The Dresden Codex is a manuscript of the mid to late Postclassic period. The difficulty in ascribing a date to it, in part, derives from the fact that it has been dated primarily by methods assessing the fit of its predictions with reconstructed astronomical events.

Apart from that data, it can be noted that the language in the Dresden Codex differs from that recorded in the hieroglyphic inscriptions of the Classic period. Alfonso Lacadena and Robert Wald find this to represent a Yucatec influence.[10] What distinguishes the Dresden Codex within the Postclassic context is that it contains 260-Day almanacs, Year Bearer rituals, *and* Long Count dates. *Prima facie*, then, it should be a very rich source for bridging the Classic-Postcontact divide.

Buried within his discussion of the Venus Table in the Dresden Codex, Thompson alludes to the calendar correlation problem. Therein, he discusses the methods that have been suggested for correcting the Venus Table, providing for its long-term usage. In order to assess various correction mechanisms, he appeals to historical data, which in turn requires the introduction of a calendar correlation. It is in attempting to match the predictions of the Table with historically reconstructed Venus periods that Thompson writes:

> However one looks at the data, if the last three entries of the table correctly register heliacal risings of Venus, as they do in terms of the Goodman-Martínez-Thompson correlation, the 9.9.9.16.0 entry must lie some sixteen days before heliacal rising; both sets of dates cannot be correct. My suggestion that it was an accumulated error of 16 days at the first date which was corrected by the addition of 16VR+16 days may be wrong, but whatever the circumstances there is no doubt that the first entry is 16 days wrong in terms of the later entries, *whatever correlation is used*, and that the Maya amended their 61 VR – 4 days and 57 VR – 8 days groupings to include this extraneous 16 VR + 16 days.[11]

Thompson notes that the correction mechanisms that he and Teeple have derived for the Venus Table's operation do not allow for both the early 'base date' of the Preface to correspond to an observable Venus event *and* for the much later corrected dates to also correspond to observable events. Rather, one of the sets must be erroneous if the other is presumed to be accurate. The key here is that Thompson then re-casts this observation as an opportunity. Thompson claims that this discrepancy will exist regardless of the calendar correlation invoked. In other words, his (and Teeple's) interpretation of the mechanism for correction should hold independently of calendar correlations. The implication is that if one calendar correlation can explain the 16-day error better than others, then that correlation has a better chance at being the right one.

Whether or not Thompson intended this as an explicit test, Lounsbury certainly seems to take it that way 10 years later. Lounsbury's abstract for his 1983 paper on the calendar correlation problem reads as follows:

> The longcount date that appears in the preface to the Venus table of the Dresden Codex poses a problem that up to the present has resisted satisfactory solution. So also does one of the intervals tabulated in the fourth tier of numbers on that same page. These problems, which are related, bear on the astronomical circumstances and the chronology of the Venus table, and indeed on Mayan chronology in general; for the interpretation accorded to them affects crucially the solution of the Maya-to-European calendar-correlation problem. A resolution of the Venus problems is now at hand; and this opportunity is taken to present it.[12]

Lounsbury has found a provocative means for addressing Thompson's concerns, which are "crucial" to the "solution" of the calendar correlation problem.

Within the text, Lounsbury clarifies his perception of the problem he wishes to address. Regarding Page 24 of the codex, Lounsbury writes that it

> highlights a day 1 Ahau 18 Kayab which it places at 9.9.9.16.0. The most natural assumption would be—and has usually been—that this must designate the primary base of the main table. The trouble with that, as Eric Thompson expressed it (1950: 226), is that 'in no correlation so far suggested, which is not derived solely from astronomical data, does 9.9.9.16.0 coincide with a heliacal rising of Venus after inferior conjunction.' Correlations can of course be coined ad hoc to accomplish this end when other pertinent evidence is ignored; but those that have taken historical evidence into account are not able to achieve it. Thompson noted that by his correlation (which is derived from post-Conquest historical data) the prediction is about sixteen days too early for the event.[13]

With this statement, Lounsbury has taken up Thompson's implicit test. Through it, Lounsbury has set up a problem in which he characterizes the GMT as a correlation derived by history but one that ambiguously meets astronomical constraints—he has subscribed to the formulation captured by Aveni's epigraph. In so doing, he is able to further refine the problem he is addressing and what may come out of it. Lounsbury goes on to lay out the desideratum for his work:

> ... why was the date 9.9.9.16.0 given such prominence and made the focus of the preface if it was not the intended base of the main table or even a historical heliacal-rising date? Its discrepancy by the Thompson correlation has posed for many a serious obstacle in the way of their acceptance of that correlation. I hope now to remove that obstacle.[14]

It is no longer a question of why a discrepancy of 16 days might exist; it is now a question of *what kind of base date* 9.9.9.16.0 must have been *given that* it was 16 days from the event it was supposed to record. Lounsbury has now transformed Thompson's implicit test into a formal problem for which he intends to provide the solution.

In order to proceed, Lounsbury borrows from his early academic training to build a very useful little mathematical instrument intended to test Thompson's correction mechanisms. Lounsbury looks at the difference between historically reconstructed first morning visibilities of Venus and its prediction by the Dresden ephemeris, having invoked the GMT. "The Thompson correlation will be assumed (in its original value: Julian day number = Maya day number + 584285), since I am convinced that it represents the truth; but it can as well be understood merely as a working hypothesis, about to be put to a test".[15] He then plots the averaged error beginning in 9.9.9.16.0, accruing linearly over periods of 104 haab', against the sawtooth function generated by Teeple's and Thompson's correction mechanism (see figure 6). For Lounsbury, this produces a very provocative result: a 'zero' error occurs on 10.5.6.4.0 1 Ajaw 18 K'ayab.

> Thus, if there was ever a heliacal rising of Venus on a day 1 Ahau 18 Kayab that motivated the ascription that is made in the Dresden Codex, and if the Thompson correlation is correct (or any correlation that respects Landa's equation), then the one of base D was it. Its date was A.D. 934 November 20 (Julian), equal to Maya 10.5.6.4.0 by the Thompson correlation. There can have been no other.[16]

That is, considering the natural variability of Venus's period along with the steadily accruing

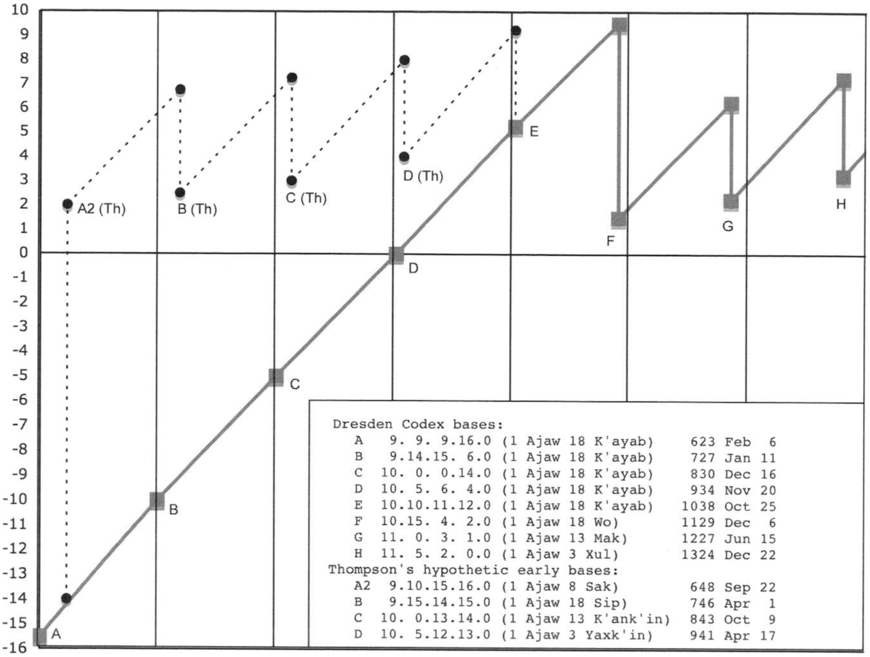

FIGURE 6. Reconstruction of Lounsbury's graph (1983) showing the 'zero error' on 20 November 934. Note that the two paths correspond to two different interpretations for implementing the correction intervals: the sawtooth function accords with Thompson's approach, while the one crossing the abscissa in AD 934 corresponds to Lounsbury's interpretation. Both plots require the assumption of the GMT.

error generated by the approximated synodic period, the heliacal rise of Venus occurs on the day predicted, with zero error: 10.5.6.4.0 1 Ajaw 18 K'ayab on November 20, 934. Precisely following Thompson, Lounsbury makes the claim that any calendar correlation must meet this constraint. That is, any correlation must put a 1 Ajaw 18 K'ayab date on the heliacal rise of Venus on AD 934, November 20. Since the GMT is the only one that does so, and because it does so so well, it must be correct.

Lounsbury then closes his article with a review of several other calendar correlations, demonstrating the similarities between them and the results he has derived, but ultimately showing that the "Thompson correlation"—the GMT—is the most compelling.

> As noted earlier, these two items [9.9.9.16.0 and 1.15.14.4.0] have posed for many scholars an obstacle in the way of their acceptance of the Thompson correlation. The solution that has been described here provides the necessary explanations for both of them. ... The problem of the Dresden Codex Venus table can no longer be held against the correlation. Rather, it may be seen now as a type case illustrating that reputed failures of this correlation may derive not from wrongness of the correlation, but from faulty analyses of some of the problems to which it has been applied.[17]

If Lounsbury was not completely assured of this solution over time, his equivocation may have been the motivation for two later articles further refining the argument. In 1992, Lounsbury published two articles on the Dresden Codex Venus Table corroborating his 1983 article. In the first he states that "[t]hough the correlation obtained from this exercise is not new, its astronomically based derivation is. I believe that this provides further assurance that one of the Thompson set of values for the correlation constant is correct".[18]

The chronology of Lounsbury's solution fits well with the developments we find in the editions of Michael Coe's introductory text, *The Maya* as well as Anthony Aveni's canonical introduction to archaeoastronomy, *Skywatchers of Ancient Mexico*. As shown in tables 4 and 5, which quote from the revised editions of both texts, Coe's and Aveni's descriptions of the calendar correlation problem follow in step with the results coming from Lounsbury's published articles.

While Aveni's revisions are separated substantially in time, Coe's provide a provocative resolution during the time that Lounsbury was working on the problem: 1980 (second edition), 1984 (third edition, specified text same as in the second edition), 1987 (fourth edition), 1993 (fifth edition, specified text same as in the fourth edition), 1999 (sixth edition), and 2005 (seventh edition, specified text same as in the sixth edition). We should be cautious, though, in readily accepting that the agreement between these two sources necessarily reflected a broad consensus in the field. In part, it may well be explained by the fact that Coe and Lounsbury were colleagues in the Yale Department of Anthropology at the time. In his own work reviewing the history of the decipherment of Mayan hieroglyphic writing, Coe implicitly describes a second, equally compelling connection. Both scholars were in the same camp when it came to the interpretation of Mayan epigraphy; out of a relatively small group of Mayanists working on the hieroglyphic script in the 1970s and 80s, Coe and Lounsbury were of the even smaller sub-group that subscribed to a phonetic hypothesis.[19]

Furthermore, this small group of epigraphers (as wonderfully told in Coe's book on the decipherment, *Breaking the Maya Code*) included others who accepted Lounsbury's 'proof' wholeheartedly. Shortly after Lounsbury published his article on the Dresden Codex and the calendar correlation, Linda Schele and Mary Miller produced *The Blood of Kings*, the first book written for a public audience that included extensive readings of Classic period hieroglyphic inscriptions based on the fledgling decipherment. Again reflecting the size of the academic community at the time, Mary Miller had recently joined Lounsbury and Coe at Yale and Coe himself wrote the Preface to the book. Therein, Coe highlighted the role of Yale researchers in the hieroglyphic decipherment, and emphasized Lounsbury's "researches into Maya calendrics and especially astronomy".[20]

The Blood of Kings focused on royal ritual texts within the corpus of hieroglyphic inscriptions, describing the recorded events as well as the actors engaging them. But it also placed these events unproblematically within Christian time. One of countless examples comes from the chapter on 'Courtly Life':

> On Piedras Negras Lintel 2 (Pl. 40), for example, Ruler 2 and seven youths celebrate what is probably an initiation ritual for young men on 9.11.6.2.1, October 24, A.D. 658. A son of Ruler 2, depicted behind the king, is named as an *ahau* of Piedras Negras in the accompanying caption.[21]

While they are tentative with the type of ritual recorded ("probably"), there is no qualification of the Christian date assigned to the Mayan Long Count. Miller and Schele's only

Edition of Aveni's *Skywatchers of Ancient Mexico*	Assessment of the Calendar Correlation Problem
Original, 1980	p. 204: "Among students of Maya calendrics, much attention (some would say too much) has been devoted to the attempt to match a given position in the Maya Long Count with a date in the Christian calendar.... We make no attempt to solve the correlation problem, which at this stage is really insoluble in the eyes of most investigators." p. 205: "Only the Spinden and the Goodman-Martínez-Thompson (GMT) correlations have ever attracted a wide following. In the last three decades the latter has emerged as the most successful of all those which have been proposed; nevertheless, the reader should be reminded that even its own proponents admit that the GMT is far from perfect."
Revised, 2001	p. 207 "While the correlation question had long been a contentious issue, developments during the final decades of the twentieth century have narrowed the span of proposed correlation constants from several centuries to a mere two days. Today, the Goodman-Martínez-Thompson (GMT) correlation constant A = 584,283 and the so-called modified GMT, with A = 584,285, emerge as the only reasonable contenders."

Table 4: Assessment of the Calendar Correlation Problem in Aveni's *Skywatchers of Ancient Mexico*.

Edition of Coe's *The Maya*	Assessment of the Calendar Correlation Problem
Second Edition, 1980	p. 160 "Some have questioned whether the movements of the planets other than Venus were observed by the Maya, but it is hard to believe that one of the Dresden tables, listing multiples of 78, can be anything other than a table for Mars, which has a synodic year of 780 days; or that the Maya intellectuals could have overlooked the fact that 117, the product of the magic numbers 9 and 13, approximates the length of the Mercury 'year' (116 days). It has even been suggested that Jupiter was of interest to [p. 161] them. They were, of course, astrologers not astronomers, and all these bodies which were seen to wander against the background of the stars must have influenced the destiny of prince and pauper among the Maya. The Chaldean and Egyptian astrologers divided up the sky in various ways, each sector corresponding to a supposed figure of stars, so as to check the march of the sun as it retrogrades from sector to sector through the year, and to provide a star clock for the night hours. The zodiac of Mesopotamia is the best known of such systems. Did the Maya have anything like it? On the subject there is little agreement, but some have seen an indication of a partial zodiac on a damaged page of the Paris Codex, which shows a scorpion, turtle, and rattlesnake pendant from a celestial band. Very little is known of star lore among the Maya, but they did have constellations called tzab ('rattlesnake rattle', the Pleiades) and ac ('turtle', made up of stars in Gemini), with which they could tell the time of night; so a 'zodiac' is quite probable."

Edition of Coe's *The Maya*	Assessment of the Calendar Correlation Problem
Fourth Ed., 1987	p. 176: They were, of course, astrologers not astronomers, and all these bodies which were seen to wander against the background of the stars must have influenced the destiny of prince and pauper among the Maya. Potentially the most significant new breakthrough along these lines has been the confirmation by Floyd Lounsbury of Yale University of the exact correlation between the Maya and Christian calendars, long a bone of contention. Any valid correlation has to fit two historical facts: one is that Bishop Landa stated that 16 July AD 1553 (Julian) was the Calendar Round day 12 Kan 1 Pop in the late Yucatecan Maya calendar (this would have been 11 Akbal 1 Pop in the Classic system); the other is that the Spanish Conquest of Yucatán began in a katun which ended on a day 13 Ahau. The two currently rival correlations are one which would have this correspond to the Long Count date 11.3.0.0.0 13 Ahau—espoused by some archaeologists working in Yucatán, but impossible since it violates the Landa equation—and one corresponding to 11.16.0.0.0 13 Ahau, long championed by Eric Thompson. That Thompson was correct is demonstrated not only by this and other historical information from the Post-Classic Yucatán, but also by the Dresden Codex itself. The eclipse predictions tables of this book forecast a solar eclipse on 9.16.4.10.8 12 Lamat 1 Muan; given the first Thompson correlation (he successively advocated three during his lifetime, each a day apart from the other), this would be 8 November AD 755 in the Julian calendar—the precise date of a lunar-solar conjunction! No other correlation satisfies this requirement. Furthermore, Lounsbury has shown that the base number of the Venus Table as given in the Dresden Codex (9.9.9.16.0 1 Ahau 18 Kayab) is contrived; as usual with such carefully chosen dates, it contains many integral multiples of important calendrical components. 1 Ahau was important throughout Mesoamerica as the conceptual heliacal rising of the deified Venus (that is, its rising just ahead of the sun on the eastern horizon following its disappearance in inferior conjunction). This contrived base date had been projected backwards in time from the real base of the Dresden Venus Table, namely 10.18.9.15.0. Using the first Thompson correlation again, this was 20 November AD 943, a red-letter day [p. 189] on which both Venus and Mars rose heliacally with each other in the east, on a day 1 Ahau 18 Kayab. Such an extraordinarily rare celestial event must have seared itself into the Maya astronomical mind. With the correlation now fixed, it should be possible, by consulting modern astronomical tables, to test the hypothesis, long held by David Kelley, that the Classic Maya inscriptions contain references to the heavenly bodies, above and beyond the lunar data which customarily follow initial Long Count dates on Maya stelae. …
Sixth Ed., 1999	p. 227: … The Maya savants were, of course, astrologers not astronomers, and all these bodies which were seen to wander against the background of the stars must have influenced the destiny of prince and pauper among the Maya. With the correlation between the Christian calendar and the Maya Long Count now fixed, it should be possible—by consulting modern astronomical tables—to test the hypothesis, long held by David Kelley, that the Classic [p.228] Maya inscriptions contain references to the heavenly bodies, above and beyond the lunar data which customarily follow initial Long Count dates on Maya stelae.

TABLE 5: Assessment of the Calendar Correlation Problem in Coe's *The Maya*.

mention of the calendar correlation qua problem comes in the Introduction where they write simply: "The correlation between the Christian and Maya calendars determined by J.T. Goodman in 1905 has held to the present day".[22] End of story.

In fact, Schele and Miller do not simply note numerous Classic period dates in the Gregorian calendar, they go so far as to record their own contemporary times as translated by the GMT. In their appendix on the Maya Calendar, they write: "The 'zero' day in the Maya calendar correlates to August 13, 3114 BC The day on which the exhibition, The Blood of Kings, opened was 12.18.13.0.3 11 Akbal 16 Uo, and it was ruled by the third Lord of the Night".[23] The solution had become sufficiently secure to use its application liberally in either direction.

Linda Schele went on to produce several other texts intended for the public with different co-authors, and in each, the books utilized the GMT without qualification.[24] Over the same time period, academic journals also began reporting the Christian equivalents to Mayan dates along with the footnoted qualification that the GMT was being used. Additionally, a new genre of articles was created, containing arguments relating the reconstructed astronomical events on any given inscriptional date recorded to interpretations of the accompanying text or imagery.[25] The inertia mobilized by the increasing number of publications generated sufficient momentum behind the acceptance of the GMT that by the monumental *Chronicle of Maya Kings and Queens* (2000), by leading epigraphers Simon Martin and Nikolai Grube, some dates were published by their Gregorian equivalents only, forsaking entirely the Long Count positions behind them.

Lounsbury's proof of the correlation had been accepted and assimilated into the fabric of further research in the field.

The Complication

So the calendar correlation problem that Thompson defined in *A Commentary on the Dresden Codex* was effectively solved by Lounsbury to the satisfaction of his contemporaries. More specifically, the *formulation* of the calendar correlation problem that Thompson called attention to in his *Commentary* was solved by Lounsbury. David Kelley, however, found this overall consideration to be less than convincing.

> It makes no sense to suggest that elaborate tables were constructed with extremely precise correction formulae, accurate to a small fraction of a day, and that the base of these tables was deliberately set inaccurately by 15 to 20 days so that the tables could be used repeatedly without correction until they finally came into step with reality. The alternative—that they were deliberately set at an inaccurate base in the past so that a derivative table (which is not given) would be in step at a contemporary date (which is not mentioned)—seems equally unconvincing, although the sophistication with which this view has been presented has tended to obscure its basic implausibility.[26]

Apart from Kelley's skepticism, the careful reader may also have noted that there is a slight problem with the problem as Thompson formulated it. As quoted above, Thompson notes explicitly: "there is no doubt that the first entry is 16 days wrong in terms of the later entries, whatever correlation is used...". As we will now see, this statement actually masks an incorrect assessment of his own interpretation of the Preface to the Venus Table.

In this quotation, Thompson's initial claim is that there are two sets of predicted observations within the Venus Table. He then observes that relative to Venus's synodic period, these two sets cannot both be right. One of them must be incorrect. What Thompson has overlooked in this statement is that the second set of dates *only* exists because he has made use of the GMT. While it is true that Page 24 lists a number of correction intervals, the Venus pages themselves do not prescribe an implementation of the correction intervals nor a set of Long Count dates for the shifted bases. In order to tie the shifted bases to specific Long Count dates, one must introduce a method for arranging the application of the correction intervals. The Dresden Codex, however, provides no clear statements about observed events. Teeple and Lounsbury agree that without any other context, the data in the Venus pages suggest that 9.9.9.16.0 should have been a first morning visibility event.[27] It is the GMT that predicts 16 days of discrepancy; the manuscript itself does not state this.

By invoking a calendar correlation, historical Venus events can be reconstructed for any given Long Count date. So it is only after a calendar correlation is introduced that a specific mechanism for correction can be entertained. It is only after a calendar correlation is applied that a second set of Venus events is generated. And this is what happened. Thompson introduced the GMT to reconstruct Venus events for the Long Count dates in the Dresden Codex. He then noticed that while the GMT places 9.9.9.16.0 1 Ajaw 18 K'ayab 16 days earlier than a first morning visibility event, it did predict an accurate first morning visibility for a 1 Ajaw 18 K'ayab date some time after that date. Specifically, 10.5.6.4.0 1 Ajaw 18 K'ayab would have corresponded to an observable first morning visibility of Venus *according to the GMT*. Thompson then adopted a version of Teeple's configuration for correction intervals in order to take the inaccurate 9.9.9.16.0 date to the accurate 10.5.4.6.0 date.[28] The upshot is that the correction mechanism was therefore constructed to accommodate the predictions of the GMT.

This by itself is fine; in fact, it is a necessary procedure for any proposed calendar correlation. Any calendar correlation must account for the Long Count dates, and the correction intervals are certainly fair game to use to support any given interpretation. The complication is that Thompson then assumes that the correction mechanism he has constructed is independent of the calendar correlation he used to produce it.

That is the critical logical shift. In effect, Thompson has created a tautology, but mistaken it for a test—he assumed his correction mechanism was built into the Venus Table, even though that mechanism was 'read' from the Table in order to correct the error introduced by his assumed calendar correlation. He then (subtly) presented the results of applying this correction mechanism as a new test for all calendar correlations. Thompson therefore suggests that he has developed a 'test' based on the Venus Table for any calendar correlation. It is this further tautology that Lounsbury took up and re-proved in his articles of 1983 and 1992. Lounsbury's 'proof', logically considered, amounts to a provocative rationalization of the inside of a tautology for the results built into the problem formulation.

But this is simply a complication. The recognition that there is a tautological argument here does not invalidate the GMT. Certainly it does limit the role of the Venus Table's correction mechanisms in providing an independent test. But this may be recognized from the nature of the data available. That is, the Venus Table provides a huge number of predicted Venus observations all according to an idealized periodicity. These can be slid arbitrarily along a sequence of Venus periods listed according to their Julian equivalents; they will match up at intervals of 584 days. Further, the correction intervals are not specified by the Dresden Codex as to the configuration by which they should be incorporated into a specific historical sequence. These, too, then, can be moved and arbitrarily rearranged to make the extended table more accurately fit any sequence of Julian-derived Venus events. In a sense, then, the entire Venus Table in all of its complexity really only amounts to a single data point. There is simply insufficient data within the rest of the Venus Table to break it up into parts and consider them independent of each other. As a result, the data within the Venus Table, like that of the Eclipse Table or the Lunar Series records, cannot generate mutually independent tests.[29]

What it can do, however, is provide a constraint to a calendar correlation derived from some other evidence. This essentially comes back to the position as Aveni cast it in the epigraph. The Venus data can be shifted around to, at some point, align a first morning visibility event with a 1 Ajaw 18 K'ayab date, so it requires some external data to constrain the set of possible Venus anchors. And in fact, this is how Lounsbury cast the problem, even though, again, it is not quite how Thompson did. That is, Lounsbury states repeatedly that Thompson's correlation came from 'historical data and amongst that, he held suspect any correlation that would require an adjustment to the Landa equation.[30]

And so to this historical data we now turn. But we will see that this too brings along another layer of complications.

Double Dates

In the problem statement of his 1983 essay quoted above, Lounsbury makes only very ambiguous reference to the non-astronomical formulation of the GMT. In the final part of the article, though, he expands the scope of the project with a comparison of his results for Venus predictions based on the GMT against the predictions of other calendar correlations. It is here that the details of what Lounsbury means by 'the historical data' become clear.

When considering "Teeple's first interpretation (1926)", for example, Lounsbury notes that Teeple himself gave up on it because it "took no account of either of the *two prime considerations* for a historically valid correlation, namely, the Landa equation and the Katun 13 Ahau condition…".[31] And Lounsbury was not alone in taking these as the important historical sources for any credible calendar correlation. In 1980, Anthony Aveni calls the "Chronicle of Oxkutzcab"'s Katun 13 Ahau double date the "principal foundation" of the GMT; Aveni then adds to this an ostensibly very impressive double date, noting that "[i]n his writings, Bishop Diego de Landa places a Maya calendar side by side with a Christian calendar. Therein he sets 12 Kan 2 Pop opposite July 16 1553".[32] To this Aveni adds that: "In the book of Chilam Balam, 11 Chuen 18, or 19 Zac, is set opposite February 15, 1544".

While the history of the interpretation of the Dresden Codex has been somewhat monotone from Förstemann's work through Lounsbury's, the historiography of these double dates is discordant at best. Yet if one follows the sequence of assessments by Eric Thompson from 1927 through 1935 and to 1950, a much more linear story is told—like that of the Dresden Codex. The key for the formulation of the calendar correlation problem is that Thompson's work became the standard set of references for the late twentieth century; and these progressively concealed important complexities.

That is, Thompson's later publications refer to his earlier publications for the detailed *contested* arguments behind his assessments of the data utilized in addressing the calendar correlation problem, but the conflict behind the earlier treatments does not show up in each successive piece.

> In a previous publication (Thompson, 1935) I have reviewed the pros and cons of the various correlations which have been propounded. I have no desire to cross that swamp again, for I still adhere to the conclusion which I then reached, namely, that the 11.16.0.0.0 correlation is the most acceptable; but I still feel that the evidence in its favor is not irrefutable. Accordingly the discussion will be confined to examination of such new evidence as has been accumulated in the past 14 years and of the new correlations proposed during that time.[33]

Thus, the old questions are left behind along with further critiques of those questions—rationalized because Thompson is still convinced of his correlation. More importantly, the contestations do not come up at all in the considerations of Lounsbury, Aveni, or the Brickers during the last few decades of the twentieth century.[34] In Bruno Latour's language, these dates have been blackboxed—arguments constituting these dates as data have been accepted on the level of assumption in later work, ignoring their complexities—and sedimented—scholars have used the work of others, which relies on the blackboxing of these dates, to advance further interpretations.[35] Thompson's assessments of the historical data had therefore been accepted even though Thompson himself recognized—as in the quote above—that the evidence was "not irrefutable". In fact, in reviewing each of the three primary data points in the order that Lounsbury presented them, we find that each one continues to rest on contested arguments.

The Landa Equation

The document containing Diego de Landa's double date has turned out to present a much more complicated source to interpret than the literature on the calendar correlation implies. As we will see, even Thompson's *Maya Hieroglyphic Writing* itself is internally inconsistent on the assessment of the data. Moreover we will find that the most recent investigations have problematized *all* interpretations of 'Landa's' Relación. In order to get there, though, it is worth tracing the argument from its source.

Herbert Spinden introduced Landa's manuscript into the calendar correlation problem in 1916 in an attempt to bolster Sylvanus Morley's extensive 1910 work culling calendric data from the Yucatec manuscripts that Daniel Brinton had collected and translated as *The Maya Chronicles*. We will address the 'other' materials below; here we focus on Landa's contribution, which took some manipulating before it even became recognized as a double date.

Landa's *Relación de las cosas de Yucatan* includes a somewhat extended description of the Yucatec calendar. In this section of the text, Landa begins with a statement regarding the accuracy of the Mayan tropical year—one that has been questioned by all his translators. Landa claims that the Yucatec practice of time keeping was to include a year of 366 days every four years exactly as the Julian calendar did.[36] He then goes on to describe the 260-Day Count, naming the Day Signs and identifying the (contemporary) Year Bearers as K'an, Muluk, Ix, and Kawak. Landa specifically describes these Year Bearers as serving the same role as dominical letters in the Christian calendar. The actual text is considered clumsy, but it is worth reviewing, as the question of dominical letters is critical within the overall consideration of the evidence. Angel Garibay records Landa's text as:

> Ya he dicho que el modo de contar de los indios es de cinco en cinco, y de cuatro cincos hacen veinte; así, en estos sus caracteres que son 20, sacan los primeros de los cuatro cincos de los 20 y éstos sirven, cada uno de ellos, de los que nos sirven a nosotros nuestras letras dominicales para comenzar todos los primeros días de los meses de a 20 días.[37]

Anthony Pagden translates the passage as:

> I have already said that the Indian method of counting is by fives and from four fives they make twenty. They then take the glyph for the first digit of each of these quinary divisions and use it as we use our dominical letters to begin every first day of each month of twenty days.[38]

But Pagden qualifies that he has provided here "an explanation rather than a translation. The Spanish is confused and fails to describe accurately the Maya calendar".[39] That the issue of dominical letters and Landa's understanding of them is important becomes clear when we return to Spinden's introduction of the manuscript into the calendar correlation question.

Spinden recognizes that the Julian day/month correlation to a Calendar Round is insufficient to serve as a double date. That is, July 16 may correspond to 1 Pop for four years in a row, but the 260-Day Count date would change from 12 K'an to 13 Muluk to 1 Ix, to 2 Kawak over the same time period. Getting the Julian year right is essential for placing the 260-Day Count. Even here, though, Spinden has to rectify a discontinuity.

> [T]he year 12 Kan ran from July 16, 1553, to July 15, 1554, the part corresponding to 1554 being placed before the part corresponding to 1553. This cutting and patching process gave a record of Mayan days equivalent to the European year except that the last day of Uayeb was a day 12 Lamat which is followed in the table by 12 Kan, an impossible situation. If we turn from 11 Eb on December 31 at the end of Landa's table back to 12 Ben on January 1 at the beginning we have two days which are really in sequence. For 12 Lamat as the last day of Uayeb terminates a year beginning with 12 Kan. Now the count of Landa's European year is continuous from January 1 to December 31 in the week day letters as in the days of the months.[40]

This much we can see within the record of Table 6. While the Julian counterpart runs from January 1 through July 15 and then continues on to July 16, ending on December 31, the Mayan accompaniment stumbles. Starting at 12 Ben 9 Chuwen assigned to January 1, the Mayan part runs continuously through the end of Kumku on July 10. It then leaves blanks for the dates corresponding to July 11 through 15, before starting up again on July 16 with 12 Kan 1 Pop. Spinden solved this riddle by first recognizing that the five missing days corresponded to the Wayeb month—in Nahuatl, the five 'nameless days' at the end of the year. Putting these days back in, he reconstructs July 15 as 12 Lamat 5 Wayeb. But this introduces the problem that we would have 12 Lamat 5 Wayeb followed by 12 K'an 1 Pop in going from July 15 to July 16—12 K'an cannot follow 12 Lamat. Spinden's solution is quite clever. He realizes that Landa has begun his count from 1 Pop in the Mayan calendar and found it to be July 16. He then adds its 260-Day Count component 12 Kan, and runs through an entire year from July 16 through the *following* July 15. Thus December 31 has progressed continuously from July 16 12 K'an 1 Pop to match up with 11 Eb 8 Chuwen. The next day is January 1 corresponding to 12 Ben 9 Chuwen, which is the first date in the table.

Dominical Letter	260 Day Count Coefficient	260 Day Count Day Sign		Dominical Letter (cont.)	260 Day Count Coefficient	260 Day Count Day Sign
ENERO	Yax					UO
a	12	Ben		g	6	Kan
b	13	Ix		…		
c	1	Men				ZIP
…				f	13	Kan
Febrero	Zac			…		
d	4	Kan		e	6	Oc
…					SEPTIEMBRE	
b	10	Akbal		f	7	Chuen
CEH				…		
c	11	Kan				TZOZ
…				e	7	Kan
c	5	Chuen		…		
MARZO				g	10	Ahau
d	6	Eb		OCTUBRE		
…				a	11	Imix
	MAC			…		
b	5	Kan		c	13	Akbal
…						TZEC
ABRIL				d	1	Kan
g	11	Akbal KANKIN		…		
a	12	Kan		b	7	Akbal XUL
…				c	8	Kan
		MUAN		…		
f	5	Akbal		NOVIEMBRE		
…				d	3	Eb
MAYO				…		
b	2	Ben				YAXKIN
…				b	2	Kan
e	12	Akbal PAX		…		
f	13	Kan		DICIEMBRE		
…				f	7	Ik
	JUNIO	KAYAB		g	8	Akbal MOL
e	7	Kan		a	9	Kan
…				…		
c	13	Akbal CUMKU		f	2	Akbal CHEN
…				g	3	Kan
f	10	Ben		…		
	JULIO			a	11	Eb
g	11	Ix				
…						
b	7	Akbal				
c		(Kan)				
d		(Chicchan)				
e		(Kimi)				
f		(Manik)				
g		(Lamat)				
		POP				
a	12	Kan				
…						
b	1	Cauac				
AGOSTO						
c	2	Ahau				
…						

TABLE 6. Abridged version of Landa's list of dates.[41] Month breaks are inserted approximately in the position shown in the manuscript. Elided portions reflect strict continuity.

This much has not been challenged since Spinden published it. The problem arises in the fact that Landa's manuscript carried another data set. According to Spinden, the additional information uniquely identifies the year of Landa's July 16.

> In connection with the orderly presentation of the days of the Mayan tzolkin occupying stated positions in Mayan and European months, Landa gives a cycle of seven letters which correspond to the days of the week, Sunday being marked by a capital A and the other days by the lower case letters b-g. The year-bearer 12 Kan has the letter A and therefore corresponds to Sunday, July 16, 1553. ... But with the day 11 Eb on December 31 being A or Sunday, the day 12 Lamat which follows it in the Mayan calendar cannot also be Sunday. This day Sunday had belonged to January 1, which preceded rather than followed the December 31 of the table. In other words, the week day letters disclose the fact that a Mayan year 12 Kan, July 16, 1553 to July 15, 1554, was set over against an almanac of the current European year 1553.[42]

Spinden claims that the dominical letter A specifies July 16 as a Sunday. This may have been the case. The practice for assigning dominical letters documented in eighteenth and nineteenth century dictionaries (and so accessible to Spinden if he was not already familiar with the practice) is that January 1 always carries the letter 'a.' The next six days are assigned b-g, and then the eighth day is assigned 'a' again. These seven letters rotate along with the days of the week through the year. The letter that falls on Sunday is called the dominical letter of the year. Therefore, if January 1 falls on a Wednesday, then the dominical letter for the year would be 'e.' Now the complication: one standard practice was to capitalize all dominical letters, A-G, starting with January 1. There was a variation, though, in which the dominical letter for the year was capitalized, and the others were all kept in lower case. This is what Spinden assumes, for he reads the capital A as specifically designating Sunday.

The further complication is that sometimes 'A' was capitalized simply because it was the first day of the year, and *not because* it fell on a Sunday. In fact, this is explicitly Richard Long's challenge in an appendix to Thompson's reconsideration of the calendar correlation problem in 1935. At Thompson's request, Long wrote "Remarks on the Correlation Question",[43] which for the most part agreed with Thompson's assessment of the problem. One significant point on which he disagreed, though, was with Spinden's interpretation of the dominical letters:

> I think there is no doubt that the year of Landa's calendar was 1553, having regard to the sequence of the year bearers given in the Books of Chilam Balam and the Chronicle of Oxkutzcab, but Spinden's supposed demonstration that it must be 1553, because the first of January is marked with the letter A, proves nothing. In the Church Calendar every first January is marked A, the first of the series of seven 'ferial' letters. If Sunday falls on A, the first of January, then the 'dominical letter' for that year is said to be A, but this has nothing to do with the invariable series of the seven ferial letters, which is all that Landa gives.[44]

In Long's assessment, then, the dominical letters cannot determine the year of Landa's double date—Spinden has misinterpreted these. Instead, Long was convinced that 1553 was Landa's intended year for other reasons related to the documents we will see below.

Unfortunately, for the question of resolution, the issue is not as simple as either side portrays it. In fact, there is evidence that yet another practice for assigning dominical letters was utilized both geographically and temporally. Howard Cline argues that the practice of assigning dominical letters was transformed for evangelical purposes in New Spain.[45] Cline claims that in some missionary practices, Spanish friars always assigned A to Sunday, not to January 1—unless, of course, the latter fell on a Sunday. This, in fact, seems to be the practice that Juan Martínez Hernández (the 'M' of the GMT) was referring to in a letter to Genet, quoted by Tozzer in the latter's heavily footnoted translation of Landa's Relación. In footnote 748, Tozzer quotes Martínez:

> … Landa, in editing his typical year, began it January 1 with the Christian dominical letter A which means Sunday. At the time of the conquest the years 1525, 1553 and 1581 alone could have begun with Sunday. The Christian solar cycle is composed of twenty-eight years. During the first Landa was not in Yucatan and in the last he was already dead. It is, then, the year 1553 which he had in mind when he drew it up. … The year 12 Kan began on Sunday, July 16, 1553. Having run through to the end of this year he returned to the beginning of the same year of 1553 instead of continuing with the year 1554. January 1, 1554 fell on Monday, Christian dominical letter G.[46]

Martínez may be following the evangelical approach here, otherwise he would not be assigning January 1 to anything but 'A'; on the other hand, he may simply have been mistaken, for even here he suggests that Monday would have been 'G,' and according to the missionary practice, G would always fall on Saturday.

Interestingly it is not this complication that makes it into later considerations. The reasoning, again, appears to depend on Thompson's 1950 treatment of the problem. That is, deep within his discussion of Year Bearers, Thompson accepts Long's objection:

> Long has shown that Landa's typical year with year bearer 12 Kan can not be placed by the European dominical letters, as Spinden had supposed, but there is *indirect evidence* that his year must be that of 1553–54. Reckoning back from one of the calendars of the present-day Indians of the Guatemalan highlands, one finds that 12 Kan fell on July 15, 1553, whereas Landa places 12 Kan first of Pop on July 16.[47]

So in the Year Bearer section of the book, Thompson gives up the 1553 dating of the Landa manuscript by the dominical letters and accepts its assignment by a one-day error between it and its projection into the twentieth century almanacs of the Guatemalan highlands.

If that were the only assessment of Landa's no-longer-double date, the issue might have ended there. This would have shifted the burden of primary evidence to the Guatemalan highlands according to Thompson and to the Oxkutzcab Chronicle and the Books of Chilam Balam according to Long. But Thompson left an equivocal record. That is, in his explicit consideration of the calendar correlation problem as an Appendix to *Maya Hieroglyphic Writing*, he does not mention Long or the deferral of legitimacy at all. Rather, he shifts the focus.

In his Appendix, Thompson states only that the "calendar is securely dated as 1553".[48] But then he provides a new twist. Here Thompson claims that Landa must have found out that July 16 was the Mayan New Year in 1551 or 1552 and recorded that in his notes. Then in 1553, he must have learned that the Year Bearer was 12 Kan. *Then* when he was writing up his manuscript, he put these two dates together (in the discontinuous way that Spinden noted) while adding the dominical letters.[49]

Thus Thompson himself discredited the 12 K'an 1 Pop = July 16, 1553 double date accuracy in *Maya Hieroglyphic Writing*. On the other hand, he shifted the weight of the argument to the Guatemalan highland almanac data, which, by the way, only took into account the 260-Day Count portion of the calendar (as we will see below). But because Thompson's summary credits Landa's equation as 'secure', it moved forward in subsequent scholarship as such. In fact, the double date became so accepted (blackboxed and sedimented) that it moved one recent scholar to suggest the same criticism that Long presented 60 years prior. The fact that in 1995 Thijs Baaijens recognized the need to raise the issue,[50] and that his peers considered it a publishable argument, speaks to the acceptance of Thompson's summary assessment, and against a direct engagement with the underlying data by the community of (calendar-correlation concerned) Mayanists during the second half of the twentieth century.

The end result in 1995, then, should have been that the Landa equation was no longer an independently stable data point. At that point, the evidence that Landa's manuscript recorded the July 16 of 1553 was as good as that behind the assignment of 12 K'an 0 Pop to July 16 of *any year* during which Landa was in Yucatan.

But this situation changed dramatically in 2002. From Spinden through Coe, the assumption had been that the Landa manuscript was actually penned by Diego de Landa in the late sixteenth century, or as Inga Clendinnen reconstructed it:

> The whole spirit and texture of the work suggests that Landa, like so many other great travelers, saw the small lost world of Yucatan the more vividly for being distanced from it, and sought to record its clear bright shapes before they were dimmed by age and failing memory.[51]

and

> Like other ageing men recalling their past, it was not the most recent years, with their bitterness, rancour, and betrayal, which compelled his attention. The world he evoked was the world which had challenged, absorbed and enchanted him in the heroic days of his youth. The *Relación de las Cosas de Yucatan* is a tender remembrance of beloved things past.[52]

In other words, despite its being a copy created by as many as three different hands, the copy remained faithful to Landa's words and intents.[53]

In 2002, though, Mathew Restall and John Chuchiak published an article demonstrating that instead, the *Relación* was assembled by multiple copyists in the seventeenth or eighteenth century, *drawing from* Landa's manuscript. Restall's and Chuchiak's investigation considered the cross-referencing of material from known sixteenth and seventeenth century authors along with what they identified as three different 'hands' behind the final version of the manuscript. They suggest further that the enigmatic reference on the last page of the manuscript regarding a *relación* on China makes perfect sense if we take the 'Landa manuscript' as part of a compilation—an encyclopedia put together from various reports in the service of the Spanish crown. In the end, Restall and Chuchiak go so far as to state:

> ... even if the Relación is viewed not as a whole but as a source on specific and isolated topics, scholars *cannot take for granted* the authorship *and dating* of particular passages—let alone the reliability of published editions.[54]

Indeed, in Restall and Chuchiak's reading:

> Its lack of overall textual integrity means that the work cannot be treated as an authentic window onto Landa's thoughts and feelings of the 1560s. We must thus view as speculative and ill-supported, albeit eloquent and tempting, Clendinnen's (1987:119) description of the Relación as "a tender remembrance of beloved things past" that, while "a very odd document" that we have in "defective form," possibly contains "allusions, omissions and emphases which could reveal something of Landa's tacit response to the terrible events of 1562."

If the 1553 dating of Landa's calendar had not been sufficiently destabilized by Long's and Thompson's acknowledgments, Restall and Chuchiak's work certainly close the door on its 'security'. If we must acknowledge the possibility that the calendar sequence in its current form reflects the misunderstandings of copyists, then we might also be forced to acknowledge the possibility that the dominical letters were not even written by Landa, but represent a later addition to the text. Without the assignment of 12 Kan 1 Pop as July 16 *in the year* 1553, the Landa calendar might find utility in providing bounds, but it cannot be utilized to argue for an anchor to the day-for-day character of the calendar correlation problem—it is certainly not the critical constraint generating an historical derivation of a calendar correlation to be tested against the astronomy in the Dresden Codex as represented by Lounsbury.

Without an anchor to the Landa equation, though, Lounsbury's work on the Dresden Codex Venus Table would still be adequately bolstered by compelling historical evidence coming from the other sources he mentions. We now turn to the Chronicle of Oxkutzcab.

Juan Xiu

We have seen that Lounsbury, Thompson, and Long referred to more than just the Landa equation as providing the historical legitimacy of the GMT, and in fact, Aveni suggested that another document was more important for it. In his 1935 review, Thompson countered the arguments of Spinden and Morley, to downplay the reliability of the Books of Chilam Balam, and raise the value of Landa's date along with a long passage within the "Chronicle of Oxkutzcab." As Aveni represents it, this document states that "a tun ended on 13 Ahau 8 Xul in the year A.D. 1539".[55] Like Lounsbury's reference to the Landa equation, though, this masks a much more complicated picture.

Thompson presents the full treatment of the Oxkutzcab material in his 1927 publication. He starts from the translation provided by William Gates:

> Page 66 of the Chronicle of Oxkutzcab
>
> 153.. The tun on 18 Yaxkin. The town was desolated because of the Maya dead in the year....
>
> .... 5 Kan being the year-bearer on Pop 1 .... Ahau the tun on 7 Yaxkin.
>
> 1535 6 Muluc the year-bearer on Pop 1 ..... the tun on 11 Ceh.
>
> 1536 7 Ix the year-bearer on Pop 1, 3 ahau on 7 Yaxkin.
>
> 1537 8 Cauac on 1 Pop, when there died the rainbringers at Otzmal, namely Ahtz'un Tutul Xiu and Ahziyah Napuc Chi, and Namay Che and Namay Tun, and the priest Evan, ... men at Mani they were, rainbringers at Chichén Itzá then, and there escaped Nahau Veeh, Napot Covoh. On 10 Zip it took place, in 12 ahau it was, the tun on 2 Yaxkin, that it may be remembered.

1538 9 Kan the year-bearer on Pop 1, when there happened a hurricane causing death. 8 Ahau the tun on 16 Xul.
1539 10 Muluc on Pop 1. 4 Ahau the tun on 11 Xul.
1540 11 Ix on Pop 1. 13 Ahau the tun on 7 Xul.
1541 12 Cauac on Pop 1. 9 Ahau the tun on 2 Xul.
1542 13 Kan on Pop 1 when the Spaniards founded the city Ti-Hoo [Merida] when they settled, and the tributes first began through those of Mani, and the province was established 5 Ahau on 16 Tzec.
1543 1 Muluc on Pop 1 when there died those of Tz'itz'omtun at the hands of the Spaniareds in a battle, their captain being Alonso Lopez. 1 Ahau it happened on 11 Tzec.
1544 2 Ix on Pop 1. 10 ahau on 6 Tzec.
1545 13 Cauac on Pop 1, when began Christianity through the friars here in the town. These were the names of the fathers, fray Luis Villapando, fray Diego de Vehar, fray Juan de la Puerta, fray Mechor de Benabente, fray Julio de Herrera, fray Angel .... They founded at the city Ti-Hoo 6 Ahau the tun on 1 Tzec.

Now on the 29th of May in the year 1685 I have copied this from an ancient book, namely in characters as they are called Anares.

I, Don Jhoan Xiu.[56]

In his analysis, Thompson's first step is to correct the errors in this text. One of these is straightforward. The progression of 260-Day Count coefficients should increase by one for each consecutive Year Bearer (365 mod 13 = 1), which is evident, for instance, in the years from 1537 through 1543, wherein the Day Signs cycle through the year-bearers, and the coefficients increase by one: 8 Cauac, 9 Kan, 10 Muluc, 11 Ix, 12 Cauac, 13 Kan, 1 Muluc. For the years 1543, 1544, and 1545 the listed dates are 1 Muluc, 2 Ix, and 13 Cauac. There should be no flags raised by the adjustment of the last 13 to a 3.[57]

The second set of 'corrections' is less straightforward. Thompson appeals to a geographical Year-Bearer discrepancy between Peten cities and the Puuc area for the difference between the haab' month coefficients recorded in this text and those corresponding to Classic period conventions. That is, as we have seen, each Day Sign may only fall on one of 4 days for any given haab' month. Here, the haab' month coefficient set for the tun ends falling in the years 1535 through 1541 do conform to the Puuc tradition of 2, 7, 12, and 17. Thompson's 'correction' then is to assume that Xiu intended all of these dates to fit within the Puuc tradition. Thompson further assumes that any deviation from the Puuc tradition represents an error and so shifts all dates into the same set. He then invokes the one-day shift between Puuc dates and Classic period dates to move them back into their Classic period 'equivalents'. Thus 13 Ahau 7 Xul becomes 13 Ahau 8 Xul.

In making these arguments, Thompson ignores the progression within the document itself. That is, a closer look reveals that Thompson's move does not require a static one-day shift, but possibly two or three shifts and the implication of more. The first date is given with a haab' collocation as 18 Yaxk'in. The 18 puts this record in the same tradition as the Classic Peten tradition. Within Juan Xiu's list, the haab' coefficients then change from the 2, 7, 12, 17 set to the 1, 6, 11, 16 set. The shift, therefore, does not occur just once as a possible accident; instead, it takes the form of a pattern, becoming consistent by the end of the sequence. In this sequence of thirteen years, there are three sets of coefficients represented. Could this have been evidence of the Mayan 'leap year' that Landa referred to? No matter; the issue is not considered. Instead, Thompson reduces the entire data set to a single data point: 13 Ajaw 8 Xul occurred in 1540.

Next, even though the Oxkutzcab manuscript makes no mention of katuns, Thompson goes further to assume that the 13 Ahau {8} Xul 'tun' end registered for the year 1540 was not simply a tun end. Thompson assumes that this tun end corresponded to a katun end. Furthermore, he invokes a 'continuity hypothesis' to suggest that it must have been the 13 Ahau 8 Xul katun end corresponding to the Long Count position of 11.16.0.0.0. Since this matched his expectations—as derived, for example, from the Landa equation—he argued that this was the Katun 13 Ahau referred to by other Colonial period manuscripts, which accordingly should have transpired sometime around 1540.[58]

These 'corrections' already leave room for debate, but there is one further move that Thompson makes to achieve continuity between the Chronicle of Oxkutzcab and the prescriptions of the Landa equation. Thompson ends the summary statement of his corrections to Xiu's chronology by noting a "changing [of] the Christian years to correspond to the beginnings instead of the endings of the Mayan years…".[59] Here Thompson is claiming that it is legitimate to shift the 13 Ajaw {8} Xul 'katun end' to the year 1539 from an explicit record placing it in 1540 by suggesting that the years given are those of the ends of the Mayan years. In other words, Thompson is claiming that Xiu knew that 11 Ix 1 Pop and 13 Ajaw {8} Xul occurred during the year 1539, but the year of the Year Bearer ended in 1540, so Xiu assigned them both to 1540. While it is clear that this move provides the results necessary for the GMT, it masks an argument that Thompson cannot really convince even himself of. Again, we do not see this internal debate until the 1950 treatment.

In his section on the Year Bearers in *Maya Hieroglyphic Writing*, Thompson starts by noting that the Aztec practice was—according to Alfonso Caso—to name the year bearer for the last day of the year.[60] Cross-culturally, this would follow the Mayan practice of naming katuns for their last days. Incommensurate with this analogy, however, Thompson states that Mayan documents unanimously place the year bearer on the first day of the year.[61] In fact, Thompson uses Xiu's "Chronicle of Oxkutzcab" as his very first example of the Year Bearer falling on the first day of the first month, and so carrying through to the following year.[62] When we get to Thompson's Table 11, however, we find that he has gone back to the change he made in the 1927 consideration. He has placed 5 K'an in 1533, which requires the Katun 13 Ahau 'correction' of the year named by its end. Of this move, Thompson states:

> The round of year bearers from 1529-30 to 1580-81 is given in Table 11, together with source materials. Note that those cases, such as the Chronicle of Oxkutzcab, which give the year in which the bearer ended his course are included.[63]

There is no justification given for this reversal—no rationale for why Xiu would have assigned the Christian year to the end of the year when the Year Bearer explicitly marked the beginning of the year. The only reasonable conclusion is that Thompson's unique characterization of the Oxkutzcab Year Bearer is specious.

Now, if 13 Ajaw 7 Xul was in 1540—that is, if we were to take the record as written—and 11 Ix was the Year Bearer at the time, then 12 K'an 1 Pop (Landa's date) would have to have occurred in July of 1554, *not* in 1553. Thus the only way Thompson can preserve his use of Landa and his hypothesis of continuity is to include internally inconsistent interpretations of the Oxkutzcab data in *Maya Hieroglyphic Writing*. Interestingly, Thompson is now in the position where his interpretation of Landa depends on his interpretation of the Oxkutzcab manuscript, but his interpretation of the Oxkutzcab manuscript is dependent on his interpretation of Landa.

While most late twentieth century scholars have accepted the Oxkutzcab double date, though, David Kelley took a radically oppositional stance. Kelley does question the progression in Xiu's chronology, but arrives at a very different conclusion.

> The scribe was writing 140 years after the latest date he gives; apparently, he did not realize that a given day name, such as Ahau, can fall only on four days of the month; he makes the year 2 Ix followed by the year 13 Cauac, although it has to be 3 Cauac (his other year-bearers are correct); and he puts the beginning of Christianity and the founding of Merida in this year 13 Cauac in 1545. 13 Cauac would actually have been either 1529 or 1581, but neither of these dates nor 1545 is correct for the founding of Merida. Such ignorance on the part of the scribe does not inspire confidence that he correctly interpreted his sources.[64]

While there is plenty of room between Thompson's and Kelley's interpretations, that space remains unexplored.[65] The net effect has been that the Oxkutzcab record remains in the literature as 13 Ajaw 8 Xul, occurring in 1539, and as evidence of continuity between it and the Landa equation, and therefore as evidence supporting the GMT.

The Katun Count

The use of the Chronicle of Oxkutzcab in the calendar correlation problem relied perhaps most heavily on the Calendar Round and Year Bearer components, but it also drew into the discussion a tremendous component of the data that has held an equivocal place in the attempts toward a solution. Namely, it brought up the Katun Counts and the use of the Books of Chilam Balam, which served as a site of contention between Thompson and his colleagues during the early twentieth century.

The Books of Chilam Balam are a collection of manuscripts coming from various towns in Yucatan. They contain some records that go back to the time of Contact and before, but they also include records from as late as the nineteenth century. The scope of the books is broad, but here we focus on the calendric material. Our focus is narrowed further by the fact that only a few of the Books were partially translated for inclusion in *The Maya Chronicles* by Brinton at the turn of the twentieth century.

For the calendar correlation problem, the debate of the early twentieth century centered on the Books' usage of the Katun Counts ubiquitous in all versions along with a double date specifically within the Tizimin manuscript. John Goodman, Sylvanus Morley, and Thompson (the 'G' and the 'T' of the GMT, but a different 'M') all recognized that there would be difficulties in utilizing this material, but they took different approaches toward handling them. Perhaps counter-intuitively, Goodman articulated an interpretation based on discontinuity, his first contribution coming as an appendix to Alfred Maudslay's *Biologia Centrali Americana: Archeology*:

> I think it is likely that each of the four ruling houses—the Itzas, Cocoms, Xius and Chels—had a chronology of its own, though using a common annual calendar, the result being that mention of the same event by members of the different houses would assign its occurrence to different ahaus and even katuns.[66]

From Goodman's perspective, then, the conflicting records found across the Books of Chilam Balam were not the result of copyist or computational errors; they spoke to different counts held by different political groups. Goodman openly questioned geographic calendric synchrony.

Goodman's conservatism went further. While he considered the contemporary Yucatec dates to be useful, he placed less credibility on the records of the deep past:

> Certain dates given in the chronicles and manuscripts enable us to align the Yucatec chronologies with ours; but this is of little service beyond dates nearly contemporaneous with the arrival of the Spaniards, as the records relating to remoter events are too broken and confused to be relied upon with anything like certainty.[67]

While his assessment may strike the reader as quite reasonable, it was not picked up by any of his far more recognized contemporaries. The others looked and argued for much greater continuity over time and space.

Sylvanus Morley, for example, argued against Goodman's fractured approach. Morley saw the Books of Chilam Balam as containing errors, certainly, but as records that were reconcilable nonetheless.

> In some places in the chronicles there are clearly breaks in the order in which the katuns follow each other. For example, in one place, a Katun 11 Ahau is followed by a Katun 8 Ahau instead of Katun 9 Ahau; and again, in another passage, a Katun 1 Ahau is followed by a Katun 6 Ahau instead of Katun 12 Ahau. Other instances where the sequence of the katuns is similarly interrupted might be cited, but these two are sufficient to show how the continuity of the sequence fails at times. The question at once arises, How are these breaks in the order of the katuns to be accounted for? How have they arisen, and how may they be obviated? In the case cited, for example, where a Katun 11 Ahau is followed by a Katun 8 Ahau, is the intervening gap to be filled by the missing katuns, 9 Ahau, 7 Ahau, 5 Ahau, 3 Ahau, 1 Ahau, 12 Ahau, and 10 Ahau? Or, are we to regard this katun 8 Ahau merely as a repetition of some former Katun 8 Ahau in the sequence, and the katuns following it, until Katun 11 Ahau is reached again, as a reduplication in the record? One of these two conditions must necessarily explain the observed breaks in the sequence, since no others are possible. A careful study of the several chronicles has convinced me that defects in the record are due to both of these causes; that sometimes katuns have been omitted, and again as clearly repeated; and that both omissions and repetitions are equally responsible for the present interruptions of the sequence.[68]

Moreover, perhaps a bit romantically, Morley saw in the Books the potential for a direct link between Long Count dates and the Katun Count.

> Apart from this question of errors, however, which may be due to inaccurate texts or faulty translations, the chronicles have in themselves many characteristics which make for their reliability. In the first place two of the chronicles at least, those from The Books of Chilan Balam of Mani and Tizimin, were composed before the close of the sixteenth century, probably by natives who had grown to manhood before the Conquest, and who had, therefore, had ample opportunity to acquire a first hand knowledge of their history before the light of the ancient learning had flickered out. Says Dr. Brinton in his connection: 'Relying on their memories, and no doubt aided by some of the ancient hieroglyphic manuscripts carefully secreted from the vandalism of the monks, they

> (the natives) wrote out what they could recollect of their national literature.' The writers of these native books were probably, in most cases, the elders of the villages, and as such vividly remembered the pre-conquest days; moreover, they may have had, as Dr. Brinton suggests, some of their old hieroglyphic manuscripts containing the very chronicles which they copied into The Books of Chilan Balam. At all events, their conditions of life were such that their authorship of the chronicles considerably enhances the value of these native manuscripts as historical sources.[69]

With direct memory and reference to hieroglyphic records girding his confidence in their accuracy, Morley saw further justification in the extent to which the various books corroborated each other in assigning specific events to the same katuns.[70] Scholars have shown since, however, that the consistency among them lies in the fact that they derived from the same textual source, and then were adapted according to the later histories accumulated in the seventeenth and eighteenth centuries.[71]

Given his confidence in the manuscripts, though, Morley was free to take the next logical step. That is, Morley noticed that the Books placed historical events at Chich'en Itza within their Katun chronicles, and Morley himself had sponsored the excavations at Chich'en Itza that revealed hieroglyphic inscriptions with dates in them. What better opportunity than to take advantage of the textual continuity between Chich'en hieroglyphic records and early Postcontact historical records referring to Chich'en history? Morley proceeded very logically to find that the date 10.2.9.1.9 9 Muluk 7 Sak had been inscribed into a lintel of the just excavated Temple of the Initial Series.[72] He then argues that this would have been assigned to the katun starting on 10.2.0.0.0 3 Ajaw 3 Keh, and so would have been referred to in the Books of Chilam Balam as a Katun 3 Ajaw. One then only needs a reference to Chich'en Itza being occupied during a Katun 3 Ajaw to establish a correlation. The one that Morley settles on is anchored to the reference to the death of Napot Xiu in the Books of Chilam Balam, occurring on a date 9 Imix 18 Zip during Katun 13 Ajaw, which "took place in the Year of Our Lord 1536".[73] This puts Copan Stela 9 (9.6.10.0.0 8 Ajaw 13 Pax) at around AD 282,74 and so the occupation of Chich'en Itza (or specifically 10.2.9.1.9 9 Muluk 7 Sak) at *ca.* AD 597.

With his elegant argument behind it, Morley's correlation (Ajaw Constant of 489,385; Spinden Correlation, A=489,384) held sway during the first decades of the twentieth century. It was upset, however, by the introduction of astronomical data by Teeple. This, of course, is where Spinden entered the debate, correcting Morley's to better account for the data available at the time, although also having to argue (along with Ludendorff) for a different interpretation of lunar moon age records.[75]

As we have seen, Thompson enters the debate in 1927, and through 1935, he does not follow Goodman, and he re-prioritizes Morley's consideration. Instead, Thompson's re-prioritization takes account of

> the undoubted fact that many errors have crept in and additions been made to the various Chilam Balams by the numerous copyists. The Chilam Balam of Chumayel contains many such errors or additions, which are on several occasions clearly self-contradictory. For example on page 17 we read that Campeche was seized in the year 1513 in Katun 13 Ahau, while on page 21 we read that Katun 11 Ahau began in 1513, and that Merida was begun in 1519. On page 86 we read that the Spaniards came to Merida in Katun 9 Ahau, whereas on page 80 we are told that the Spaniards first arrived in the first Tun of Katun 11 Ahau.[76]

As a consequence of his assessment of their unreliability, Thompson re-calibrates the source material to emphasize the Landa and Xiu data (reviewed above). He then, only appeals to the Books of Chilam Balam when they can provide 'confirmatory evidence'.[77] Such is the case, apparently for one date from the Book of Chilam Balam of Tizimin—the last date that Aveni referred to in 2001 as critical to the legitimacy of the GMT. Therein, Thompson accepts Martínez's extraction of a double date: 11 Chuwen 18 or 19 Sak on February 25, 1544.[78]

> Martinez was the first to discover the passage in the Chilam Balam of Tizimin which correlates 11 Chuen 18 Zac with February 25, 1544. This, however, he corrects to February 28, 1544, on the perfectly plausible grounds that the Indians, although well aware of their own year, were not sufficiently well acquainted with the Christian year at such an early date as 1544, and for that reason made an error of three days. With this correction the 11 Chuen 18 Zac date is brought into accord with his equation 12 Kan 1 Pop equals July 23, 1553. Thereby the Ahau equation 584281 is obtained.[79]

While there is a minor discrepancy between the Martínez Ajaw equation noted here and the 584,283 constant that Thompson later espoused, this is not the discrepancy that leads to Thompson's later disavowal of the date's accuracy. For that, we must introduce a mid-century challenge to the GMT.

During the early twentieth century, the full Tizimin manuscript was only available through direct consultation with the original, which is what Brinton obtained in the late nineteenth century for inclusion in *The Maya Chronicles*. This changed, though, with the work of Ralph Roys, who published a partial English translation in 1949. The astronomer and then amateur linguist and Maya hobbyist, Maud Makemson, who also had been working with the original manuscript, took the opportunity of Roys's translation to launch an attack on the GMT. She writes:

> Roys' translation ends with the following sentence from page 13: 'I completed putting it in writing on 18 Zac, on 11 Chuen .... On the 15th day of February in the year 1544.'
>
> This 'double date,' *which is entirely inconsistent with the calendar of the previous pages*, has been often quoted as a corroboration of the Goodman-Thompson correlation. Roys, however, appends the wise caution: 'I do not know how early Maya began to be written in European letters; the first example we know is dated 1557. Certainly it was not done as early as 1544, and a correlation of Christian and Maya dates at this time seems quite impossible.'.[80]

First, then, Makemson points to the readily recognized but unreferenced fact that this double date does not fit into any kind of continuous relationship with the Katun Count records in the same manuscript. Then she reinforces her own deduction that the 1544 date must have been erroneous by giving Roys's own assessment amounting to as much. Makemson utilized this to argue for her own calendar correlation, which differed significantly from the GMT.

In fact, this constituted an interesting reversal of opinion. Makemson's first work in Maya Studies, sensible given her background in astronomy, was to consider the Venus Table of the Dresden Codex. In her first publication on it, she championed the GMT, and, according to Linton Satterthwaite, while Makemson

> avoided the claim, one of the soberest and keenest of Middle Americanists considered that she had definitely established the Thompson solution as correct (R.C.E. Long, The Venus Calendar of the Aztec [Carnegie Institution of Washington, 1944]). The vexed problem seemed solved at last.[81]

In some odd non-linear fashion, Makemson had anticipated Lounsbury and—according to Long, anticipating Coe—"proved" the GMT using the Dresden Codex Venus Table. But it must have been tenuous in her own mind since in her 1946 publication, Makemson "abandoned" that interpretation to introduce a new correlation entirely.[82]

This reversal, perhaps not surprisingly, did not go unreprised. Michael Coe's characterization of Thompson's argumentative style, when backed into a corner,[83] is on display again in his treatments of Makemson's publications. Regarding Benjamin Whorf's 1930s engagement with the hieroglyphic script, Coe writes that Thompson

> went for the jugular, taking three of Whorf's weakest cases, and worrying them to death, while at the same time deliberately skirting the truly important part of the Whorfian message, his general statements about the probable nature of the script. On the unwary or unwise, this methodology makes a great impression—you attack your opponent on a host of details, and avoid the larger issues.[84]

Similar to the strategy marshaled against Whorf, Thompson conceded the point regarding the Tizimin double date,[85] but he joined Long in an attack on Makemson's work. In fact both Long and Thompson postured as champions of the Maya themselves, arguing that Makemson's correlation required that the Maya be ignorant of their own calendar, forced to follow the errors of copyists of Landa's manuscript in attempting to write their own chronicles.[86] Thompson may have had to concede the Tizimin double date in the process, but he ensured that the credibility of Makemson's work would pay a price.

The end result of the Tizimin double date discrediting was that Long, Satterthwaite, and Thompson all conceded that it lacked independent authority, but they fell back on the seemingly powerful 'continuity' data suggesting that the 260-Day Count had continued 'unbroken' from ancient times into the early twentieth century in the Guatemalan Highlands. In the end, the Books had proven too complicated to cleanly integrate into a compelling solution. Again, we may turn to David Kelley's view, which points to an extreme. Of the Books, Kelley writes:

> There are too few chronicles and they give too little detail to reconstruct various calendars with any assurance, but the nature of the variations suggests calendrical differences, as well as copying errors, and confusions. Kirchhoff, in an unpublished 1949 study, maintained that 13 separate katun counts were operating in Yucatan; that is, every katun would have every possible name in some part of the area.[87]

Without the independent stability of the Landa equation, the Chronicle of Oxkutzcab, or the Tizimin double date, we are left to follow Thompson and turn our attention to Guatemala.

Continuity with the Guatemalan Highlands

A far cry from its late twentieth century portrayal, for Thompson the historical data was

Begin	End	Katun	Begin	End
1599.2.14	1618.10.31	3 Ajaw	1618.10.31	1638.7.17
1579.5.30	1599.2.13	5 Ajaw	1599.2.13	1618.10.30
1559.9.12	1579.5.29	7 Ajaw	1579.5.29	1599.2.12
1539.12.26	1559.9.11	9 Ajaw	1559.9.11	1579.5.28
1520.4.9	1539.12.25	11 Ajaw	1539.12.25	1559.9.10
1500.7.23	1520.4.8	13 Ajaw	1520.4.8	1539.12.24
1480.11.5	1500.7.22	2 Ajaw	1500.7.22	1520.4.7

TABLE 7. Katun 13 Ajaw with Fuensalida and Orbita's date at the beginning or end of Katun 3 Ajaw.

ambiguous. As we have seen, he had to fight with the Landa data in two different directions, and he was forced to make several 'corrections' for the Chronicle of Oxkutzcab material to fit with his interests—this all on top of the various arguments he marshaled against the legitimacy of other historical dates. But these machinations were justified to him by the larger frame of continuity.

By including the data supplied by the ethnographic research of his contemporaries, Thompson was reassured of his data manipulations. This long-term continuity data came in two forms. On the one hand, he referred again to Spanish historical records.

> The second statement which clearly has not been tampered with or altered by copyists is that a Katun 3 Ahau was running its course when Fathers Orbita and Fuensalida reached Tayasal late in October of 1618. … It has been suggested that the Katun count might have broken down in Yucatan during the period of confusion and strife following the fall of Mayapan. However, the Itza of Tayasal had left Yucatan prior to this period and, therefore, before their calendar could have been affected by the unrest in the north. Since the Tayasal Katun endings are in agreement with those of Yucatan, one can assume that there was no break-down in the count of the Katuns in Yucatan in the period subsequent to the fall of Mayapan. …
>
> If a Katun 3 Ahau was running its course October 31, 1618, the Katun 13 Ahau of the Conquest ended somewhere between July 22, 1500, and December 24, 1539. This is in agreement with the deduction from the Landa statement that the Katun ended late in the fall of 1539.[88]

Examining the bounds of Thompson's statement proves insightful (see table 7). If October 31, 1618 was the last day of Katun 3 Ajaw, then Katun 13 Ajaw would have ended on April 8, 1520. Clearly this would violate Thompson's use of Landa, which necessitates a Katun 13 Ajaw to be still running in the autumn of 1539. On the other hand, if October 31, 1618 was the first day of Katun 3 Ajaw, then Katun 13 Ajaw would have begun on April 8, 1520 and ended on December 24, 1539. This is the scenario that provides continuity with Landa. Within a 40-year range, Thompson has found a 3-month window for meeting his continuity criterion. Notice, though, that Xiu's double date in the Chronicle of Oxkutzcab would have violated this periodization if it were taken as written. There is no way that a Katun 3 Ajaw could have been running in October of 1618 if Katun 13 Ajaw ended in 1540, as long as we subscribe to a continuity hypothesis.

Not all scholars treating the historical or ethnographical records accepted continuity. We saw very early on, for example, that Goodman considered the real possibility of political difference serving as an obstacle to continuity. Having worked through "Yucatec, Cakchiquel, and Inscriptional" material first hand, Goodman resisted the temptation to

	Landa	Aztec	Ixil	K'iche' 1	K'iche' 2	K'iche' 3
Anchor	12 K'an 1 Pop = July 16, 1553	1 Couatl =	6 Kaban 1 Pop = March 10, 1940	7 Ben 1 Pop = March 15, 1927	12 Etz'nab 1 Pop = March 13, 1932	4 Ik' 1 Pop = March 2, 1977
Projection to July 16, 1553 (Julian)	12 K'an 1 Pop	13 Chikchan	1 Kimi 5 Sip	1 Kimi 4 Sip	1 Kimi 4 Sip	13 Chikchan 4 Sip
Error	0	1 day	2 days**	2 days*	2 days*	1 day***

*There are 2 days between 12 K'an and 1 Kimi; note, however, the difference of 43 days in the haab'.
**Here again, there are 2 days between 12 K'an and 1 Kimi, but the haab' has slipped one day between the Ixil and the K'iche' counts.
***Here the one day slippage is only in the 260-day count, while the haab' count remains consistent over a fifty-year period during the 20th century.

TABLE 8. Continuity evidence.

consider it consistent:

> In any attempt to deal with the Maya chronology it will be found expedient to arrange the subject under several separate heads in order to avoid confusion, as different systems prevailed not only at different centers of their civilization, but varying styles were concurrently made use of in the same place.[89]

Goodman's assessment is particularly sensible given his struggles reconciling the distinction between the 360-day 'tun' and the 365-day Year Bearer sequence. Having pulled these apart and then made sense of Landa's discussion of the calendar, Goodman is frustrated by his inability to extend them directly into applicability for the Inscriptional period.[90]

> But, though confident that I had discovered the secret of the ahau and katun count, when I tried the plan on the dates and reckonings of the inscriptions it proved totally inapplicable. … It was discouraging, but I did not lose faith in my discovery. The inapplicability of the Yucatec scheme to the reckonings of the inscriptions, probably, was simply owing to different methods of computing the ahaus and katuns. There was no alternative but a patient and exhaustive analysis of the Archaic dates and time reckonings.[91]

Goodman, as we saw in the last section, took a more conservative approach than his successors in treating the various calendric records available. Goodman considered each independently, attempting to find its sense within its local context. If this reconstructed sense did not fit with that of other contexts, he did not force the issue; instead, as we have seen above, he allowed for diversity in practice. The opposite practice—that of assuming continuity and then looking for evidence to support it—has prevailed, though, as addressed explicitly in Kelley's epigraph.

As early as the 1920s Goodman's contemporaries encountered data with the potential to speak to the continuity hypothesis. This is the data that led Aveni to report in 2001 that "all the historically surviving almanacs from the highlands of Guatemala show not a single day break from the archaic calendar (Thompson 1950, p. 310)".[92] J. Steward Lincoln, Oliver La Farge, Samuel Lothrop, and Robert Burkitt had all ventured into the Guatemalan highlands in their ethnographic investigations and all returned with data to fuel the fire. Consulting Ixil and K'iche' daykeepers, they brought back calendric information that was then tested against the various correlations of the time. Thompson summarized this data in 1950, which may be reduced as in table 8. His focus in 1950, though—having struggled with his other historical data—is now to cast his net more widely. In 1950, he argued for considerable continuity between known Aztec 'double dates', the Guatemalan highland data, and the Landa equation.[93] While the Aztec data proved somewhat inconsistent, he emphasized a "1 Couatl date, given by three independent native sources, [which] leads to 13 Couatl (13 Chicchan) on July 26, 1553…".[94]

Here, then, is only a one-day discrepancy between the Aztec calendar (putting July 26 (Gregorian) on 13 Chikchan) and Landa's equation, which put July 26 (Gregorian) on 12 K'an.

On its surface table 8 suggests a reasonable argument for continuity. But a lack of break in the calendar, or a discrepancy of only one or two days depending on the acceptance of corrections, is predicated on the specific components of the calendar being considered. It is also based on a larger assumption that has not held up against the accumulation of data over time—the latter a complication explicitly acknowledged by Thompson himself.

First, scholars have argued along with Alfonso Caso that although there may not be commensurability between the 365-Day Counts across Mesoamerica, the 260-Day Count must have been inviolate throughout the region.[95] The continuity between the Aztec tonalpohualli and the Guatemalan *chol qiij* stood as the primary data supporting this notion, augmented by (a corrected) Landa's equation. Yet such a provision breaks down with the inclusion of further data. Cline, for example, states as fact that multiple calendars were in operation concurrently, as the rule when a larger mechanism such as the Long Count was not present:

> One of his conclusions was 'that any correlation of the Aztec and Christian calendars must be based on the 1 Couatl [Snake] August 13, 1521 equation, and the agreement of the Aztec date with the Maya material makes it unlikely that there were other calendars in Central Mexico which would fail to agree with the above equation.' While perhaps a useful hypothesis in 1955, the Thompson conclusion now is incorrect. … The Thompson equation assumes a unitary Mexican system analogous to the Mayan.
>
> That view, generally shared by Caso and others trained in the Eduard Seler tradition, has become increasingly untenable as the pluralistic nature of the Mexican calendric usages has since 1940 been conclusively established. … There is now no reasonable scientific doubt that at the coming of the Spaniards distinct functioning calendrical systems co-existed in Mexican communities.[96]

Thompson hinted at the beginning of a possible concession in the Preface to the 1960 version of *Maya Hieroglyphic Writing*.

> One final matter before leaving the present subject. On page vi of the Preface to the Second Edition, I briefly mentioned the discovery of a Mixe 260-day almanac which I said was synchronous

> with surviving highland Maya almanacs. Later information makes clear that the almanacs are not synchronized; the Mixe count, in fact, varies from village to village. In one center it differs by five days from the highland Maya almanacs.[97]

With data contradicting the assertion that a single 260-Day Count was used throughout Mesoamerica—i.e. arguing against what Makemson called the intertribal tzolkin—we are left to wonder whether the 1 to 5 day errors are really that, or whether they have resulted from various shifts over time that produced a net '1 to 5 day error' given an appropriate selection of data.

Moreover, the statement that no break has occurred in the calendar is misleading. While we may find only a difference of one day in the 260-Day Count between Landa's equation and the Guatemalan highland data, this would not take into account the fact that the 365-Day Count was still being used in some form during the twentieth century. Why leave this aspect out? Why assume that the 365-Day Count can be so arbitrarily pushed around and that the 260-Day Count is inviolate? Part of the rationale may lie in the fact that including the 365-Day Count generates an difference of 43 days or more, since continuity from the sixteenth century would place what the highlanders are calling the first day of the year on the third day of the seventeenth month (the 323rd day of the year). But it would be equally inaccurate to suggest that this amounts to an error of 43 days over four hundred years since we are now working in a Calendar Round space. We cannot take each element independently; we have to look at the difference between, for example, the recorded 7 Ben 1 Pop and the reconstructed 5 Chuwen 3 K'ayab. While it looks like a slip of two days in the chol qiij, or a slip of 43 days in the haab'', when we consider the Calendar Round as a unit, the difference becomes an 'error' of 2,600 days (i.e. ten 260-Day Counts later, 5 Chuwen falls on 1 Pop). Taking all of the data into account, then, we may find an error of 2 days, 43 days, or 2,600 days between the Landa equation and the calendars of the twentieth century Guatemalan highlands, depending on what we mean by 'continuity'. Once again, the answer depends on the specific formulation of the problem and the assumptions underlying it.

Lounsbury's Proof—Take II

To this point, we have spent an inordinate amount of time on the consideration of only four data points specifically used to support one calendar correlation. With over 50 calendar correlations proposed during the twentieth century,[98] and twice that many data points used to support them, this may strike the reader as a poor strategy for reviewing the history of the calendar correlation problem. The counterargument, though, is simply that: i) the one correlation we have focused on has been considered proven since the last few decades of the twentieth century; and perhaps more importantly, ii) the rest of the data used for any other correlation does not differ substantially from that considered here—this is the 'best' of available data. That is, other correlations differ (as we saw in Morley's case) in the relative weight given to one or another subset of the data, but they do not introduce data of different types.

When we step back, then, and look at Lounsbury's proof in the last few decades of the twentieth century along with his peers' acceptance of it, it appears that—to a degree—they have been guilty of the same charges leveled against Morley for his archaeological work in the early twentieth century. Coe, for example, complains that Morley only recovered and published the portions of the hieroglyphic texts that recorded calendric information, ignoring the rest. This impaired the eventual decipherment of the hieroglyphic script by leaving out a tremendous amount of relevant data.[99] Similarly, scholars of the late twentieth century have focused on the double date calendric components of the Postcontact period, disregarding the larger textual and historical contexts in which they were found. In so doing, they have solved the calendar correlation problem to their satisfaction, but perhaps only to the same degree that Morley proved that the ancient Maya were obsessed with astronomy and the keeping of time.

The Inscriptional Period

Apart from the specific data pointed to by Aveni,[100] Lounsbury,[101] Bricker and Bricker,[102] and Thompson,[103] there have been other forms utilized in the consideration of the calendar correlation over the last century. None of the following evidence has been utilized on its own or as the primary data supporting any calendar correlation with a substantial following, but much of it has been and continues to be used in 'corroboration' arguments. Principal here are celestial corroborations, and some of these come from lunar records.

For all impressions that the Maya were known for being great astronomers, one might be puzzled as to why, apart from the Dresden Codex, so little part of the hieroglyphic record can be unequivocally identified as celestial. The tremendous exceptions from the Classic period, of course, are lunar records. Hundreds of lunar records have been identified within the corpus of hieroglyphic inscriptions, the basic interpretation of which was provided by Teeple in the late 1920s as reviewed above. Further details have been worked out since, around the turn of the twenty-first century.[104]

Early on in the debate on the calendar correlation problem, these lunar records provided an important check on the numerous calendar correlations that had been proposed. Thompson, for example, used Teeple's work to weed through them principally in his first treatment.[105] As noted above, that is, even though there was some variation to the records, the great majority could be anchored to a progression of 29.53-day cycles. If a calendar correlation generated the historical placement of lunar records that did not come within a few days of the records in the inscriptions, that correlation could be rejected outright. In fact, this is the factor that gave Thompson ammunition against Bowditch and Vaillant, shifting the major contenders to Thompson's and Spinden's.

Like the Venus Table, though, the lunar records present a single check. Once a correlation satisfies one Moon Age, it essentially satisfies them all. Kelley is of similar opinion:

> We still do not have a clear understanding of the correction values implied by the multiplication tables [in the Eclipse Table preface], hence the Maya parameters may vary substantially from ours. Adoption of the principle of a formal eclipse table does not have as clear results for the correlation problem as the parallel case of the Venus table, and probably many correlations might be justified by suggesting minor changes in the Maya values for lunations or draconitic node passage intervals. A slight preference might be given to correlations that agree precisely with our formulae, but a lack of agreement should not be considered significant.[106]

What would be necessary to go beyond a single anchor here is a second type of information, such as the unambiguous date of an historical eclipse. Naturally, this should bring along the Dresden Codex Eclipse Table as an important element for consideration, but as we have seen and as Aveni elucidates nicely, the table cannot be matched with any historical pattern of eclipses, and so it looks more like a warning table.[107] Scholars, including Thompson, have been content to note that the base of the Eclipse Table 9.16.4.10.8 is predicted to be very close to New Moon according to the GMT.

That said, there is one Classic period record that ostensibly should be of some value. The glyph understood to represent eclipses in the Dresden Codex also shows up on an isolated Classic period monument. Thompson describes it thusly:

> It has been claimed that Stela 1 at Poco Uinic records an eclipse in the Goodman-Martinez correlation. The date in question reduces to M.D. 1425516, which with the Martinez equation 584281 becomes J. D. 2009797. According to the Oppolzer tables the eclipse, which was total in Central America, occurred on J. D. 2009802. It is clear that the Martinez equation shows an error of five days if this date is meant to record the eclipse in question.[108]

The one record from the Classic period, then, with the potential for identifying a unique date astronomically does not conform to any version of the GMT.[109] Rather than call into question the GMT, this has led to speculations about the authenticity of the record itself; more often than not, however, the Poco Winik data is left outside of the discussion.[110]

Planetary Events

There have been countless arguments connecting planetary positions—relative to each other or relative to the stars—and the dates recorded in the inscriptions since the beginning of the twentieth century. From Robert Willson at the turn of the twentieth century, to Lounsbury at the end of the twentieth century, planetary conjunctions, maximum elongations, heliacal rises, and more have been proposed as the explicit or implicit referent behind inscriptional dates.[111] Such events are often portrayed as evidence corroborating the validity of the GMT (or whichever correlation is being used), but as Kelley remarks in the epigraph to this essay, we have reason to be cautious with such arguments.

Astronomical event based arguments generally take the form found in Thompson's *Maya Hieroglyphic Writing*. First Thompson qualifies the data:

> There are few, if any, references to observed positions of Venus in the hieroglyphic texts of the stelae. If one takes all the Venus glyphs in the inscriptions and computes the positions of the planet, no pattern will emerge whatever correlation is used.[112]

Despite his initial caveat, he goes on to examine an exceptional case.

> Three texts commemorate 9.10.0.0.0 1 Ahau 8 Kayab, but two of these are badly eroded. The only one in good condition is the so-called lintel re-used in the hieroglyphic stairway of Naranjo. This carries the following arrangement of dates:
>
> 9.7.14.10.8 3 Lamat 16 Uo
> \+ 2.5.7.12
>
> ————
>
> 9.10.0.0.0 1 Ahau 8 Kayab

> The distance number reduces to 16,352 which is equal to 28 synodical revolutions of Venus. Furthermore, 41 synodical revolutions of Jupiter reach 16,353.5 days. Therefore, on the two dates both Venus and Jupiter would have been in the same positions in the sky. The presence of a Venus glyph and the fact that a day Lamat and the day 1 Ahau are involved in the calculation make it fairly certain that the astronomical values of the distance number are not fortuitous.
>
> At both dates, according to the Goodman-Thompson correlation, Venus and Jupiter were morning stars. The former was approximately 40 degrees above the horizon at sunrise; the latter approximately 20 degrees. There was nothing outstanding about the planets on those dates, although sun, Jupiter, and Venus, evenly spaced in the dawn sky, are ever a sight to rejoice one's heart. I think, therefore, the Maya recorded this appearance of the two planets because their thoughts were turned to Venus by the fact that the katun they were commemorating ended on 1 Ahau. Furthermore only after 28 revolutions of Venus and 41 of Jupiter will the cycles of the two planets come within a day or two of coincidence.[113]

Thompson's inscriptional evidence, then, amounts to an interval made up of an integer multiple of 584-day periods, which also intercedes between a Lamat Day Sign and a 1 Ajaw 260-day count date. Jupiter comes along with the invocation of the GMT, even though there is no celestial 'event' occurring on either date.

While the 1 Ajaw date may indeed have been recognized as associated with Venus during the Classic period, there are other reasons for its record on this lintel. First of all, the date 1 Ajaw 8 K'ayab commemorated the end of the tenth k'atun, as the text states explicitly (G3), so we do not have to infer a connection to Venus since k'atun ends were important enough in their own right. Second, Thompson was mistaken in stating that a 'Venus glyph' is present in the inscription; the sign taken to be a Venus glyph is actually the logographic element **EK'**, referring more generally to celestial bodies.[114] In this case, it is part of a historical person's name: Na Batz' Ek' ('Lady Monkey Star', (C4)).

More interesting, though, is the fact that this text names historical rulers of the city of Caracol, but was found broken and used within a hieroglyphic stairway at Naranjo.[115] This narrative fragment helps to fill out the bellicose history between these two cities and the larger political drama involving Tikal and Calakmul—the 'superpowers' of the Classic period (see figure 7).[116] The upshot is that while the integer multiple of 584 days is interesting, there are far more reasons to find historical purpose behind the dates recorded and the historical figures referred to than those conjectured by Thompson's astronomical hypotheses.

During the latter half of the twentieth century, Lounsbury contributed to two similar appeals connecting astronomy to inscriptional dates. The first concerned a series of verbs that contained within them the EK' ('celestial body,' or 'star') icon. Kelley and Lounsbury noted that a collection of these verbs fell on dates that were separated by Venus periods.[117] Since it was fashionable at the time to read the EK' icon as Venus, these records formed the basis of the 'Star War' interpretation, i.e. warfare ritually timed by the positions of Venus.[118] Subsequent research aimed at bolstering the placement of these Venus events increased the ambiguity of the association between glyph and astronomical event.[119] Finally, the historical contexts of the 'Star War' records were taken into account, revealing the lack of consistency by any individual patron behind the events.[120] The result here is that the astronomically driven pattern was not corroborated by the increased contextual data made available by the hieroglyphic decipherment.

Finally, a similar argument by Lounsbury was that a text from Palenque recorded an impressive and rare planetary conjunction. Schele and Freidel added to the interpretation,

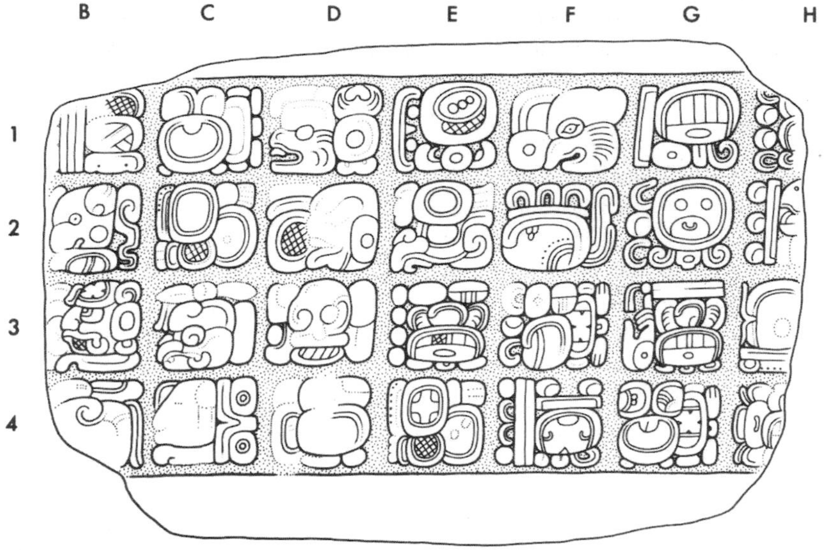

FIGURE 7. Naranjo Lintel 1 (reproduced by permission of the Peabody Museum of Archaeology and Ethnology, Harvard University).

suggesting that the hieroglyphic text actually used a term that could be translated as 'conjunction'.[121] While this reading has been de-bunked by Stephen Houston,[122] the celestial affiliation of the date has been retained into the later literature.[123]

The overall trend, then, is that with the continuing advance in the hieroglyphic decipherment, various astronomical interpretations are becoming increasingly difficult to accept.

Other Data

There are two other forms of data that have bearing on the calendar correlation problem generally, though they do not contribute much to the day-for-day formulation of the problem. Both ceramic sequencing and C-14 data have played important roles in the debate, without necessarily deciding the issue. David Kelley has summarized the contribution as: "The majority of C-14 dates would support a correlation between 470000 and 605000, but if there are systematic differences between areas (even if those are only in probability and kind of contamination), a 'majority vote' is not a useful approach".[124]

When C-14 was introduced to the field at mid-century, though, the complications seemed more dramatic. Thompson provides a comfortably smug version of the history in the Preface to the Third Edition of *Maya Hieroglyphic Writing*:

> With regard to the correlation question, a factor not known when that problem was so to the fore in the earlier part of this century was Carbon 14. The few sporadic first readings supported the

> Spinden (12.9.0.+0.0) correlation, a matter which filled me with dismay. However, I felt that all other lines of evidence so strongly supported the Goodman-Martínez-Thompson (11.16.0.0.0) correlation, as is made clear in Appendix II, that one must not act hastily, but wait to see how this new technique developed. New processes or new machines, from the latest detergent to the slickest computer, have their teething troubles—and how consoling to be able to envisage a computer so human and defenseless as to suffer the pangs of teething. To change the simile, I suspected that this new model would soon require adjustments to steering mechanism, brakes, or gearbox.
>
> . . .
>
> That hesitation to accept unreservedly the new technique proved wise. Later refinements, including the gas process, provided more reliable readings. Above all, the need for multiple runs of a single beam or charcoal to eliminate maverick readings became apparent. Multiple runs of samples taken from the outer edges of beams at Tikal carrying dates in the Maya calendar overwhelmingly supported the 11.16.0.0.0 correlation (Satterthwaite and Ralph, 1960; Ralph 1965). Samples are now taken from as close to the outer edge of a beam as possible because a tree dies from the center outward. Sapodilla is long-lived, with the result that a sample from the center of a log or beam may be nearly two centuries earlier than the date at which the tree was felled; disregard of that factor had significantly distorted early readings in favor of the Spinden correlation.
>
> It is pleasant that Carbon-14 readings now fall into line with the other factors which so strongly support the 11.16.0.0.0 correlation. In my opinion there is now no serious doubt that it is the correct answer.[125]

He included a much more entertaining version in a letter he wrote to Coe in 1957:

> Well, the old bull ought to be at bay, but he isn't; he's just quietly chewing the cud out at pasture. I seem to remember two years ago everyone was saying its [[sic]] all up with old J.E.S.T.; C-14 has blown his correlation sky high, and he's the only one that doesn't know it... Well, looks to me now that with the new C-14 readings the old 11.16.0.0.0 correlation is right back on top, where it obviously had to be for historical, astronomical, archaeological and every other reason.[126]

In *Maya Hieroglyphic Writing*, Thompson conceded that the ceramic data fit better with an 11.3 correlation, but since that would have violated continuity, he adhered to 11.16.

Other Calendar Correlations

If Lounsbury solved the calendar correlation based on Thompson's Venus tautology and if the security of i) Landa's equation; ii) the Oxktuzcab Chronicle katun end; and iii) the Tizimin double date are all called into question, then it would appear that we are now back to the early twentieth century state: the problem appears under-constrained and unsolved. This, then, opens the door to considering alternatives to the GMT.

Some of David Kelley's assessments we have already seen. He was unconvinced by the Xiu Chronicle, for example, as well as the use of the Dresden Codex Venus Table. But in his own words, the "tropical year criterion was the final factor in convincing me that neither the Spinden nor the Thompson correlation could be correct".[127] Namely, Kelley found to be convincing several records identified by Spinden as falling on solar partition intervals. These did not match up with the corresponding positions according to the Spinden or GMT correlations, so Kelley began looking for more criteria along with alternative correlations.

In the end, Kelley's method was to focus on Jupiter-Saturn conjunctions and their purported recording in Classic period hieroglyphic texts.

> In view of the rarity of Jupiter-Saturn conjunctions (19 to 20 years apart) and the variability of the period, such conjunctions seemed to suggest possible correlations more than such short-term variable phenomena as lunations, Mercury conjunctions, specified tropical year positions, or even eclipses.[128]

This criterion is reasonable enough, although one might be concerned with the lack of explicit record that the dates in question were related to either Jupiter or Saturn. Nonetheless, with this criterion, Kelley finds two correlations that match the Jupiter-Saturn data. The first he discards because it fails the lunar constraints: "The remaining correlation, 663310, is the only one that seems to fit, though sometimes rather roughly, all the criteria I accept at this time".[129] Among these criteria, for instance, are that Chan Bahlum (now known as Kan B'ahlam, 10th ruler of Palenque) was born on an eclipse that was visible in Mexico; that Kelley's expected equinoxes and solstices fell on historical equivalents; that planetary conjunctions are found among the dates of the inscriptions; and that his explanations of the Venus and Mars tables are met. Moreover, with this alternative, "[a]ll dates are 216 years later than they are in the Thompson correlation, closely matching my estimate, based on the historical epigraphic evidence, of about 200 years after Thompson".[130]

While his critique of the data supporting other correlations is strong, Kelley's replacement criteria rely excessively on the inference of astronomical relevance within hieroglyphic inscriptions. This in itself might not be sufficient to dissuade the open-minded researcher, but Kelley's corroborating arguments do require some leaps of faith. For one, Kelley is reluctant to give up the notion of an inviolate 260-Day Count throughout Mesoamerica over time. In fact, he accepts only a single revision—one he identifies in the Mixtec codices, following a version of Alfonso Caso's interpretation.[131] This gives Kelley a calendar reform in AD 934. The attentive reader will recall that Lounsbury put the 'true' use of the Dresden Codex Venus Table at 934, which Kelley accepts as the Mayan adoption of the Mixtec reform.

Here again, a single pan-Mesoamerican calendar reform may not seem outlandish. Where Kelley pushes the envelope, however, is in his appeal to trans-Pacific contact for the basis of the Mayan and Aztec calendars.

> I have also argued that the ideas and calendar systems incorporated in the new calendar were largely of Eurasian origin and that they probably first came together not earlier than the first century B.C., probably in northern India (Kelley 1960, 1972, 1974, 1975; Moran and Kelley 1969). ... In India the last of these [four world ages] was thought to have begun at a date used by astronomers as an era base, the so-called Kaliyuga era of 17 February – 3101 (3102 B.C.), calculated by the Hindus as a mass planetary conjunction in zero degrees of Aries (Ginzel 1906/58, vol 1:[p.201]337-38) and regarded in the conjunction astrology of the Persians as the date of the great Flood (Pingree 1963:243, Kennedy and Pingree 1971:187-89).[132]

Unfortunately, the extreme character of this part of his argument and the substantial deviation of his correlation from the GMT have left Kelley's more salient criticisms to fall on mostly deaf ears.

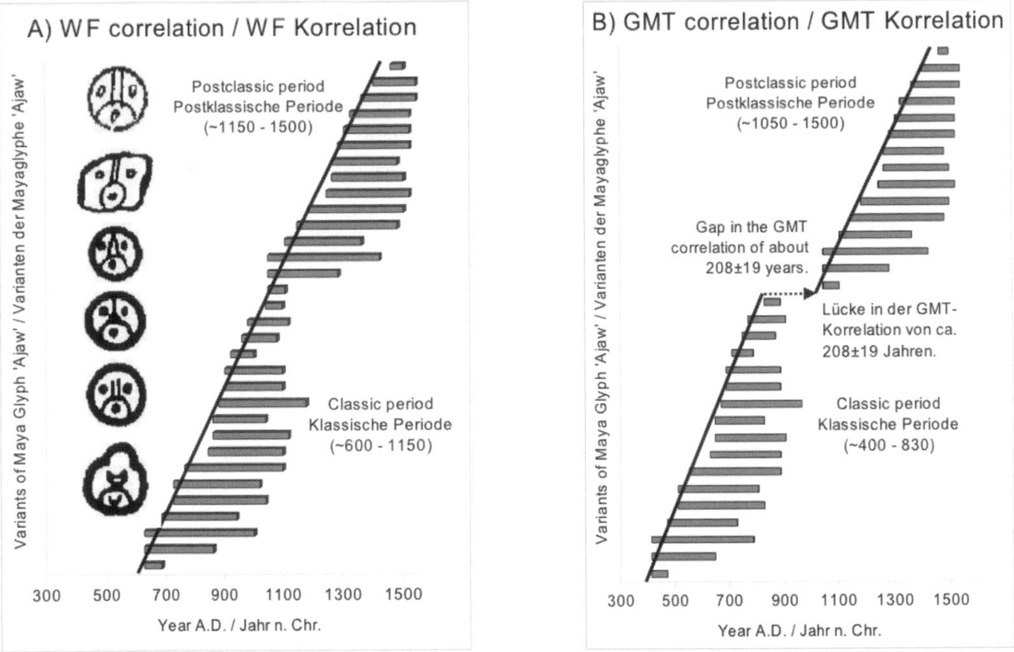

FIGURE 8. Fuls's graphic representation of Lacadena's hypothesized change in the hieroglyphic depiction of AJAW over time (reproduced by permission of Andreas Fuls).

There have been some, however, who have seen the logic in Kelley's critique, and used it for alternate means. Most recently, Andreas Fuls and Brian Wells have taken up perhaps the most concerted challenge to the GMT, first using a best-fit approach to the astronomical data, then Fuls followed up with a refinement of the argument on his own.[133] Fuls goes so far as to claim that his is the "correct solution" to the Calendar Correlation problem,[134] which has even made it into the popular media given the public interest in 2012.[135] Accordingly, Fuls does not expend much effort arguing for the error of the GMT. Rather, he aims to show simply that his correlation fits more data better.

In part, his interpretations of the 'raw' data do differ from traditional twentieth century interpretations; for example, Fuls does not accept Thompson's interpretations of the corrections for the Dresden Codex Venus Table. Instead, Fuls takes the original 9.9.9.16.0 1 Ajaw 18 K'ayab as a legitimate date for a Venus heliacal rise.[136] He also incorporates what he interprets to be solar station records, though these differ from the ones identified by Kelley.[137] Finally, Fuls explicitly addresses the Poco Winik eclipse record, although his correlation puts the Long Count date one day before a partial eclipse, one which would not have been visible from Mesoamerica.[138] Whilst it is one thing to argue that the scribes at Poco Winik made an error in recording a visible eclipse—as GMT proponents suggest—it seems something quite else to argue that the scribes were monumentalizing an eclipse they did not see.

Perhaps most interestingly, though, Fuls, for the first time in decades, introduces a new data set into the consideration. Fuls turns to Alfonso Lacadena's work on stylistic changes in the representations of specific glyphs over time (see figure 8).[139] On the one hand, Lacadena's is in the same vein as Proskouriakoff's work that dated inscriptions by carving style. Here, though, he has shifted the analysis to focus on the rate at which styles change. Lacadena finds a relatively consistent rate of change, for example, in the depiction of the Ajaw glyph. Fuls jumps on this data since Lacadena's analysis argues that the GMT requires a break in the rate of change. This break is removed, however, with the WF correlation. While Fuls's WF correlation has not found ready acceptance, neither does it seem to have been seriously entertained by Mayanists, largely because the vast majority considers the GMT to have already been proven. On the other hand, a 'best-fit' approach does bring to bear a host of complications regarding how certain types of data should be weighted against others—again, factors which may betray specific biases, removing them from view in the analysis. Certainly it lacks the elegance and authority of an analytic solution.

Conclusion

One of the results of this history of the calendar correlation problem is the recognition that Thompson has had a tremendous effect on its consideration since mid-century. In part, as Coe ably demonstrated,[140] this reflects his own academic work and positioning within the politics of the field. But we also would do well to recognize that other scholars actively engaged and furthered Thompson's self-portrayal, acting out of self-interest. Lounsbury, for example, found in Thompson's work a problem he was able to solve and which he considered to be worth solving. It may be that, on one level, we here confront evidence of Aveni's 2001 caveat that the more technical astronomy and calendric analyses that make up treatments of the calendar correlation problem are often accepted without consideration by "anthropologists" because they are framed "in the scientific jargon of their specialty".[141]

On the other hand, Lounsbury's proof created a new pressure for the further acceptance of the GMT. That is, through an accepted GMT, scholars encountered a charter for a new area of legitimized scholarship. With a growing field thanks, for instance, to the Mayan Heiroglyphic Writing workshops offered by Schele (the so-called 'Texas Meetings')—themselves uncritically utilizing and in some ways canonizing the GMT—and a growing profession overall,[142] the ideal scenario for the sedimentation of Lounsbury's proof came together. The GMT was accepted because it was accepted by well respected authorities in the field—not because it had been uncontrovertibly proven.

Naturally, though, this leaves an open question. If the problem is essentially underconstrained—that is, if there is insufficient data to provide a unique solution—is there any reason not to find a consensus on a 'best' solution and utilize it as a working hypothesis?

My own sense is that this is justifiably contested territory. If it were taken as a working hypothesis, the resulting work might be different. But as we have seen, it has been taken as secure—and in anecdotal cases, belligerently so. And even if it were taken tentatively, we can readily see the potential pitfalls in the late twentieth century hypothesis of the Mayan Star War (as noted above) that might result. That is, we run the risk of developing interpretations of cultural practices and even historical events based on erroneous analyses of the data.

Yet there is a much larger question to consider here. It seems intuitive to think that during the Classic period, the Long Count was intended to produce a linear chronological record not unlike the Julian or Gregorian systems. But once a given community has deviated from that construct, what evidence is there that subsequent calendric constructs were intended to function in similar ways? In order for us to address this question rigorously, of course, we would have to take into account Mayan conceptualizations of time and history. While it is convenient to simply invoke a model of cyclicity or linearity or some 'hybrid' spiral time, is there any evidence that any of these is warranted? How do we substantiate a 'cyclical' view of time represented in the Books of Chilam Balam? Is it enough to find a representation of a 'katun wheel'? Why should a katun count in Postclassic Yucatan be ideologically or philosophically dependent upon the Long Count of the Classic Peten? Certainly such assumptions are convenient but, again, that has the potential to lead us to interpretations that are self-serving and little else. Is there any reason that Mayan scribes of either period would be interested in maintaining an 'objective chronology' for times into the distant past? While our Post-Enlightenment, Post-Modern, Postmodern common sense suggests that it would be most straightforward to presume that Mayan scribes would have preferred to maintain continuity in their chronology, there is no direct evidence to support or refute such an assertion.

The alternative, it seems to me, is not unreasonable. Certainly some investigations do require the specific reconstructions of historical night skies, but there is a substantial number of others that do not. My sense is that significant work remains to be done in documenting and reconstructing Mayan astronomical methods, which may be investigated independently of any correlation. Architectural alignments, for example, do not require a calendar correlation, nor do investigations into astronomical references in the hieroglyphic record relative to each other. No doubt the invocation of a calendar correlation is convenient for some research, but convenience should probably not be the primary motivation. Perhaps counter-intuitively, then, the more intellectually conservative approach is the research that proceeds without assuming a calendar correlation.

Notes

1. Aveni (2001), p. 207.
2. Coe (1992), p. 114.
3. I use the term "artefact" following Latour's description of the reversible movement of concepts from artefact to fact. See Latour (1987).
4. Novick (1994), pp. 1–17.
5. Thompson (1950), pp. 69–93; Tedlock (1992), pp. 107–131.
6. See, e.g., Aveni (2001), pp. 288–293.
7. Aveni (1980), p. 205.
8. There has been some debate over time whether moon ages were computed based on an idealized progression, or whether they were simply records of observed phases. Some of this debate plays out in the exchanges between Thompson and SpindenŞthe former arguing for observed moons, and the latter for computed records (Thompson (1935), p. 78). Satterthwaite (1957) went through a large number of records for his dissertation, and while his results were mixed, he concluded that the vast majority may well have been directly observed.
9. Aveni (2001) pp. 173–181.
10. Lacadena (2006); Wald (2006).
11. Thompson (1972), pp. 63–64).
12. Lounsbury (1983), p. 1.
13. Lounsbury (1983), p. 4.
14. Lounsbury (1983), p. 5.
15. Lounsbury (1983), pp. 5–6.

16. Lounsbury (1983), p. 11.
17. Lounsbury (1983), p. 24.
18. Lounsbury (1992a), p. 204.
19. Coe (1992), p. 197–201.
20. Schele and Miller (1986), p. 3.
21. Schele and Miller (1986), pp. 136–137.
22. Schele and Miller (1986), p. 21.
23. Schele and Miller (1986), p. 319.
24. Schele and Freidel (1990); Freidel, Schele, and Parker (1993); Schele and Mathews (1999).
25. See, e.g., Dutting and Aveni (1982); Dutting (1985); Tate (1985); Closs (1994).
26. Kelley (1983), p. 174.
27. Teeple (1931); Lounsbury (1983), p. 4.
28. Thomspon (1972), pp. 63–64.
29. This is not to say that the Eclipse Table is dependent on the Venus Table. These two are mutually independent data sets and can be used against the other to provide checks. Either of these in isolation, however, cannot be checked against itself.
30. Thomspon (1983), p. 19.
31. Lounsbury (1983), p. 19; emphasis added.
32. Aveni (1980), p. 207 and (2001), p. 208–209.
33. Thompson (1950), p. 303.
34. Lounsbury, for example, seems to get his confirmation of the Landa equation from Tozzer, and thus missed entirely its problematization by Long (Lounsbury (1992a), p. 205, note 3).
35. Latour (1987).
36. Tozzer (1975), p. 134; Garibay (1973), p. 60; Pagden (1975), p. 96.
37. Garibay (1973), p. 61–62; identical to Pérez Martínez (1938), p. 143.
38. Pagden (1975), p. 97.
39. Pagden (1975), p. 97.
40. Spinden (1916), p. 85–86.
41. Garibay (1975) pp. 160–203.
42. Spinden (1916), pp. 85–86.
43. Long (1935).
44. Long (1935), p. 97.
45. Cline (1973), p. 18.
46. Tozzer (1975), p. 151, footnote 748.
47. Thompson (1950), pp. 126–127; emphasis added.
48. Thompson (1950), p. 304.
49. Thompson (1950), p. 304.
50. Baaijens (1995).
51. Clendinnen (1987), p. 118.
52. Clendinnen (1987), p. 119.
53. Clendinnen 1987), p. 117.
54. Restall and Chuchiak (2002), p. 664; emphasis added.
55. Aveni (2001), p. 208.
56. Thompson (1927), pp. 6–7.
57. Thompson (1927), p. 7; cf. Kelley (1983), p. 166.
58. Thompson (1935), pp. 57–58.
59. Thompson (1927), p. 7.
60. Thompson (1950), p. 125.
61. Thompson (1950), p. 125.
62. Thompson (1950), p. 125.
63. Thompson (1950), p. 127.

64. Kelley (1983), p. 164.
65. It would be interesting, for example, to consider the possibility that Xiu was simply projecting back in time based on an early seventeenth century subscription to leap-year calendrics.
66. Goodman (1974[1897]), p. 2.
67. Goodman (1974[1897]), p. 2.
68. Morley (1911), p. 198.
69. Morley (1911), p. 203.
70. Morley (1911), p. 203.
71. Brotherston (1992); Parker (1996).
72. Morley (1910), p. 201.
73. Morley (1910), p. 196.
74. Morley (1910), p. 204.
75. Spinden (1935), p. 78.
76. Thompson (1935), p. 57.
77. Thompson (1935), p. 57.
78. Thompson (1935), pp. 55–56.
79. Thompson (1935), p. 74.
80. Makemson (1950), p. 168; emphasis added.
81. Satterthwaite (1947), p. 678.
82. Satterthwaite (1947), p. 678; Makemson (1946).
83. Coe (1992), pp. 139, 152.
84. Coe (1992), p. 139.
85. Thompson (1950), p. 305.
86. Thompson (1950) pp. 306–307; Long (1947), pp. 107–108.
87. Kelley (1983), pp. 166.
88. Thompson (1935), p. 59.
89. Goodman (1974 [1897]), p. 1.
90. Goodman (1974[1897]), p. 12.
91. Goodman (1974 [1897]), pp. 12–13.
92. Aveni (2001), p. 208.
93. Thompson (1950), p. 303–304.
94. Thompson (1950), p. 303.
95. Caso (1967).
96. Cline (1973), pp. 9–10.
97. Thompson (1950), p. vii-viii.
98. Kelley (1983), p. 157.
99. Coe (1992), p. 129; also Newsome (2009), p. xv.
100. Aveni (1980, 2001).
101. Lounsbury (1983, 1992a,b).
102. Bricker and Bricker (2007).
103. Thompson (1927, 1935, 1950).
104. Schele et al (1992); Linden (1991); Aldana (2006).
105. Thompson (1927), p. 11.
106. Kelley (1983), p. 178.
107. Aveni (2001), pp. 179–181.
108. Thompson (1935), p. 74.
109. It has been suggested that a day or two of error for this record is reasonable since it may have resulted from a prediction. The trouble with such interpretations is that the monument narrative provides the eclipse record retrospectively on its way to commemorating the following period end.
110. cf. Aveni (2001); Lounsbury (1983, 1992a); Bricker and Bricker 2007).
111. e.g. Willson (1924); Lounsbury (1989); Dutting (1985); Tate (1985); Schele and Freidel (1990).

112. Thompson (1950), p. 227.
113. Thompson (1950), pp. 227–228.
114. Aldana (2005).
115. Martin and Grube (2000), p. 73.
116. Martin and Grube (1998); Aldana (2006).
117. Kelley (1977); Lounsbury (1982).
118. e.g. Schele and Freidel (1990); Lounsbury (1982); Martin (1996); Closs (1978); Coe (1995).
119. Aveni and Hotaling (1994); Nahm (1994).
120. Aldana (2005).
121. Schele and Freidel (1990), pp. 473–474.
122. Houston (1996).
123. Aveni (2001), p. 169.
124. Kelley (1983), p. 162.
125. Thompson (1950), pp. vii–viii.
126. Coe (1992), p. 161.
127. Kelley (1983), p. 184.
128. Kelley (1983), p. 203.
129. Kelley (1983), p. 204.
130. Kelley (1983), p. 204.
131. Kelley (1983), p. 167–168.
132. Kelley (1983), p. 200).
133. Wells and Fuls (2001), Fuls (2008).
134. Fuls (2008), p. 144.
135. Maloof (2010).
136. Fuls (2008), p. 137.
137. Kelley (2008), pp. 140–141.
138. Fuls's WF correlation places 9.17.X.X.X on 27/5/998; see Fuls (2008). A partial solar eclipse occurred on 28/5/998, visible in northernmost North America; see Espanek (2010).
139. Fuls (2008), p. 143.
140. Coe (1992), p. 123.
141. Aveni (2001), p. 4.
142. The SAA Census shows a spike in the number of PhDs awarded in archaeology in the U.S. in the 1970s relative to the 1960s. The near 400% increase of the 70s continued at a rate of about 150% into the 80s and 90s. The numbers here are based on a voluntary census with a response rate of only 30%. On the other hand, the trend clearly indicates one of substantial growth.

References

Aldana, G., 2005, "Agency and the 'Star War' Glyph: An Historical Reassessment of Classic Maya Astrology and Warfare", *Ancient Mesoamerica* 16:2, 305–320.

——, 2006, "Lunar Alliances: Conflicting Classic Maya Hegemonies", in Bostwick, T. W. and Bates, B. (eds.), *Viewing the Sky Through Past and Present Cultures: Selected Papers from the Oxford VII International Conference on Archaeoastronomy*, Pueblo Grande Museum Anthropological Papers 15 (Phoenix: City of Phoenix Parks Recreation and Library), 237–258.

Aveni, A. F., 1980, *Skywatchers of Ancient Mexico* (Austin: University of Texas Press).

——, 2001, *Skywatchers: Revised Edition of Skywatchers of Ancient Mexico* (Austin: University of Texas Press).

——, and Hotaling, L., 1994, "Monumental Inscriptions and the Observational Basis of Maya Planetary Astronomy", *Archaeoastronomy* 19, *Supplement to the Journal for the History of Astronomy* 25, S21–S54.

Baaijens, T., 1995, "The Typical 'Landa Year' as the First Step in the Correlation of the Maya and the Christian Calendar", *Mexicon* 17, 50–51.

Bricker, H. and Bricker, V., 2007, "When was the Dresden Codex Efficaceous?", in C. Ruggles and G. Urton (eds.), *Skywatching in the Ancient World: New Perspectives in Cultural Astronomy Studies in Honor of Anthony F. Aveni* (Austin: University of Texas Press), 95–120.

Brotherston, G., 1992, *Book of the Fourth World: Reading the Native Americas through their Literature* (Cambridge: Cambridge University Press).

Caso, A. 1967, *Los Calendarios Prehispánicos* (México: Universidad Autónoma de México).

Clendinnen, I., 1987, *Ambivalent Conquests: Maya and Spaniard in Yucatan, 1517–1570* (Cambridge: Cambridge University Press).

Cline, H., 1973, "The Chronology of the Conquest: Synchronologies in Codex Telleriano-Remensis and Sahagun", *Journal de la Société des Américanistes* 62, 9–34.

Closs, M., 1994, "A Glyph for Venus as Evening Star", in M. G. Robertson and V. M. Fields (ed.), *Seventh Palenque Round Table, 1989* (San Francisco: Pre-Columbian Art Research Institute),

——, 1978, "Venus in the Maya World: Glyphs, Gods and Associated Astronomical Phenomena", in M. G. Robertson (ed.), *Tercera Mesa Redonda de Palenque, Volume IV* (Palenque: Pre-Columbian Art Research Center), 158–163.

Coe, M., 1992, *Breaking the Maya Code* (London: Thames and Hudson).

——, 1993, *The Maya* (London: Thames and Hudson, Fifth Edition).

——, 2005, *The Maya* (London: Thames and Hudson, Seventh Edition).

Dütting, D., 1985, "Lunar Periods and the Quest for Rebirth in the Mayan Hieroglyphic Inscriptions", *Estudios de Cultura Maya* 16, 113–147.

——, and Aveni, A. F., 1982, "The 2 Cib 14 Mol Event in the Palenque Inscriptions", *Zeitschrift für Ethnologie* 107, 233–258.

Espanek, F., 2010, NASA Eclipse Web Site, http://eclipse.gsfc.nasa.gov/SEsearch/SEsearchmap.php?Ecl=09980528

Freidel, D., Schele, L. and Parker, J., 1993, *Maya Cosmos: Three Thousand Years on the Shaman's Path* (New York: William Morrow and Co.).

Fuls, A., 2008, "Reanalysis of Dating the Classic Maya Culture", *Amerindian Research*, Band 3/3, Number 9, 132–146.

Goodman, J. T., 1974, Appendix to A. P. Maudslay *Archaeology*, Volume VI (New York: Milpatron Publishing Corp.).

Houston, S., 1996, "Symbolic Sweatbaths of the Maya: Architectural Meaning in the Cross Group at Palenque, Mexico", *Latin American Antiquity* 7, 132–151.

Kelley, D., 1977, "Maya Astronomical Tables and Inscriptions", in A. F. Aveni (ed.), *Native American Astronomy* (Austin: University of Texas Press), 57–74.

——, 1993, "The Maya Calendar Correlation Problem", in R. Leventhal and A. Kolata (eds.), *Civilization in the Ancient Americas: Essays in the Honor of Gordon R. Willey* (Albuquerque: University of New Mexico Press), 157–208.

Lacadena, A., 2006, "Passive Voice in Classic Mayan Texts: CV-h-C-aj and –n-aj Constructions", in S. Wichmann (ed.), *Linguistics of Maya Writing* (Salt Lake City: University of Utah Press), 165–194.

Landa, Diego de., 1938, *Relación de las cosas de Yucatán*, translated by Héctor Pérez Martínez (México: Editorial P. Robredo).

——, 1973, *Relación de las cosas de Yucatán*, translated and introduced by Angel Ma. Garibay K. (México: Editorial Porrúa).

Latour, B., 1987, *Science in Action* (Cambridge, MA: Harvard University Press).

Linden, J.. 1996, "The Deity Head Variants of Glyph C", in M. G. Robertson (ed.), *Eighth Palenque Round Table, 1993* (San Francisco: Pre-Columbian Art Research Institute), 343–356.

Long, R. C., 1935, "Appendix III: Remarks on the Calendar Correlation", in *Maya Chronology: The Correlation Question*, Contributions to American Archaeology, No. 14 (Washington D.C.: Carnegie Institution), 97–100.

——, 1947, "The Maya Correlation Problem by Maud Worcester Makemson. Book Review", *American Journal of Archaeology* 51/1, 107–108.

Lounsbury, F., 1978, "Maya Numeration, Computation, and Calendrical Astronomy", in C. C. Gillispie (ed.), *Dictionary of Scientific Biography* (New York: Charles Scribner's Sons), Volume 15, 759–818.

——, 1983, "The Base of the Venus Table of the Dresden Codex, and its Significance for the Calendar-Correlation Problem", in A. F. Aveni and G. Brotherston (eds.), *Calendars in Mesoamerica and Peru: Native American Computations of Time*, BAR International Series 174 (Oxford: Archaeopress), 1–26.

——, 1989, "A Palenque King and the Planet Jupiter", in A. F. Aveni (ed.), *World Archaeastronomy* (Cambridge: Cambridge University Press), 246–259.

——, 1992a, "Derivation of the Mayan-to-Julian Calendar Correlation from the Dresden Codex Venus Chronology", in A. Aveni (ed.), *The Sky in Mayan Literature* (New York: Oxford University Press), 184–206.

——, 1992b, "A Solution for the Number 1.5.5.0 of the Mayan Venus Table", in A. F. Aveni (ed.), *The Sky in Mayan Literature* (New York: Oxford University Press), 207–215.

Makemson, M. W., 1950, "The Katun Calendar of the Book of Tizimin", *American Antiquity* 16/2, 166–168.

Maloof, A., 2010, "2012: Countdown to Armageddon", http://channel.nationalgeographic.com/episode/2012-countdown-to-armageddon-4438/maloof-maya-calendar

Martin, S., 1998, "Tikal's Star War Against Naranjo", in M. Macri and J. McHargue (eds.), *Eighth Palenque Round Table, 1993* (San Francisco: Pre-Columbian Art Research Institute), 223–236.

Martin, S. and Grube, N., 2000, *Chronicle of the Maya Kings and Queens: Deciphering the Dynasties of the Ancient Maya* (London: Thames & Hudson).

Maudslay, A. P., 1974, *Archæology*, Facsimile edition with introduction by Dr. Francis Robicsek (New York: Milpatron Publishing Corp.).

Morley, S. G., 1910, "The Correlation of Maya and Christian Chronology", *American Journal of Archaeology* 14/2, 193–204.

——, 1911, "The Historical Value of the Books of Chilan Balam", *American Journal of Archaeology* 15/2, 195–214.

Nahm, W., 1994, "Maya Warfare and the Venus Year", *Mexicon* 16, 6 –10.

Newsome, E., 2001, *Trees of Paradise and Pillars of the World: The Serial Stelae Cycle of "18-Rabbit-God K," King of Copan* (University of Texas Press, Austin).

Norvick, P., 1994, *That Noble Dream: The Objectivity Question in the American Historical Profession* (Cambridge: Cambridge University Press).

Pagden, A. R. (ed. and trans.), 1975, *The Maya: Diego de Landa's account of the affairs of Yucatán* (Chicago: J. P. O'Hara).

Parker, M. 1996, *The Story of a Story Across Cultures: The Case of the Doncella Teodora* (New York: Tamesis).

Restall, M. and Chuchiak, J., 2002, "A Reevaluation of the Authenticity of Fray Diego de Landa's Relación de las cosas de Yucatán", *Ethnohistory* 49:3, 651–669.

Satterthwaite, L., 1947, "The Maya Correlation Problem by Maud Worcester Makemson", *The Hispanic American Historical Review* 27/4, 677–679.

Schele, L. and Freidel, D., 1990, *A Forest of Kings: The Untold Story of the Ancient Maya* (New York: William Morrow).

——, Grube, N., and Fahsen, F., 1992, *The Lunar Series in Classic Maya Inscriptions: New Observation and Interpretations*, Texas Notes on Precolumbian Art, Writing, and Culture, No. 29.

——, and Mathews, P., 1999, *The Code of Kings: The Language of Seven Sacred Maya Temples and Tombs* (New York: Simon and Schuster).

——, and Miller, M., 1986, *The Blood of Kings* (New York: George Braziller Inc.).

Spinden, H., 1924, "The Reduction of Maya Dates", *Papers of the Peabody Museum of Archaeology and Ethnology* 6/4.

Tate, C., 1985, "Summer Solstice Ceremonies Performed by Bird Jaguar III of Yaxchilan, Chiapas, Mexico", *Estudios de Cultura Maya* 16, 85–112.

Tedlock, B., 1982, *Time and the Highland Maya* (Albuquerque: University of New Mexico Press).

Teeple, J., 1931, *Maya Astronomy, Contributions to American Archaeology*, Volume I, Nos. 1 to 4 (Washington: Carnegie Institution).

Thompson, J. E. S.. 1927, *A Correlation of the Mayan and European Calendars*, Field Museum of Natural History, Anthropological Series, Publication 241, Vol. XVII, No. 1 (Chicago: Field Museum of Natural History).

——, 1935, *Maya Chronology: The Correlation Question*, Contributions to American Archaeology, No. 14 (Washington D.C.: Carnegie Institution).

——, 1950 [1971], *Maya Hieroglyphic Writing: An Introduction* (Norman: University of Oklahoma Press)

——, 1972, *A Commentary on the Dresden Codex*, Memoirs of the American Philosophical Society 93 (Philadelphia: American Philosophical Society).

Tozzer, A., 1975, *Landa's Relación de las Cosas de Yucatan: A Translation*, Papers of the Peabody Museum of American Archaeology and Ethnology, Harvard University, Volume XVIII (New York: Kraus Reprint Co.).

Wald, R. F., "The Languages of the Dresden Codex: Legacy of the Classic Maya", in S. Wichmann (ed.), *Linguistics of Maya Writing* (Salt Lake City: University of Utah Press), 27–60.

Wells, B. and Fuls, A., 2000, *The Correlation of the Modern Western and Ancient Maya Calendars*, Monograph No. 5, Early Site Research Society.

Willson, R., 1924, *Astronomical Notes on the Maya Codices*, Peabody Museum of American Archaeology and Ethnology Papers, 6, 3.